D0875449

Property of
St. John Fisher College
Lavery Library
Rochester, N.Y. 1461

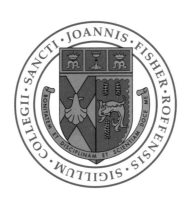

Lavery Library

St. John Fisher
College

Rochester, New York

Trust under Pressure

Trust under Pressure

Empirical Investigations of Trust and
Trust Building in Uncertain Circumstances

Edited by

Katinka Bijlsma-Frankema

*Associate Professor of Organization Theory, Free University,
The Netherlands*

Rosalinde Klein Woolthuis

*Assistant Professor of Organization Sciences, Free University,
The Netherlands*

Edward Elgar

Cheltenham, UK • Northampton, MA, USA

© Katinka Bijlsma-Frankema and Rosalinde Klein Woolthuis 2005

All rights reserved. No part of this publication may be reproduced, stored in a retrieval system or transmitted in any form or by any means, electronic, mechanical or photocopying, recording, or otherwise without the prior permission of the publisher.

Published by
Edward Elgar Publishing Limited
Glensanda House
Montpellier Parade
Cheltenham
Glos GL50 1UA
UK

Edward Elgar Publishing, Inc.
136 West Street
Suite 202
Northampton
Massachusetts 01060
USA

A catalogue record for this book
is available from the British Library

Library of Congress Cataloguing in Publication Data
Trust under pressure : empirical investigations of trust and trust building in
  uncertain circumstances / edited by Katinka Bijlsma-Frankema, Rosalinde
  Klein Woolthuis.
    p. cm.
  Includes bibliographical references.
    1. Industrial organization—Social aspects. 2. Trust—Economic aspects.
  3. Business ethics. 4. Organizational behavior. I. Bijlsma-Frankema, Katinka,
  1946– II. Woolthuis, Rosalinde Klein, 1970–

  HD2326.T78 2005
  302.3'5—dc22

                                                                    2005051825

ISBN 1 84542 311 9

Printed and bound in Great Britain by MPG Books Ltd, Bodmin, Cornwall

Contents

Contributors

Katinka Bijlsma-Frankema is Associate Professor of Organization Theory at the Free University Amsterdam and Professor of Organization Sciences at the European Institute for Advanced Studies in Management (EIASM). She received her Masters degree in Sociology from the University of Groningen, the Netherlands, and her PhD in Organization Sciences from the University of Amsterdam. Current research interests include frictions between organizational cultures and structure, learning processes within and between teams, managerial cognition and trust, control and performance within organizations. She is chair of the First International Network on Trust (FINT), in which scholars from 21 countries participate. She has recently published in *Research Method Forum*, *Personnel Review* and the *Journal of Strategic Change*. Together with Paul Koopman, she was (guest) editor in 2003 of a special issue on trust within organizations of *Personnel Review* and of a special issue on managerial control of the *Journal of Managerial Psychology* in 2004. Together with Ana Cristina Costa she is currently guest editor of special issues on trust and control of International Sociology and of Group and Organization Management.

Kirsimarja Blomqvist is Professor of Knowledge Management, part-time director at TeliaSonera Chief Technology Office, and vice-director for Telecom Business Research Center at Lappeenranta University of Technology. Formerly she has worked as a corporate analyst for technology-based firms. Her research interests include trust and social capital in knowledge creation and innovation, R&D and innovation management, strategic alliances and intra-organizational collaboration. Her PhD published in 2002, 'Partnering in the Dynamic Environment – The Role of Trust and Technology in Asymmetric Technology Partnership Formation', was given a special 85-year award for its contribution to management by the Finnish Foundation for Business Education. She has published in *R&D Management*, *Technovation*, *Scandinavian Journal of Management*, *Journal of Strategic Change* and has book chapters in several books.

Gerhard van de Bunt is Assistant Professor at the Department of Social Research Methodology of the Faculty of Social Sciences of the Free

University Amsterdam. He received his Masters degree in Sociology and Methodology and his PhD in Sociology from the Interuniversity Center for Social Science Theory and Methodology (ICS, University of Groningen, The Netherlands). The title of his dissertation was 'Friends by choice: an actor-oriented statistical network model for friendship networks through time'. He has published on friendship, statistical network models, and trust within organizations. His current research interests are the evolution of intra- and inter-organizational networks, friendship strategies, trust, solidarity, and social capital. Since January 2004 he has been editor of *International Sociology*. Furthermore, he is a board member of The Netherlands Organization for Methodological Research in the Social Sciences, and the secretary of the Dutch Research Group on Social Network Analysis.

Bruno Busacca is Full Professor of Corporate Economics and Management at the Faculty of Business Administration at Bocconi University (Milan, Italy). He is also Director of the Corporate Executive Education Division and Member of the Executive Committee and Management Board at SDA Bocconi School of Management. He attended the International Teachers Programme (Centre HEC-ISA, Jouy-en-Josas, Paris, 1986). In 1990, he was Research Associate at the University of California at Berkeley, School of Business Administration. His research interests concern consumer behaviour, brand management, market-based asset and pricing strategies; his research work on these topics has been published by several academic journals and publishers. Other research-related activities include: membership of the editorial boards of several academic journals, membership of the Council of Presidency of the Italian Marketing Society (SIM) and membership of FINT – First International Network on Trust. He is advisor of the Italian Ministry of Education, University and Research.

Hans Caljé is co-ordinator of Communication Research and Senior Advisor for Strategic Communication at the Dutch Ministry of Traffic, Water Management and Public Works. As a research coordinator, he is involved in the organization of public opinion research, media analysis and monitoring studies. After studying Personality Psychology at the University of Groningen, he received his PhD in Social Sciences on mass media effects of newspapers on public opinion about environmental issues at Twente University. Following that, he worked as a lecturer in Communication Science at The Free University of Amsterdam at the Faculty of Social Sciences, Department of Political Science and Policy Studies.

Sandro Castaldo is Full Professor of Management at Bocconi University (Milan, Italy) and Chairman of the Marketing Department at SDA Bocconi

School of Management (Milan, Italy). He received his PhD in Management at Bocconi University. In 1993 he was visiting Professor at the University of Florida. He teaches at graduate and post-graduate levels in marketing, channel and relationship management. His research interests lie in the fields of trust, inter-organizational relationships and distribution channels. He is a member of the Academy of Management, European Academy of Management, EAERCD and FINT – First International Network on Trust, and member of the editorial committee and referee for many journals. He has published articles, chapters and books on *Trust in Market Relationships*, *Loyalty Management in Retailing*, *New Products Development*, and *Channel Collaborative Relationships*.

Dick de Gilder is Assistant Professor of Public Administration and Organization Science at the Faculty of Social Sciences of the Free University Amsterdam (The Netherlands). He received his PhD in Social Psychology from the Faculty of Social Sciences, University of Groningen, The Netherlands. His research interests lie in the fields of social identity theory, error management, contingent work and management of research groups. He has recently published in *Personnel Review*, *Academy of Management Review* and *British Journal of Social Psychology*.

Andreas Hoecht is a senior lecturer in the Department of Strategy and Business Systems at Portsmouth Business School, University of Portsmouth (UK). He holds a PhD in Economics from Budapest University and an MA in Political Science from the University of Hamburg. His research interests include the role of trust and the relationship between trust, risk and control in inter-organizational relations. He is also interested in the role of trust within organizations, in particular the link between trust, control, accountability and professional autonomy in public sector organizations such as universities.

Rosalinde Klein Woolthuis is Assistant Professor of Public Administration and Organization Science at the Faculty of Social Sciences of the Free University Amsterdam, The Netherlands. She holds a doctorate in business administration from the University of Twente, the Netherlands. Her research interests lie in the fields of interorganisational collaboration and innovation, systems of innovation and innovation policy, and institutional theory. She has recently published in *Organization Studies* and *Technovation*, and has contributed chapters to a number of books.

Peter Kerkhof is an Assistant Professor at the Department of Communication Science of the Free University Amsterdam, The Netherlands. He received his PhD in 1997 at the Department of Social Psychology at the same university. His research focuses on the effects of the internal and external communication of organizations.

Torsten M. Kühlmann is Chair of Human Resource Management at the University of Bayreuth, Germany. He holds a doctorate in business administration from the University of Erlangen-Nürnberg. His research and teaching interests lie in the fields of (international) human resource management. Other interests include entrepreneurship, opportunism in networks, and corruption in transnational business relationships. He is actively involved in international executive education and has consulted with a variety of organizations. Recently he has published a book on expatriation management.

Guido Möllering is a Researcher at the Max Planck Institute for the Study of Societies in Cologne, Germany. He holds a PhD in Management Studies from the University of Cambridge, UK. His research is generally in the area of interorganizational relationships with specific interests in trust, boundary spanning, supply networks and, more recently, collective institutional entrepreneurship. He has published articles in leading journals such as *Organization Science* and *Sociology* among others. Together with Jörg Sydow, he is co-author of the German textbook *Produktion in Netzwerken* and for the *Journal of Managerial Psychology* he guest-edited, with Reinhard Bachmann and Soo Hee Lee, a Special Issue on the micro-foundations of organizational trust.

Elena Rocco is Assistant Professor at the Department of Business Economics and Management of the University of Venice (Italy). She holds a Ph.D. from the Department of Management of the University of Udine (Italy), and a post-doctoral degree from the University of Michigan. Her research interests are the effects of information technology on organizations and markets, cooperation and negotiation within and between organizations, and organizational evolution. She conducts experiments and field studies on trust, negotiation and reputation.

Bastiaan W. Rosendaal is a lecturer at the Free University Amsterdam, Department of Public Administration and Organization Studies. His major fields of research are Organizational Learning and Knowledge Development. Prior to this he worked at the University of Amsterdam in the Department of Adult Education and that of Organizational Sociology. In addition to his academic career he worked for 13 years as an independent researcher and consultant in the field of human resources development and knowledge support systems.

Andrej Rus is Associate Professor of Sociology and Organizations at the University of Ljubljana and the head of the Centre for Strategy and Evaluation at the Institute for the Social Sciences at the same university. His empirical research has dealt with organizational responses to privatization in Eastern Europe, the social and institutional barriers to the SME development in the Balkans, and the dynamics between formal and social structures in organizations. Currently, he is working in the area of public management seeking to apply network analysis to the study of co-ordination between organizations in public and private sectors.

Malin Tillmar is Associate Professor at the Department of Management and Economics at Linköping University (Sweden), as well as researcher at the National Institute for Working Life. She received her PhD at Linköping University in 2002 for her dissertation titled 'Swedish Tribalism and Tanzanian Agency: Preconditions for trust and cooperation in a small-business context'. Her research interests include trust and cooperation, entrepreneurship and small businesses. Currently, she is engaged in a project on entrepreneurship in the public sector.

Nadine Vahstal-Lapaix is an Account Coordinator at an advertising agency and design studio. She received her Masters degree in Policy, Communication and Organization at the Faculty of Social Sciences at the Free University Amsterdam, The Netherlands.

1. Trust under pressure: trust and trust building in uncertain circumstances

Katinka Bijlsma-Frankema and Rosalinde Klein Woolthuis

INTRODUCTION

Changes in the structure of societies, organizations, and exchange relationships have placed issues of trust solidly on the research agenda. Within organizations, changes to flatter organizations, participative leadership styles and virtual teams, for instance, have increased the complexity of direct supervision and hierarchical control (Sheppard and Tuschinsky 1996; Grey and Garsten 2001; Sydow 2001; Tyler 2003; Bijlsma and Koopman 2004). Between organizations, the increased number of inter-organizational and cross-border relationships, the greater importance of collaborative innovation and the increased importance of intangible resources in learning and innovation, have narrowed the basis for formal control and shifted the attention to trust as an alternative governance mechanism (Lane and Bachmann 2001; Nooteboom 2002). Trust is taken to signify and represent a coordinating mechanism supporting collaboration within uncertain environments (Reed 2001), that is in situations in which rational predictions are hard to make (Luhmann 1979; Barber 1983; Gambetta 1988; Lane 2001) and risk is present (Rousseau et al. 1998; Ring and van de Ven 1994; Dyer and Chu 2003). It is especially in those situations that trust becomes relevant, as it can enable a 'leap of faith' beyond that which reason alone would warrant (Lewis and Weigert 1985; Bradach and Eccles 1989). Building upon this conceptualization of trust, trust appears to be of great importance in relationships that are staged within environments where a solid basis for control – for instance in well-developed institutional structures, complete contracts and hierarchies – is lacking.

Although some attention has been paid to situations where the basis for control is narrow due to the international character of relationships or lacking institutional structures supporting exchange (see Child 2001; Humphrey 2001), most literature on trust is still grounded on theoretical and empirical work that 'tended to focus on societies where trust relations are firmly embedded in institutional frameworks and established practices. Trust relations are sustained by institutional mechanisms and the "taken-for-granted" nature of relationships' (Humphrey 2001: 216). Reed argues that as a result of this focus on these 'well backed-up' trust relationships, most scholars have actually researched institutionalized trust 'that is, trust tied to formal societal and organizational structures that shape interactional patterns' (2001: 203). This book takes a different turn. It aims to shed light on exactly those situations where institutional, taken-for-granted, or rational bases for control and trust are lacking. The chapters in this book focus on relationships in which partners have little to fall back upon to make their 'leap of faith': actors are from different organizations, tribes or countries; relationships are not embedded in a shared institutional structure, common culture, or networks; and transactions are not backed up by contracts, monitoring and/or sanctioning systems. How will actors go about this lack of embedding structures? Will they enact trust in an interplay of social and discursive structures? Will they build up a 'common ground' or embedding structure to construct a springboard for their 'leap of faith'? It is this question of how actors build trust under pressure that is explicitly or implicitly addressed in the studies brought together in this book.

SHIFTS IN GOVERNANCE

A central observation in this book is that in a context in which economies are globalizing and de-localizing, relationships are becoming more distant, both in a metaphorical and geographical sense (Dicken 1992; Castells 2000). This has far-reaching consequences for how relationships can be governed, both from a formal control and trust perspective. Formal control needs a solid basis to be able to function. First, formal control is based on specification and codification *ex ante* (Boisot 1995). This requires programmability of behaviors and measurability of outcomes. However, in many cases, activities and transactions have become harder to specify and codify. In high-tech or knowledge-intensive industries, the pace of technological developments is high, and business processes are complex and often unpredictable. As a result, task programmability and outcome measurability are low (Nooteboom 1999; Das and Teng 2001). This implies that contracts will be hard to specify and enforce. Moreover, if parties would want to specify everything *ex ante*, this would raise transaction costs to an unsound level and could slow down business processes to such an extent that accurate appropriation of opportunities would be impossible. Furthermore, competitiveness in these industries is increasingly determined by intangible resources (Von Krogh 1998; Lekanne Deprez and Tissen 2002) which are hard to codify or specify, and as a result hard to safeguard by contracts or hierarchical structures (Powell 1990, Grey and Garsten 2001).

Second, formal control requires the possibility of monitoring to determine if actors deviate from the formally specified agreements (Nooteboom 1999). This implies that parties must either be in close contact so they can directly supervise the agreement's execution, or have intelligent monitoring systems that enable distant monitoring. Due to the de-localization and globalization of markets, and inherent rise of cross-boundary collaborations between actors from different countries, business contacts have become spread beyond closed groups like organizational teams and local business communities (Dicken 1992). Monitoring as a result becomes problematic. Due to large geographical distance, close monitoring will be expensive and time-consuming, or otherwise incomplete. Cultural differences and language barriers will add to this (Child 2001; Humphrey 2001). Difficulties with monitoring can also occur as a result of large cognitive distances (Nooteboom 1999). Whereas successful collaboration and innovation requires complementarity of partners, too large differences in knowledge between partners from, for instance, different scientific or technological communities, may inhibit monitoring due to difficulties in understanding the other's activities, competences and intentions (Klein Woolthuis 1999).

Third, if formal control is to effectively safeguard against opportunism, it should include mechanisms to enforce an agreement, that is an opportunity to penalize opportunistic behavior or unjust execution of the agreement. Otherwise, no credible threat can be made (Williamson 1985). This requires a suitable juridical structure, including well-functioning courts, to enforce contracts in inter-firm as well as intra-firm relationships. However, if relationships take place across organizational and geographical borders, a uniform institutional infrastructure is not available to fall back upon. Formal institutions, such as contract law and regulations, may be different in the actors' various home bases, and relationships are hence embedded in different institutional frameworks simultaneously. Consequences of globalization also include doing business with partners in countries where institutional structures are non-existent or poorly functioning. For instance, in transition economies like China and former communist states in Eastern Europe, property rights and contract law have only recently been developed. Effective courts to appeal to in case of contract breach may also be missing, making safeguarding of relationships through formal means impossible. Furthermore, other forms of retaliation will be narrowed too as a result of de-localization of exchange relationships, since the relationships with partners outside the realm of ongoing business relationships within local communities will tend to lack both social and temporal embeddedness (Granovetter 1985; Blumberg 2001). This implies that opportunistic behavior cannot be punished by, for example, reputation effects or gossiping as to limit a partner's room to maneuver (Nooteboom 1999). All these difficulties with formal control would call for a shift to alternative forms of governance that are better suited to govern relationships under the uncertain circumstances that increasingly characterize our international and knowledge-intensive economies.

FROM FORMAL CONTROL TO TRUST-BASED GOVERNANCE

Many authors have claimed that, partly due to these developments, trust is a superior governance mechanism because it is considered to rest on different bases than control, and to have a positive effect on relationship development and outcome. This is because trust has the following divergent characteristics from formal control.

First, trust is not based on strict codification and specification *ex ante* of formal agreements which might reduce transaction costs (Sako 1992, Sydow 2001). Not only because one needs not specify everything *ex ante*, but also because trust enables open communication and problem solving (Zand 1972; Dirks 1999, Klein Woolthuis 1999) thereby reducing *ex post* transaction costs in the form of haggling and conflict (Dyer and Chu 2003). Within organizations, and in agency relationships, less specified contracts, resting less on control and more on spontaneous trustful reciprocity, even appear to be more effective and efficient (Chen 2000; Fehr et al. 2001). However, much in line with the bases for formal control, trust also needs alignment of goals and expectations. This alignment can be based in explicit interaction between transacting partners, but can also more implicitly find its roots in a common ground: social or clan-like structures in which expectations are aligned through a socialization process (Ouchi 1980). This can be recognized in a common culture, and shared norms and values (Eisenhardt 1985). If these embedding structures that provide a basis for trust are lacking, trust has to be developed at a cost. A large part of this trust-building process will be devoted to developing a shared language and understanding of each other, and of vision and goals regarding the collaborative venture (Larson 1992; Ring and van de Ven 1994). This will also be more difficult when relationships are becoming more international as 'Cultural and associated language differences tend to impede communication and easy understanding, and may therefore stand in the way of affect based trust' (Child 2001: 246). On the other hand, trust-based relationships do seem more suitable to sustain relationships in which intangible resources, tacit knowledge, learning and innovation play an important role. Because agreements are not lived to the letter but more to the goals and intentions, trust-based relationships provide more room for the openness, creativity and flexibility needed to make these relationships successful.

Second, trust, very much like the monitoring function in formal control structures, needs close and repeated interaction to build up. Parties learn about each other's competences and intentions (Nooteboom 2002) in repeated interactions in which the strategic importance of the transactions slowly builds up (Lewicki and Bunker 1996). In cross-border relationships, virtual teams and, for example, e-business relationships, this requirement will not be easily met. In other words, the basis for trust is in this respect narrowing in the same manner as the basis for formal control. On the other hand, and crucially different from the formal control meaning of the word monitoring, monitoring in a trustful relationship can actually contribute to the trust building process. Monitoring can be interpreted as a sign of involvement, care and concern, rather than as a check on opportunism or inability, that is a sign of distrust (Bijlsma and van de Bunt 2003).

Third, although trust is not based on the explicit threat of enforcement of an agreement through legalistic sanctions, social control does imply the threat of social sanctioning if breach of trust is observed. If parties live up to expectations, this will further positive expectations, enhance the level of trust, and promote actors' willingness to cooperate (Lewicki and Buncker 1996; Buskens 1999; Gautschi 2002). However, such mechanisms for social sanctioning are only possible if parties are embedded in communities in which reputation mechanisms can support exclusion or other social sanctions as gossip or loss of future business relationships. This embedding structure of informal institutions made up of shared norms, values, standards, codes of conduct and so on will deteriorate as communities de-localize. In this respect, the basis for trust – in the form of social sanctioning – is like the basis for formal control narrowing as a result of de-localization. Furthermore, although the sanctioning function of formal institutions (for example regulations, courts) might not be of direct importance for trust, they *are* as a general basis to start building trust from.

As organizations increasingly need to move toward network forms and alliances (Piore and Sabel 1984; Best 1990; Sheppard and Tuschinsky 1996) and these cooperative relationships take place across organizational and geographical borders, it is more difficult to fall back upon an institutional infrastructure. Actors' multiple embeddedness in different institutional structures causes trust to be problematic because it will be harder for the interacting actors to understand each other's background and consequent behavior. For instance, parties from countries in which formal institutions are hardly developed will value the opportunity to sanction differently than actors from countries where these institutions are taken for granted. The 'rules of the game' that the other party abides by, will be hard to know and to interpret, whereas mutual understanding is often mentioned as key to establishing trustful relationships (Bradach and Eccles 1989; Nooteboom 2002). Moreover, actors might get involved in business relationships with countries in which the informal institutional context is counterproductive to trust, for instance due to political struggles or war. This might jeopardize the build up of trust.

TRUST UNDER PRESSURE

All in all we conclude that, as a result of the internationalizing economies and the changing nature of industries, trust will – like formal control – become harder to establish, although sometimes for different reasons. Lack of shared formal and informal institutions, different cultural backgrounds, large geographical distance, intangible resources, fast moving technologies and markets, and virtual relationships, all reduce both the bases for formal control and trust. So, whereas trust becomes more important because the bases for formal control are weakening, the bases for trust are also narrowing. It is because of this development that we (with Lane 2001: 2) conclude that trust is becoming more important and more problematic at the same time.

This raises the question of how actors go about these situations. How are relationships built and sustained when the basis for both formal control and trust is thin? Very little attention has been devoted to this question, whereas it is especially in those situations where the 'taken for granted' bases of trust and control are lacking that one wonders how actors make their leap of faith and engage in productive business relationships. Some first attempts have been made to describe how actors build trust under such uncertain circumstances. Child and Mollering (2003) described how standardization of business systems between Hong Kong and Chinese business partners served as a means to actively build trust. Here the standardization of systems provided a perceived 'common ground' to fall back upon. Bacherach and Gambetta (2001) described how trust could be built by signaling behavior; that is, how actors can mimic behavior or looks, or otherwise give trustworthy cues, to actively win the other's trust. This behavior is especially relevant when more solid sources for trust are absent, that is, when the person who has to make the decision whether to trust or not, has very little ground to base trust on. Although these studies offer some preliminary insight into how trust is built and sustained under pressure, there is still much to be explored.

This volume therefore brings together a collection of empirical studies that deal with 'trust under pressure': it sketches the problems partners are facing in building up a cross-border alliance between German and Mexican businessmen, the struggle people have to go through in building up trust and collaboration between partners from different tribes in Tanzania, the difficulties of knowledge protection in industries where resources purely reside in the heads of the beholders, and the challenge of building trust when there is no time to 'earn it' or where hard and soft institutions are lacking to support it. In all cases, actors use different tactics and strategies to govern their transactions and build up trust. By describing the bases for trust that parties can partly fall back upon, but that are often also actively and creatively constructed, this volume contributes to insights on how trust can be built and sustained under uncertain circumstances. It furthermore sheds light on what mechanisms and artifacts actors recognize as 'ready to use', and which 'building blocks' they actively construct, to build trust. It also illuminates the partially conscious and unconscious processes that enable actors to construct a basis for trust that they perceived to be solid enough to engage in transactions, that is, to make their leap of faith.

STUDIES IN THIS VOLUME

The empirical studies presented in this book are conducted by scholars with a wide variety of disciplinary backgrounds, employing insights from many fields, including organization theory, knowledge management, sociology, psychology, economics, management, human resources management and communication sciences. Empirical data were gathered in twelve different countries, including Eastern European countries, Mexico and Tanzania as well as Western European countries. The studies were conducted in a variety of contexts: relations both within and between organizations and within and between nations, in contexts that can be typified as uncertain because institutional, taken-for-granted, or rational bases for control and trust are weak or lacking. In studying trust and trust building under pressure, the conceptualization of trust used by most authors in this volume was rather open so as not to limit the room for exploration. Although the authors do not agree on an exact definition of trust, most seem to agree on two characteristics that are worded in the definition of Rousseau et al. (1998, pp. 217–18), 'trust is a psychological state comprising the intention to accept vulnerability based on positive expectations of the intentions or the behavior of another'. According to most authors trust is an expectation, and trust is a way to deal with perceived risk (Gambetta 1988; Luhmann 1988). What bases underlie this expectation is left open, and explored rather than defined. In this way, room was left to 'discover' sides of trust and the trust-building process that would be left untouched if trust was strictly defined *ex ante* and studied under stable circumstances only.

Chapters 2–5 of this volume illuminate how actors build trust under conditions where formal institutions are precarious or lacking: sound institutional frameworks do not exist, courts are absent or malfunctioning, laws and regulations are ill-developed or relationships are embedded in different institutional structures simultaneously. There is hence no uniform, stable framework to fall back upon to support either trust building or formal control. Whereas the studies of Möllering and Kühlmann concentrate on the problems of trust-building and collaboration across countries and cultures, that is where relationships are multiply embedded, the studies of Tillmar and Rus focus on the role of trust in countries where stable institutions are lacking.

Chapter 2 by Möllering is a theoretical analysis of types of trust. He distinguishes three ideal types of trust: rational trust, institutional trust and active trust. Rational trust is looked at as a prudent choice based on the perceived trustworthiness of the trustee and is paradigmatic for much of the trust literature to date. Institutional trust is discussed using phenomenological and neo-institutional theory to suggest a more unusual explanation of trust that rests on the taken-for-grantedness in the trustor's natural propensity towards social, reciprocal behavior. Third, given the limitations of the first two ideal types, active trust is illuminated as a highly experimental and reflexive form of trust. It highlights the challenges of trust development that is typical of the ostensibly short-lived and fast-changing social relations in late modernity. Active trust involves a process of familiarization, by discovering 'common ground' or by creating new similarities in interaction with others. On the basis of this creative process, trust is built, and serves as a mechanism for the suspension of doubt.

In the chapter by Kühlmann, the build up of a German–Mexican business relationship is examined. Kühlmann emphasizes that in international and hence intercultural relationships, trust is of crucial importance since contractual agreements are difficult to design and implement because the relationship is embedded in different constitutions (different laws and regulations). Formal safeguarding of the relationship would not only be costly and time-consuming, but also difficult to enforce since monitoring at such distance would be impossible. However, as Kühlmann contends, trust is also difficult to build because actors: cannot monitor the other's behavior;

have limited understanding of the other's values, norms and culture; lack knowledge of the business partner's institutional framework; have no (or little) information on the partner's reputation; and have to deal with the different ways trust is conceived and given value in the different countries. The questions that Kühlmann asks to find out how actors deal with these difficulties and uncertainties in building up trust and collaboration focus on the specific mechanisms that business partners use or construct to build up trust, how they use these mechanisms to build trust, and how the trust mechanisms are combined with more formal mechanisms for governance and control. Kühlmann examines 30 German–Mexican business relationships, mainly in sales, to answer these questions.

Chapter 4 by Tillmar investigates how cooperation between small entrepreneurs in Tanzania can be arrived at, especially across tribal borders. In this country, reliable formal institutions are not well developed. No one trusts the police or courts; often these institutions are corrupt or do not offer help when needed. Rather people base their trust in the indigenous institutions such as tribalism and witchcraft. Moreover, Tillmar contends that in Tanzania trust – and also distrust – is not general (based on institutions), nor personal, but rather based on categories of people: women, immigrants, tribes and so on. As a result, trust is almost only viable within tribes, because within the tribes there are elected leaders that are respected by all and take care of arbitration. Within these tribes, the indigenous legal-like mechanisms of sanctions and safeguarding enable collaboration between their members. However, inter-tribe relationships are very difficult to establish because they are not supported by institutions and are mainly characterized by distrust. This is a major obstacle for economic development since it limits the scope of economic activities to a great extent. Tillmar studies how the Tanzanian Chamber of Commerce, Industry and Agriculture tries to break down the barriers between the tribes to stimulate economic development. The chapter describes how a cooperative Savings and Credit Society is established to form the 'common ground' that people from different tribes can fall back upon, and how courses on accounting bring people together that would otherwise not meet, in an attempt to build collaboration and stimulate business activity.

The chapter by Rus studies the effect of trust on business development as he observes that trust, or social capital, by scholars and practitioners alike (for example the World Bank) is viewed as key to economic development. To stimulate trust and social capital within less-developed countries, the development of social infrastructures is hence considered crucial. He reports on a comparative study of small and medium enterprises (SME) development survey among almost 800 SMEs in Bosnia, Macedonia and Slovenia in which he examines not only how social capital stimulates cooperation and therewith SME growth, but also how well developed institutional structures (legal system, laws, regulations) underlie the degree to which social capital is present in SME relationships. He distinguishes three types of trust: interpersonal trust that 'sticks to' strong ties; network trust that may travel through weak ties; and institutional trust that is easily transferable as it is public information and requires no ties. Rus examines how these various forms of trust are present in the three countries, and how these forms of trust stimulate or inhibit SME cooperation and growth.

In the next two chapters of this volume, the studies by Hoecht and Blomqvist focus on knowledge-intensive industries. In these industries, exchange of knowledge, often with new or external partners, is crucial to spur creativity and innovation. However, as a result of the intangible nature of the resources involved, the low level of task programmability and outcome measurability, and the risk of information leakage, these partnerships are hard to govern by formal control, because the codifiable and enforceable aspects of agreements are limited.

Chapter 6 by Hoecht focuses on collaborative R&D projects with externally hired specialists in the flavor and fragrance industry in the UK. In these industries, external linkages are needed to promote creativity and innovation, while these linkages also increase the risk of intentional or accidental disclosure of sensitive information. Since information leakage, especially by external workers, is hard to monitor, and punishment is always too late to repair the potential damage, traditional legal and bureaucratic control mechanisms are unsuitable to control this risk. Hoecht describes how in this industry legal remedies are considered too slow, and that secrecy clauses in contracts are hence not considered protective. The study examines which alternative mechanisms actors use to govern these relationships, and specifically how social and formal control mechanisms complement each other in doing so.

Chapter 7 by Blomqvist sheds light on trust building in partnership formation between large and small firms in the high-tech ICT industry. In this sector, the market does not allow actors to slowly build up trust before they engage in IT partnerships or joint business projects. Furthermore, because resources are mainly intangible or devaluate swiftly as they become outdated in this fast-moving industry, capabilities play a much larger role than resources in choosing a partner. Blomqvist describes how the trust literature is dominated by the idea that trust must be built up slowly, in a process in which actors can get to know the other's competences and intentions. In the ICT industry, though, actors do not have time for this and hence have to select a partner without having an elaborate exchange history to derive some 'well informed' choice to trust from. The future does not provide many leads either: due to the high complexity and uncertainty of technological and market developments, predictions are hard to make and hence the suitability of a business partner can only partly be appraised. Still, trust is claimed to play an important role by the actors that actually do business and collaborate in these highly volatile markets. Blomqvist examines how business partners build this trust, and build it fast. She examines the role that personal affection and shared excitement play in triggering almost instant trust, and describes the tactics that actors use to test whether affection and excitement can be shared with a potential partner to support trust.

The remaining chapters of this volume focus on 'trust under pressure' within organizations. Due to fast-moving markets and more flexible, even virtual organizational forms, relationships between individuals (customers, employees) and organizations have become looser, more distant and less easy to monitor and control by traditional means. At the same time, these organizations have become more dependent on the intangible resources that these individuals hold, that is, the capabilities of their employees and possibly external experts. Knowledge, expertise and capabilities are key to gaining and maintaining competitive advantage. The question raised in this part of the book is how organizations deal with this challenge. The studies focus on how trust and loyalty is built between companies and their customers – a process that is increasingly difficult because trends and hypes dominate markets, and because different product characteristics increasingly require custom-made strategies to build trust. Furthermore, these relationships are more and more of a virtual nature as the internet takes over much of earlier face-to-face contacts.

In Chapter 8 by Busacca and Castaldo relationships and trust are studied from a 'resource-based view' (RBV) perspective. Seen from this perspective, they claim that trust does to external relationships what knowledge does internally to the firm, that is it creates value, not only in an abstract manner, but also in a concrete, economic sense by creating shareholder and customer value. They examine how the level of consumer trust creates relationship stability and thereby net present shareholder value. This value, they suggest, results from the customer's willingness to pay a premium price, and from reduced entrepreneurial risk (for example by decreasing the costs of capital). Because of this, firm profitability can increase. They also examine how trust relates to the firm's shareholders' and customers' value by comparing marketing relationships in several highly differing markets in Italy: financial services, meat, university undergraduate training and consumer electronic appliances. Most interesting, though, is that Busacca and Castaldo distinguish which sources of trust actually lead to this value. In other words, they examine whether value-creating trust relationships have different antecedents in different markets and customer relationships.

This sheds light on how trust-building is not only an interactive process, but may also to a great extent be co-determined by the environment and context in which it takes place, and by the process and/or product which it concerns.

Kerkhof, Vahstal-Lapaix and Caljé also emphasize the value creation side of trust in Chapter 9. They analyse how reputation and trust relate in situations where there is no face-to-face contact between buyer and seller in Internet shops. In most of these situations there is neither common ground, nor a shadow of the past to base trust on. The question then arises, how can trust be built? The authors examine how – without interacting with the customer – trust can be built by actively making use of reputation effects, a form of trust that is easily transferable. They therefore study whether a group of respondents place trust in a (for them) unknown company, based on the (indirect) trust they have in the Internet shop that presents the unknown party, or based on the advertisement banners shown at the unknown party's website that present well-known companies with a good reputation. In this way it is examined how parties that have very limited possibilities to build trust in a direct manner can actually construct trust by giving credible cues and signals.

Chapter 10 by Rocco sheds light on the question of how trust can be built within cross-border teams. She studies an international team of ICT professionals. The team is virtual in the sense that its team members are all working for the same organization, but located in three different countries. Hence, members cannot meet regularly, or face-to-face. This implies that both control and trust will be hard to establish: geographical distance complicates not only the process of getting to know and understand each other, it also hinders monitoring activities, and implies cultural differences and potential misunderstanding. Rocco examines the obstacles of trust development under these circumstances, by examining the build-up of 'common ground', that is the sum of mutual ideas, beliefs and assumptions upon which a group of individuals bases its choices and coordinates activities. She pictures common ground as the springboard of trust development. Common ground is discussed as flowing from three sources: community membership, that is being a member of the same community; linguistic co-presence, that is the ability to communicate using the same language/vocabulary; and physical co-presence, that is the ability to meet each other in person to be able to communicate and develop mutual understanding. The main research question is how these sources of common ground function when the actors that have to build trust are located at great geographical distance. In this way she contributes to the question of which sources actors can fall back on in the globalizing economy in those situations where actors share little, and have no exchange history, which renders them a very narrow basis for trust.

In Chapter 11 Bijlsma, Rosendaal and van de Bunt examine to what degree perceived organizational support (POS) affects team performance indirectly via vertical and horizontal lines of trust, selfish behaviors of colleagues, and heedful interrelating. More specifically, they examine in which way trust in managers (vertical) and trust in colleagues (horizontal) within teams of knowledge workers affect heedful interrelation within the team and team performance. They examine these relationships by comparing a research organization, which can be characterized as a professional bureaucracy, and a network organization active in ICT and e-business. By comparing these organizations, their chapter also gives insight into how the formal structure of an organization affects both the level of trust and the consequences of trust. Two structural equation models were fitted to the data.

Chapter 12 by de Gilder examines how the loosening of relationships between employees and their employers influences trust. This question is relevant as employee–employer relationships are becoming more flexible, and contingent work and temporary work relationships are increasingly common. De Gilder examines how trust develops by focusing on differences in organizational citizenship behavior (OCB) between temporary contingent workers and core employees. In his study, he describes the differences in trust, commitment and justice perceptions in two hotels, and their effect on OCB/work behaviors. He examines whether contingent workers have a lower commitment to the team and to the organization, and how this relates to their behavior towards the organization and their 'core employee' colleagues. The insights contribute to the question of how a feeling of being part of an organization, and thus sharing the organizational culture, provides a basis for trust and positive behaviors.

REFERENCES

Bacherach, M. and D. Gambetta (2001), 'Trust in signs', in K.S. Cook (ed.), *Trust in Society*, New York: Russel Sage Foundation, pp. 148–84.

Barber, B. (1983), *The Logic and Limits of Trust*, New Jersey: Rutgers University Press.

Best, M.H. (1990), *The New Competition: Institutions of industrial restructuring*, Cambridge: Polity Press.

Bijlsma, K.M. and G.G. van de Bunt (2003), 'Antecedents of trust in managers: a "bottom up" approach', *Personnel Review*, **32**(5), 638–64.

Bijlsma, K.M. and P.L. Koopman (2004), 'The oxymoron of control in an era of globalisation: vulnerabilities of a mega myth', *Journal of Managerial Psychology*, **19**(3), 204–17.

Blumberg, B.F. (2001), 'Co-operation contracts between embedded firms', *Organizations Studies*, **22**(5), 825–52.

Boisot, M.H. (1995), *Information Space: A framework for learning in organizations, institutions and culture*, London: Routledge.

Bradach, J.L. and R.G. Eccles (1989), 'Markets versus hierarchies: from ideal types to plural forms', in W.R. Scott (ed.), *Annual Review of Sociology*, **15**, 97–118, Palo Alto: CA, Annual Reviews Inc.

Buskens, V.W. (1999), *Social Networks and Trust*, Amsterdam: Thela Thesis.

Castells, M. (2000), *The Rise of the Network Society: The information age*, Vol. 1, New York: Blackwell Publishers.

Chen, Y. (2000), 'Promises, trust, and contracts', *The Journal of Law, Economics, & Organization*, **16**(1), 209–32.

Child, J. (2001), 'Trust and international strategic alliances: the case of Sino–foreign joint ventures', in C. Lane and R. Bachmann (eds), *Trust Within and Between Organizations: Conceptual issues and empirical implications*, New York: Oxford University Press Inc., pp. 241–71 [first printed 1998].

Child, J. and G. Mollering (2003), 'Contextual confidence and active trust development in the Chinese business environment', *Organization Science*, **14**(1), 69–80.

Das, T.K. and B-S. Teng (2001), 'Trust, control and risk in strategic alliances: an integrated framework', *Organization Studies*, **22**(2), 251–83.

Dicken, P. (1992), *Global Shift: The internationalization of economic activity*, 2nd edn, New York: Guilford; London: Paul Chapman.

Dirks, K.T. (1999), 'The effects of interpersonal trust on work group performance', *Journal of Applied Psychology*, **84**(3), 445–55.

Dyer, J.H. and W. Chu (2003), 'The role of trustworthiness in reducing transaction costs and improving performance: empirical evidence from the United States, Japan and Korea', *Organization Science*, **14**(1), 57–68.

Eisenhardt, K.M. (1985), 'Control: organizational and economic approaches', *Management Science*, **31**(2), 134–49.

Fehr, E., A. Klein and K.M. Schmidt (2001), 'Fairness, incentives and contractual incompleteness', Working paper no. 72, Institute for Empirical Research in Economics, University of Zurich.

Gambetta, D. (1988), *Trust: Making and breaking co-operative relations*, Oxford: Basil Blackwell.

Gautschi, T. (2002), *Trust and Exchange: Effects of temporal embeddedness and network embeddedness on providing a surplus*, Amsterdam: Thela Thesis.

Granovetter, M.S. (1985), 'Economic action and social structure: the problem of embeddedness', *American Journal of Sociology*, 78, 481–510.

Grey C. and C. Garsten, (2001), 'Trust, control and post-bureaucracy', Organization Studies, **22**(2), 229–50.

Humphrey, J. (2001), 'Trust and the transformation of supplier relations in Indian industry', in C. Lane and R. Bachmann (eds), *Trust Within and Between Organizations: Conceptual issues and empirical implications*, New York: Oxford University Press Inc., pp. 214–40 [first printed 1998].

Klein Woolthuis, R.J.A. (1999), *Sleeping with the Enemy: Trust, dependence and contracts in interorganizational relationships*, Enschede: Twente University.

Krogh, G. von (1998), 'Care in knowledge creation', *California Management Review*, **40**(3), 133–53.

Lane, C. (2001), 'Introduction: theories and issues in the study of trust', in C. Lane and R. Bachmann (eds), *Trust Within and Between Organizations: Conceptual issues and empirical implications*, New York: Oxford University Press Inc., pp. 1–30 [first printed 1998].

Lane, C. and R. Bachmann (2001), *Trust Within and Between Organizations: Conceptual issues and empirical implications*, New York: Oxford University Press Inc. [first printed 1998].

Larson, A. (1992), 'Network dyads in entrepreneurial settings: a study of the governance of exchange relationships', *Administrative Science Quarterly*, **37**, 76–104.

Lekanne Deprez, F. and R. Tissen (2002), *Zero Space: Moving beyond organizational limits*, San Francisco: Berrett-Koehler.

Lewicki, R.J. and B.B. Bunker (1996), 'Developing and maintaining trust in work relationships', in R.M. Kramer and T.R. Tyler (eds), *Trust in Organizations: Frontiers of theory and research,* Thousand Oaks: Sage, pp. 114–39.

Lewis, J.D. and A. Weigert (1985), 'Trust as a social reality', *Social Forces*, **63**(4), 967–85.

Luhmann, N. (1988), 'Familiarity, confidence, trust: problems and alternatives', in D. Gambetta (ed.), *Trust: Making and breaking co-operative relations*, Oxford: Basil Blackwell.

Luhmann, N. (1979), *Trust and Power*, New York: John Wiley and Sons Ltd.

Nooteboom, B. (1999), *Inter-firm Alliances: Analysis and design*, London: Routledge.

Nooteboom, B. (2002), *Trust: Forms, foundations, functions, failures and figures*, Cheltenham, UK; Northampton, MA, USA: Edward Elgar.

Ouchi, W.G. (1980), 'Markets, bureaucracies and clans', *Administrative Science Quarterly*, **25**(1), 129–43.

Piore, M.J. and C.F. Sabel (1984), *The Second Industrial Divide: Possibilities for prosperity*, New York: Basic Books.

Powell, W. (1990), 'Neither market nor hierarchy: network forms of organizations', *Research in Organizational Behaviour*, 12, 295–336.

Reed, M.I. (2001), 'Organization, trust and control: a realist analysis', *Organization Studies*, **22**(2), 201–28.

Ring, P. and A.H. van de Ven (1994), 'Developmental processes of cooperative interorganizational relationships', *Academy of Management Review*, **19**(1), 90–118.

Rousseau, D.M., S.B. Sitkin, R.S. Burt and C. Camerer (1998), 'Not so different after all: a cross-discipline view of trust', *Academy of Management Review*, **23**(3), 393–404.

Sako, M. (1992), *Prices, Quality, and Trust: Inter-firm relations in Britain and Japan*, Cambridge: Cambridge University Press.

Sheppard, B.H. and M. Tuschinsky (1996), 'Micro-OB and the network organization', in R.M. Kramer and T.R. Tyler (eds), *Trust in Organizations: Frontiers of theory and research,* Thousand Oaks, CA: Sage, pp. 140–66.

Sydow, J. (2001), 'Understanding the constitution of interorganizational trust', in C. Lane and R. Bachmann (eds), *Trust Within and Between Organizations: Conceptual issues and empirical implications*, New York: Oxford University Press Inc., pp. 31–63 [first printed 1998].

Tyler, T.R. (2003). 'Trust in organizations', *Personnel Review*, **32**(5), 556–68.

Williamson, O.E. (1985), *The Economic Institutions of Capitalism: Firms, markets, relational contracting*, New York: The Free Press.
Zand, D.E. (1972), 'Trust and managerial problem solving', *Administrative Science Quarterly*, **17**(2), 229–39.

2. Rational, institutional and active trust: just do it!?

Guido Möllering

INTRODUCTION

Confucius, 551–479 BC, already held the view that trust is a precondition and basis for all worthwhile social relations (Hann 1968). This insight is popular again, but while we can easily relate to it from everyday experience, we still find it difficult to grasp the phenomenon of trust in abstract terms. The question of what trust *is* and whether it may be amenable to management can only be assessed on the basis of a differentiated concept of trust, showing different sides of the phenomenon instead of taking in everything at once.

Hence I distinguish three ideal types of trust, each representing corresponding parts of the trust literature. Particular attention shall be given to the concept of *active trust* and the leap of faith that all trust requires as these have been underplayed in previous work. First, though, I will look at the ideal type of *rational trust* as a prudent choice based on the perceived trustworthiness of the trustee which is paradigmatic for much of the trust literature to date. Second, the ideal type of *institutional trust* will be discussed, using phenomenological and neoinstitutional sociology to suggest a more unusual explanation of trust that rests on taken-for-grantedness in the trustor's natural attitude towards social interactions. Third, given the limitations of the first two ideal types, *active trust* as a highly demanding experimental and reflexive form of trust is introduced to highlight challenges for trust typical for the ostensibly short-lived and fast-changing social relations in late modernity.

While trust in practice will always be a combination of the three ideal types, my analysis reveals that the essential accomplishment and defining feature of all trust is the suspension of doubt. I illustrate my overall argument towards the end of this chapter discussing the notion of *swift trust* as introduced by Meyerson et al. (1996).

17

The main point that trust researchers might agree on is that they disagree about concepts and definitions of trust. However I concur with Rousseau et al. (1998, p. 395) that fairly broad consent could be obtained for their definition of trust as 'a psychological state comprising the intention to accept vulnerability based upon positive expectations of the intentions or behavior of another'. Moreover the conditions under which the problem of trust arises are basically agreed on: it is a social phenomenon involving two or more actors who are embedded in a social context. At least one of the actors is vulnerable to the actions of another actor whose behaviour cannot be fully controlled. The problem of trust therefore arises due to the other's principal freedom to act in a way that benefits or harms the trustor. Whether or not, and to what extent, the trustee can harm the trustor depends on the latter's own action. By definition enacting trust means that the trustor increases her vulnerability towards the other's uncertain actions (Baier 1986; Gambetta 1988). The 'trust game' (Figure 2.1) is a useful way of illustrating the conditions for trust to become problematic (Dasgupta 1988; James 2002).

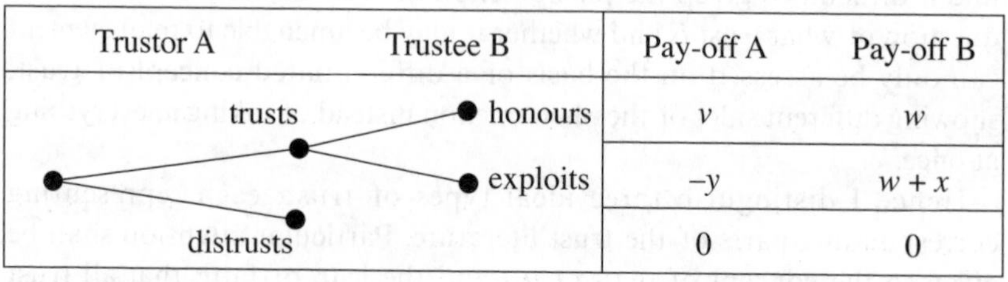

Trustor A	Trustee B	Pay-off A	Pay-off B
trusts	honours	v	w
	exploits	$-y$	$w + x$
distrusts		0	0

Figure 2.1   The trust game

The set-up is similar to the classic prisoner's dilemma (Luce and Raiffa 1957, p. 95). The trustor A's move precedes that of the trustee B, but A has to consider B's options and likely behaviour while making her own choice. For B the question of honouring or exploiting trust only arises if A trusts. Assuming a single interaction and all variables are positive, then B not only has an interest in being trusted, but also in exploiting that trust, because $w + x > w$. This is anticipated by A who therefore distrusts in order to avoid a loss of y. As a result neither A nor B wins or loses anything. However they can both see that the trust–honour sequence would be preferable, since it promises the pay-offs v and w respectively. The trust game is therefore a social dilemma as long as $x > 0$ and $-y < 0$. We might now say that the essence of trust is to overcome this dilemma by placing trust *nevertheless*.

RATIONAL TRUST

The kinds of considerations about the trust problem just introduced are characteristic for the ideal type of *rational trust*. In this ideal type, however, the trustor could not go against the rational choice suggested by the pay-offs and *just do it* anyway. Rather research on *rational trust* aims to show how the game can be devised in such a way that the preferable trust–honour sequence of interaction will arise without making the actors' choices irrational or imprudent (James 2002). If all actors are intendedly rational, predominantly self-interested, know the pay-off structure of the game and know that everybody else assumes all of this, too, then it is only prudent to trust, if it is not in the trustee's interest to exploit trust. In other words, whether or not the trust–honour sequence materialises depends on the trustworthiness of the trustee. As long as $x > 0$, the trustee B is untrustworthy, not because she is malicious, but because rational self-interest dictates that she should exploit A's trust, if it were placed in her. In the following, I present a number of classic suggestions for how and why placing trust may still become rational.

Probability

Suppose that irrespective of B's pay-offs as such, a probability p for her honouring A's trust could be estimated reliably. In that case, as Coleman (1990) suggests, the trustor's decision is essentially like placing a bet on the basis of Bayesian expected values. Trust should be placed if the probability that B will be trustworthy relative to the probability that she will exploit trust is greater than A's potential loss relative to her potential benefit. That is, A will trust, if $p/(1 - p) > y/v$. The same consideration applies, according to Dasgupta (1988), if a proportion p in the population of potential trustees is trustworthy ($x < 0$) while everybody else is untrustworthy ($x > 0$). Hardin (1993) refines this, describing the trustor as an 'instinctive Bayesian' who continuously updates her p estimates for individuals (Coleman) or a relevant population (Dasgupta) on the basis of past experiences.

There are at least two problems with this solution. First, in practice it will be very difficult for the trustor to have reliable p estimates. Second, it needs to be explained why a rational trustee should be trustworthy sometimes although $x > 0$ or why sometimes and only for some rational actors $x < 0$ and whether the trustor can recognise this.

Encapsulated Interest

Hardin (1993) favours the solution that trust can be placed in dilemma-type situations, if the trustee's interest encapsulates that of the trustor. In other words, B's pay-off is a function of A's pay-off, that is $w = f(v, y)$. In that case, by harming the trustor the trustee would harm herself unless the extra pay-off x overcompensates this effect. Hence the encapsulation of interests can make B trustworthy. This is a plausible and classic solution, especially in principal–agent contexts (Jensen and Meckling 1976; Eisenhardt 1989), although it equally raises questions about how the encapsulation can be ascertained.

Modified Pay-offs

All solutions that produce *rational trust* essentially aim to recalibrate the actors' pay-offs in such a way that the trust–honour sequence in Figure 2.1 represents the rational choice for all actors. The simplest solution to this effect is to ensure that $w > w + x$, that is $x < 0$, thus making B trustworthy from A's point of view. But why should x be negative? Even some economists suggest that B might experience a negative utility like guilt from exploiting A's trust and gaining an unfair extra pay-off (Frank 1987). This gives a formally plausible solution, but raises questions such as how B's emotions can be factored into A's pay-off calculations.

Emotions may not be necessary, however, as explanations in rationalist accounts of trust, because the pay-offs can also be modified by 'hard' incentives. For example, a contract between A and B could devise rewards and penalties for honouring and exploiting trust respectively (Levinthal 1988). Another solution suggested is that potential trustees could invest in signalling their trustworthiness, which may work if a 'truly' trustworthy actor can afford to send such a signal while an untrustworthy impostor could not: 'No poisoner seeks to demonstrate his honesty by drinking from the poisoned chalice' (Bacharach and Gambetta 2001, p. 159). Without going through each formal argument here, it can be shown that contractual provisions and signalling can be devised, in theory, in such a way that the trust–honour sequence should be chosen as long as the costs of modifying and monitoring the game do not consume the potential benefits of a successful trust–honour interaction.

This solution is plausible, but only if the basic assumption that the actors know each other's pay-off structure applies, which in practice is highly questionable. Moreover, if the modification removes the dilemma, we can only call A's choice 'trust', if there is still a possibility that B acts unreasonably from A's point of view. Otherwise, we would simply explain cooperation with no need for trust (Kee and Knox 1970).

Shadow of the Future

So far I have referred to Figure 2.1 as if the trust game were only played once. However, if there is a chance that A and B meet again and repeat the game, then B might be trustworthy today simply to prevent that A distrusts her tomorrow. Let us assume for simplicity's sake that future interactions are considered just as important as immediate ones and are therefore not discounted. Thus, if $w > x$, for example, even two trustful interactions will be better for B than a single exploitative interaction and no further interactions. Actors should therefore consider a series of interactions. This is challenged by the notorious backward-induction argument (Luce and Raiffa 1957) which entails that this solution only works if interactions are to be repeated indefinitely, because otherwise the trustee's incentive to cheat on the last interaction means, in effect, that the trustor should not even trust her on the first interaction.

The backward-induction argument is too narrow-minded, though, for if in a series of n interactions B cheats m times, then the trustor should keep placing trust as long as $(n - m)v > my$ instead of ending the interaction: 'It is happier to be cheated sometimes than not to trust' (Deutsch 1973, p. 143, quoting Samuel Johnson's *The Rambler*). Equally it may suffice that the probability q of one more future interaction is high enough, specifically $q>x/(w+x)$. The formal arguments are highly simplified here, as I only intend to show that the pay-off matrix in Figure 2.1 can be modified by factoring in potential future interactions, the famous 'shadow of the future' (Axelrod 1984), and thus bring about the trust–honour sequence. Whether in everyday situations actors can get the maths and the data right is highly questionable and there are additional problems, for example that actors have to be able to recognise each other in the future, but the general proposition that the prospect of future beneficial interactions prevents actors from exploiting trust in the present is quite plausible.

Collective Rationality

Let us assume that all the modifications suggested above can actually be applied by actors in practice. It may then still be the case that the pay-off matrix represents a social dilemma. Does this make the trust–honour sequence impossible? Not necessarily, according to Hollis (1998) who proposes that once the actors involved stop reckoning their own individual pay-offs and instead consider their collective aggregate pay-off, they should obviously place and honour trust, unless $v < x - y$. However, because the subsequent redistribution of the aggregate pay-off only brings about further trust games and free-rider problems, this solution only works if actors genuinely ask 'What is good for *us*?' and not 'What is good for *me*?' As Hollis himself concedes, in Rousseau's words, such a transition from a 'me' rationality to an 'us' rationality would require 'a remarkable change in man'. And it would still require the actors to make trusting choices as long as there are still some opportunists and free-riders left. Nevertheless, one explanation for why A and B accomplish the trust–honour sequence in spite of the social dilemma could be that they have established a collective rationality between them.

In concluding this section, I would characterise the ideal type of *rational trust* as utilitarian in the sense that it is motivated by pay-offs. The trustor's choice is made with reference to a particular trustee and pay-off structure in a particular time and place. The reference for *rational trust* is therefore local rather than global and, for the same reasons, its validity must be specific, because A's trust in B cannot be transferred or generalised to another trustee C without recalculating the game. The rationally trusting actor uses an inductive method, as she assembles observable data on the basis of which she reaches a more general conclusion about the trustee's trustworthiness in the interaction. She perceives the inherent risk of her trust decision as low, since by taking the logical course of action she minimises her Type I and II errors of wrongly trusting or distrusting. Thus she will also accept automatically the increase in vulnerability, if and when she trusts.

It is important to note that this is the description of an *ideal type*. If the ideal type were empirical reality, then trust would be a fully rational bet and therefore an obsolete category (Williamson 1993; James 2002). The difference between the ideal type and trust in reality is that an actor basing social interactions on notional pay-off matrices will quickly realise the rational limits of this method, *but often trust nevertheless*. In other words, her utilitarian considerations help her up to a point, but then she still has to deal with the fact that by placing trust she makes herself vulnerable to the ultimately uncertain actions of another. This is the case because in practice the trustor may be intendedly rational, but at the same time aware of the boundaries of her rationality (Simon [1947] 1997). She can never rule out the possibility that her trust might be based on mistaken or misguided pay-off and probability estimates.

INSTITUTIONAL TRUST

In this section the issue at stake continues to be how a successful trust–honour sequence in the trust game of Figure 2.1 can be accounted for, but I will look for a radical alternative explanation to the basically game-theoretical perspective presented above. In a nutshell the ideal-type of *institutional trust* that I present here rests on the idea that actors place and honour trust, because they take it for granted. In other words, *institutional trust* means that actors look at a trust game, recognise it as such and then act in a predetermined way without even thinking about the values of the variables. *Institutional trust* emphasises the process whereby actors socially construct and maintain the game. If actors regularly enact the trust–honour sequence, then they may just play the game in the normal way. Trust is then simply an institutionalised interaction rather than a rational decision. To trust in this way, however, also increases vulnerability, because there is no absolute guarantee that the normal sequence unfolds. This crass view should be supported by powerful theoretical concepts which I shall now present.

The 'Natural Attitude'

The concept of 'institution' that underlies *institutional trust* is borrowed here from sociological neoinstitutionalism and in particular those authors who are interested in organisation theory and in the phenomenological roots of neoinstitutionalism (Powell and DiMaggio 1991). In this view, 'trust is a set of expectations shared by all those involved in an exchange' including both 'broad social rules' and 'legitimately activated processes' (Zucker 1986, p. 54). When the actors involved in an exchange share a set of expectations constituted in social rules and legitimate processes, they can trust each other with regard to the fulfilment and maintenance of those expectations. Trust hinges on the ability to have, and rely on, a world in common with others. For Garfinkel (1963), trust means to expect (a) the rules to frame a set of required alternative moves and outcomes, (b) the rules to be binding to all other players, and (c) the other players to equally expect (a) and (b). These 'constitutive expectancies' match what Schütz ([1932] 1967) calls the 'natural attitude': most of the time actors take their everyday world and the fact that they are engaged in social relations for granted.

I cannot go into any detail here at all, except to note that Schütz's theoretical insights not only inspired Garfinkel's ethnomethodology but also Berger and Luckmann's (1966) social-constructionist sociology of knowledge and, subsequently, neoinstitutionalist organisation theory. What is important here is that the 'natural attitude' of taking the social world for granted implies that actors are both empowered and constrained by institutions as routine-reproduced systems of rules (Jepperson 1991) and that they are also part of the process of institutionalisation: '*Society is a human product. Society is an objective reality. Man is a social product*' (Berger and Luckmann 1966, p. 61; original emphasis).

In terms of the trust game this means that when a trust–honour sequence is institutionalised actors will follow that sequence and, notably, not out of utility considerations, but because it defines them as actors and to them 'it may be literally unthinkable to act otherwise' (Zucker 1986, p. 58). As Lane and Bachmann (1996, p. 370) point out, the 'first problem is not how to select profitable occasions for trust investment but, above all else, to establish shared meaning as a fundamental precondition of the possibility of social action'. In the natural attitude, trust rests on the taken-for-granted expectations that are shared, fulfilled and maintained by those involved in an interaction and that may still be disappointed, but *nevertheless* form the basis of trusting action.

Institutional Isomorphism

How actors come to follow institutionalised patterns of trusting interaction can be elucidated by the mechanism of *institutional isomorphism* introduced by DiMaggio and Powell (1983). Isomorphism generally refers to the force that makes one unit in a population resemble other units that face the same environment. In this sense, isomorphic trust would mean to place and honour trust, because everybody does it. There are three forms of institutional isomorphism: coercive isomorphism stems from external pressure, mimetic isomorphism is the copying of others' behaviour in an ambiguous or uncertain context, and normative isomorphism means similar behaviour due to socialisation and learned roles. Generally, institutional isomorphism is sustained by the legitimacy that can be gained from compliance with institutions.

However, actors are not fully determined to comply or at least they may decouple their actions and merely pretend or dramatically enact institutional compliance (Meyer and Rowan 1977). What to the observer look like successful trust–honour sequences could just be 'façades of trust' (Hardy et al. 1998). While it often makes and gives sense to the actor to blend in, she still has 'agency' (Beckert 1999) in many respects. In conclusion trust–honour sequences may stem from institutional isomorphism and, in this sense, they are explained by external pressures to conform, the imitation of others in the face of uncertainty, or internalised norms and roles. However they are not due to utilitarian motives, but to the empowering taken-for-grantedness of institutions. Sanctions guide action more than they deter it.

Rules, Roles and Routines

To give more plasticity to the idea that trust can be based on institutions, let us consider how rules, roles and routines on the one hand constrain the actor, but on the other hand enable her to have expectations, find meaning and thus become socially active in the first place. Rules, for example, whether laid down in contract and law or left unwritten and subtle, not only give legitimacy and imply sanctions that could be understood in rational utilitarian terms, but more importantly define a part of social reality and the social identity of the actors therein. As Garfinkel (1967) shows in his (in)famous breaching experiments, actors regularly rely on the normalcy of the situation and the validity of basic rules. They actively 'normalize' and redefine events that fall outside of the rules in order to maintain the game and thereby accomplish a social world.

In a similar vein roles enable the individual to become socially active, but the institutions that prescribe roles are like an 'unwritten libretto' which only exists empirically if it is realised by actors (Berger and Luckmann 1966, p. 75). Seligman (1997) objects that trust is about role negotiability rather than role expectations, but he also accepts that roles give confidence and that not all roles can be negotiable all the time all at once. Finally, as with rules and roles, 'the reality of everyday life maintains itself by being embodied in routines, which is the essence of institutionalization' (Berger and Luckmann 1966, p. 149; see also Giddens 1984, p. 60). Routines can be seen as a basis for trust, since, for example, most parents will not fret every morning when their child leaves for school, as entrusting the child to the care of bus drivers, teachers and others is part of a daily routine.

Yet once again this brings up higher-order problems of trust, first of all in the reliability of the routine and in the motivation and ability of the actors involved not to deviate from the programme of action – for whatever reason. Rules, roles and routines are bases for trust in so far as they represent taken-for-granted expectations that give meaning to, but cannot guarantee, their own fulfilment in action.

Trust in Institutions

If the idea of institution-based trust as such is convincing, at least as a partial explanation for trust–honour sequences in dilemma-beset situations (Zucker 1986), then this raises at least one further issue, namely the problem that institution-based trust requires trust in those institutions. They are both *sources* and *objects* of trust (Sydow 1998). That this is a crucial point is demonstrated by Walgenbach (2001, p. 696) who finds in a sample of German companies that 'the adoption of the ISO 9000 standards and the certification of the quality system did not, as was intended, result in trust in inter-organizational relationships. On the contrary, it produced distrust in the ISO 9000 certification.' Obviously, institutions cannot be effective bases for trust, if they are not trusted themselves (Child and Möllering 2003).

Unlike Shapiro (1987, p. 652) who worries about an 'inflationary spiral of escalating trust relationships' due to the requirement of guarding the guardians, Luhmann ([1968, 1975] 1979) and Giddens (1990) propose that trust in institutions as abstract systems is possible indirectly. The upshot of both Luhmann and Giddens's ideas, which I cannot review in detail here, is that trust in an institution means confidence in its reliable functioning but has to be based mainly on trust in visible controls or representative performances rather than on internal workings of the institution as a whole. It follows that there remains vulnerability and uncertainty in *institutional trust*, too.

Altogether, I would describe *institutional trust* as being ontologically motivated, because this ideal type emphasises that the actors' existence as social beings hinges on their successful performance of trust–honour sequences, if and when these are institutionalised. The ideal type of *institutional trust* draws on 'disembedded' (Giddens 1990) social practices as global points of reference. It is therefore also rather generically valid from the trustor's point of view, because it can be transferred to other trustees. As the corresponding rules, roles and routines are generic, the method of *institutional trust* can be called deductive. With a high degree of institutionalisation, the perceived risk will be low. As pointed out before, a leap of faith will be required in this form of trust, too, but it should be very habitual as the trustor simply follows the usual procedure.

Once again, if the ideal type were empirical reality, the category of trust would not be required as trust–honour sequences could be fully explained as enactments of institutional requirements. In conclusion, the ideal type of *institutional trust* offers a genuine alternative to *rational trust*, but institutions as bases for trust also help the trustor only up to a point. She still needs to deal with irreducible vulnerability and uncertainty.

ACTIVE TRUST

The point of departure for the third ideal type, called *active trust* here, is that the actors are unable to refer to anything like Figure 2.1 in their interactions. There are no defined rules, roles and routines and no corresponding estimates of pay-offs either, meaning that in this extreme scenario neither *rational* nor *institutional trust* would be possible. There is no game to start with! I borrow the concept of 'active trust' from Giddens (1994, pp. 186–7) who introduces the term to describe how close relationships need to be actively cultivated in complex and fast-changing late-modern societies. According to Giddens, actors are nowadays increasingly unable to maintain a natural attitude and take their everyday world for granted as a world known in common with others. Similarly Luhmann (1988, p. 105) observes 'an increasing diversification and particularization of familiarities'.

If the actors facing such a situation interact, nevertheless, then I would call this *active trust*, because they actively create through their interaction the trust–honour sequence which initially they are not even able to describe meaningfully or calculate rationally. In *active trust* the actors *just do it*!

Instead of allowing social complexity to paralyse them, they experiment and continuously communicate about the changing game conditions. Thus, a mutually beneficial sequence just like the trust–honour sequence may emerge, although – and because – the actors make themselves vulnerable while finding out if it does. In many ways, this resembles what Zucker (1986) calls 'process-based trust'. Zucker, however, means that trust is produced over time on the basis of positive experiences. In *active trust*, however, the actors cannot extrapolate, because both the past and the future are uncertain. That 'active trust development' is a meaningful and real possibility has been demonstrated in our study of trust in the management of Mainland Chinese Operations from Hong Kong (Child and Möllering 2003).

By way of illustration, consider the scenario captured in Defoe's ([1791] 1994) *Robinson Crusoe* and imagine that the protagonist finds out that the island is inhabited. He can hardly be familiar with the institutions or pay-offs that guide the interactions of people living in this world and in particular he does not know which treatment they give stranded strangers. One day he approaches the islanders for the first time. It does not take much imagination to see the willpower this takes, how risky it feels, which hopes and fears will be in his mind simultaneously and how this *active trust* might either go horribly wrong for him or initiate a reflexive process of interaction that promotes his rescue from the island or even his integration into the island community. I will now consider a few concepts that should make this combination of pragmatism and reflexivity in *active trust* clearer.

Familiarity, Unfamiliarity and Familiarisation

According to Luhmann (1988, p. 95) 'trust has to be achieved within a familiar world' and while familiarity is an unavoidable fact of life and a precondition for actors having a life-world to start with, building on familiarity in trust is contingent and risky (Luhmann [1968, 1975] 1979; Schütz [1932] 1967). If an actor considers something as familiar, she presumes the unfamiliar, too. Everything could be different: You never know. At the same time what is familiar to her and what unfamiliar also depends on herself. From within her familiar life-world she can transfer the unfamiliar into the familiar, but thereby needs to draw reflexively on what she is already familiar with. By introducing part of the unfamiliar into the previously familiar her life-world changes. The main point for *active trust* here is that actors engage in familiarisation as the transfer between the unfamiliar and the familiar. Thus, if trust generally builds on familiarity with, for example, institutions or potential pay-offs, then *active trust* in a relatively unfamiliar context builds on reflexive familiarisation.

Principle of Gradualness

Actors do not heroically or foolishly increase their vulnerability totally all at once, exposing themselves to the uncertain actions of unfamiliar others. Instead *active trust* would set off according to something like the 'principle of gradualness' that Luhmann ([1968, 1975] 1979, p. 41) recommends for trust development, meaning that at first fairly short trust games with relatively small stakes are initiated, hopefully establishing and at some point even institutionalising a trust–honour pattern while gradually expanding the time horizon and increasing the degree of vulnerability. This principle does require, though, that at least one of the actors involved is prepared to take the first step, often without being able to know how big or small this step really is. Robinson, for instance, may be warmly welcomed or hotly boiled by the islanders. Hence *active trust* can be regarded as experimental and innovative in the sense of trying out something previously unknown, but even small initial experiments might not be safe. Gradualness also highlights that *active trust* is a more processual category in comparison to the more structural and immediate *rational* and *institutional trust*.

Continuous Communication

Another key aspect in Giddens's (1994) concept of 'active trust' is the fact that late-modern actors are not only aware how limited their familiarity is in relation to the infinite unfamiliarity out there, but that what may be taken for granted and familiar today may not be the same anymore tomorrow. *Active trust* therefore requires actors to continuously and intensively communicate in order to maintain reflexively the constitution of their social world, including the trust games played in social interaction. In the conditions of late modernity *active trust* is therefore more than an initial process that is only required as long as a trust game with stable institutions and pay-offs is still being gradually established. *Rational* or *institutional trust*, in this scenario, may never replace *active trust* eventually, if the trust game has to be recreated before every interaction in an ongoing process. Every move is a first move, because the players and rules keep changing.

Summarising the features of *active trust* as an ideal type, I describe the motive behind this form of trust as pragmatic, as the actor wants to avoid social paralysis or paranoia, but proceeds rather tentatively. Her point of reference, in the extreme, is individual in the sense that she needs to fall back on her self-trust, because due to the presumed unfamiliarity she can draw neither locally on potential pay-off and trustworthiness estimates, nor globally on institutionalised rules. Her trust as an expectation towards the trustee has to be ambiguous, in terms of validity, because in the ideal-typical case her placement of trust is an experiment without a predictable outcome. This means that she uses an experimental method that I would prefer to call innovative, if only to highlight the fact that *active trust* means experimenting with new trust games. Even though the principle of gradualness suggests that the stakes can be kept small, the perceived risk in *active trust* should be high, definitely in comparison to the other two ideal types, because the actor is quite aware of the ambiguous and experimental nature of her trust placements. This also implies that the trustor must bring herself to take the trust initiative, and her leap of faith is thus rather active.

The ideal type of *active trust* is certainly just as extreme as the other two ideal types and it is equally unthinkable to be found in a pure form in empirical situations, for it is impossible that an actor faces a totally unfamiliar world. As long as there is some familiarity, there will at least be some background expectations on which to initiate a new trust game. As Simmel ([1908] 1950, p. 318) points out, complete ignorance would make trust an obsolete category just as much as complete knowledge would do. In the end active trust gives a third, distinct explanation for why trust–honour sequences come about, but to say that the trustor should pragmatically *just do it* also helps her only up to the point at which she might then overcome at least momentarily her worries about making herself more vulnerable.

Table 2.1   Three ideal types of trust

	Rational Trust	Institutional Trust	Active Trust
Motive	utilitarian	ontological	pragmatic
Reference	local	global	individual
Validity	specific	generic	ambiguous
Method	inductive	deductive	innovative
Perceived Risk	low	low	high
Leap of Faith	automatic	habitual	active

SUSPENSION: THE LEAP OF FAITH

Table 2.1 summarises the characteristic features of the three ideal types of trust that I have presented in the previous sections. I would like to stress that these types of trust are indeed ideal types and therefore exaggerated for analytical purposes. At the same time, however, they do represent three broad streams in trust research which emphasise respectively the *rational*, *institutional* or *active* element in trust. While sometimes these streams flow together in the literature, they certainly combine in empirical manifestations of trust where it may be difficult, albeit not impossible, to judge how much of an observable trust–honour sequence can be explained in terms of rational, institutional or active trust. Hence, I would not engage in partisan arguments about which type of trust is the main one. And we should also be open to further ideal types, perhaps *emotional trust* (Lewis and Weigert 1985).

However, I do think that there is one element in all types of trust which runs the risk of being explained away by ideal-type concepts of trust and this element is the leap of faith. It is required for all trust, if we want to retain that part of the definition of trust which expresses that to trust means to be vulnerable to the ultimately uncertain actions of others. I propose that this element not only needs to be acknowledged as an inconvenient residual (Elster 1989), but must be examined more carefully, if trust research is to contribute something meaningful that most economists, institutionalists or pragmatists do not already know.

Just to recapture briefly I have argued that neither rational grounds nor institutional grounds nor tentative experimentation can produce trust without the actor having to somehow deal with irreducible vulnerability and uncertainty. Many authors recognise this, mostly implicitly, when they say along the lines of Lewis and Weigert (1985, p. 969) that 'to trust is to live *as if* certain rationally possible futures will not occur'. The denotation of the *as if* must not be underestimated. How can a trustor be aware that her pay-off estimates may be completely wrong, that an institutionalised routine may fail, or that a seemingly harmless experimental interaction may be disastrous – and still act on trust *as if* this were unproblematic? This further element that I am after is described by Simmel as 'a further element of socio-psychological quasi-religious faith' ([1900] 1990, p. 179; see also Möllering 2001).

In line with Simmel I would say that, as suggested by the ideal types above, trust rests on good reasons up to a point but then requires faith in order to be realised. Giddens (1991) expresses this view explicitly when he says that trust 'presumes a leap to commitment, a quality of "faith" which is irreducible' (p. 19) and defines trust as 'the vesting of confidence in persons or abstract systems, made on the basis of a "leap into faith" which brackets ignorance or lack of information' (p. 244).

The leap of faith is a very disconcerting notion in Kierkegaard's ([1843] 1985, pp. 83–95) *Fear and Trembling* where it refers to Abraham's 'teleological suspension of the ethical' as he is supposed to sacrifice his son Isaac by God's will. It has been adopted in trust research without the full weight of Kierkegaard's analysis not only by Giddens but also for example by Seligman (1997), Zaheer et al. (1998) and Sztompka (1999). The leap of faith is very instructive in capturing the further element in trust, because it contains both the irreducible and unjustifiable quality of 'faith' on the one hand, and the 'leap' as a reflection of the actor's agency on the other.

Other attempts at capturing the Simmelian 'further element' draw on the vocabulary of phenomenology and talk about suspension and bracketing. The suspension of doubt about the reality of the life-world defines the Schützian 'natural attitude' and the idea of bracketing goes back even further to the phenomenological method where putting something into brackets means not to deny its reality in order to be able to analyse how it is experienced (Schütz [1932] 1967). Again the notion of suspension, or bracketing, is highly instructive for the further element in trust. It is probably even more useful than the leap of faith, because suspension connotes that the trustor's doubts about whether she should really increase her vulnerability are not eliminated but transcended for the time being. This matches Luhmann's ([1968, 1975] 1979, p. 79) usage of suspension in the Hegelian sense of *Aufhebung* where a synthesis transcends thesis and antithesis, thereby simultaneously preserving and rescinding them. As with the leap of faith, suspension retains an element of agency on the part of the actor who could, in principle, question everything, but in practice overcomes her doubts and arrives in trust at what Simmel ([1908] 1950, p. 318) calls 'a hypothesis certain enough for practical conduct'.

In conclusion, trust not only relies to a greater or lesser extent on available good reasons, but also on a kind of tranquiliser (Beckert 2002). Against this background we can appreciate the following provocative claim by Giddens (1990, p. 33): '*All* trust is in a certain sense blind trust!' I would take this to mean that all trust is *partially* blind, because Giddens certainly does not mean that from the trustor's point of view trust is random. The same applies to Frankel's (1977, p. 36) statement that trust enters 'where more exact knowledge is not available' and Lewis and Weigert's (1985, p. 976) remark that '[t]rust begins where prediction ends'. In both sources it is assumed that the actor looks for good reasons first, but that the *interesting* or *essential* element of trust is the further element which I prefer to call suspension and which, notably, is only one element of trust, but one that always has to be present in all trust. This means that not only *active trust* but effectively all trust requires that trustors *just do it*.

AN ILLUSTRATION: SWIFT TRUST

The well-known study on *swift trust* by Meyerson et al. (1996) can serve as an illustration of how the trust concept proposed in this chapter applies to management practice. The authors look at the problem of trust specifically in temporary work groups and teams. These are typically formed in order to accomplish a specific, often complex and critical project through the collaboration of specialists who possess very different but interdependent skills. It is kind of surprising that temporary work groups can operate very quickly as if team members trust each other although, at first sight, there seems to have been no opportunity to establish bases for trust, while incentives for opportunistic behaviour do exist. Hence Meyerson et al. speak of 'swift trust'.

Each of the three ideal types of trust that I have introduced offers a partial explanation for this *swift trust*. It could be explained as *rational trust*, for example, because the team members realise immediately that their interests are encapsulated and that there is a shadow of the future, if not in the sense of repeated interaction, then at least in the sense of having to lose a professional reputation. However, encapsulation of interest might not be enough to prevent free-riding in a group. And the shadow of the future can lose its power, if a team member is not professionally committed or if the potential gain from exploiting trust is large enough for her, all of which the other team members probably cannot know for sure.

Alternatively, *swift trust* could be explained as *institutional trust*, for example, because team members will take many written and unwritten rules for granted and because they are assigned specific roles on the team. According to Meyerson et al., trust in temporary teams is enhanced by role clarity and by people dealing with each other more as roles than as individuals. In other words, the natural attitude in temporary teams may be to comply with the usual rules and roles which institutionalise trustful interaction. Nevertheless this can only be a partial explanation, too, because there is no certainty for the trustor that everybody on the team knows the rules and roles and is competent and willing to fulfil them.

Third, *active trust* offers another explanation for *swift trust*. Meyerson et al. (1996, p. 170) observe that 'people have to wade in on trust rather than wait while experience gradually shows who can be trusted and with what'. The teams have to get on with it and not let themselves be impressed by the unfamiliarity of some team members or the given task. At the same time, as the study shows, the team members tend not to commit themselves too much in the beginning. They follow the principle of gradualness and maybe it just so happens that quite often the first collaborative experiments succeed and that within hours of working together *active trust* builds up reflexively. On projects team members also need to communicate frequently which, as I would argue with Giddens, makes it possible to maintain trust even in a rapidly changing context. However, there are also quite a number of projects that go wrong, especially in early phases, and turn a cooperative team into a competitive one, which is a threat faced by all team members in every project, meaning that they cannot count on *active trust* to always succeed.

As cursory as this illustration may be I believe it shows that all three ideal types of trust offer plausible but partial explanations for swift trust. Putting them all together will give an aggregate explanation that could be more complete, but could also contain some irreconcilable contradictions, given the disparate basic assumptions underlying the three ideal types. If we asked the team members directly, they would surely be able to give us reasons for their swift trust (Luhmann [1968, 1975] 1979, p. 26) but, more likely than not, those reasons will not be more compelling than what can be inferred using ideal types. In the end, if trust 'may rest upon particular reasons, but is not explained by them' (Simmel [1900] 1990, p. 179), the conclusion is bound to be that notwithstanding some good reasons for swift trust people *just do it*. In the future this should not be the point at which trust research wraps up, but where it begins to become interesting and challenging: what does it mean to *just do it*? If it means a leap of faith, then we may not ask about the faith, but about the leap. If it means suspension, then we may find out what is bracketed and what causes doubts to return. These kinds of issues should let trust research come into its own. My feeling, however, is that there will remain the 'brute fact' of a fairly large 'unknown residual' and not only 'for the time being' (Elster 1989, p. 150). We might treat this residual as an inconvenience, or we might regard it as a symbol for the gap that the leap of faith has to cross and begin to investigate how this is accomplished, thereby getting closer to the essence of trust.

CONCLUSIONS

In this chapter, I bring together three very different views of trust that are more or less common and popular in the trust literature. I conceptualise them as the ideal types of *rational, institutional* and *active trust* to bring out the differences, only to conclude later on that all three contribute to the explanation of trust. However, in as much as they all provide good reasons for trust both for trustors and for observers, we always reach a point where the defining element of trust as an acceptance of vulnerability in the face of another's uncertain actions will not be explained away, but needs to be overcome by a suspension of doubt or leap of faith. I therefore define trust as a process of building on available good reasons and suspending irreducible social vulnerability and uncertainty *as if* they were favourably resolved. While I can only offer preliminary thoughts on suspension, I am convinced that any major contribution to our understanding of trust has to take it seriously. *Just do it.*

ACKNOWLEDGEMENTS

A first draft of this chapter was based partly on an article in German which benefited a lot from constructive comments by Jörg Sydow. At EURAM 2002 in Stockholm, I received helpful suggestions especially from my discussant Antoinette Weibel. This final draft owes much to Katinka Bijlsma-Frankema who was very enthusiastic and supportive and raised a number of points which have led me to revise the chapter substantially. If she does not recognise it anymore, this is also due to the fact that I have included additional ideas from my doctoral thesis (Möllering 2003).

REFERENCES

Axelrod, R. (1984), *The Evolution of Co-operation*, New York: Basic Books.
Bacharach, M. and D. Gambetta (2001), 'Trust in Signs', in K.S. Cook (ed.), *Trust in Society*, New York: Russell Sage Foundation, pp. 148–84.
Baier, A. (1986), 'Trust and antitrust', *Ethics*, **96** (2), 231–60.
Beckert, J. (1999), 'Agency, entrepreneurs, and institutional change. The role of strategic choice and institutionalized practices in organizations', *Organization Studies*, **20** (5), 777–99.
Beckert, J. (2002), 'Vertrauen und die performative Konstruktion von Märkten', *Zeitschrift für Soziologie*, **31** (1), 27–43.
Berger, P.L. and T. Luckmann (1966), *The Social Construction of Reality*, Garden City, NY: Doubleday.
Child, J. and G. Möllering (2003), 'Contextual confidence and active trust development in the Chinese business environment', *Organization Science*, **14** (1), 69–80.
Coleman, J.S. (1990), *Foundations of Social Theory*, Cambridge, MA: Harvard University Press.
Dasgupta, P. (1988), 'Trust as a Commodity', in D. Gambetta (ed.), *Trust: Making and Breaking Co-operative Relations*, Oxford: Basil Blackwell, pp. 49–72.
Defoe, D. ([1791] 1994), *Robinson Crusoe*, London: Penguin Books.
Deutsch, M. (1973), *The Resolution of Conflict*, New Haven: Yale University Press.
DiMaggio, P.J. and W.W. Powell (1983), 'The iron cage revisited: institutional isomorphism and collective rationality in organizational fields', *American Sociological Review*, **48** (2), 147–60.
Eisenhardt, K.M. (1989), 'Agency theory: an assessment and review', *Academy of Management Review*, **14** (1), 57–74.
Elster, J. (1989), *The Cement of Society: A Study of Social Order*, Cambridge: Cambridge University Press.
Frank, R.H. (1987), 'If homo economicus could choose his own utility function, would he choose one with a conscience?', *American Economic Review*, **77** (4), 593–604.
Frankel, S.H. (1977), *Money: Two Philosophies*, Oxford: Basil Blackwell.

Gambetta, D. (1988), 'Can We Trust Trust?', in D. Gambetta (ed.), *Trust: Making and Breaking Co-operative Relations*, Oxford: Basil Blackwell, pp. 213–37.

Garfinkel, H. (1963), 'A Conception of, and Experiments with, 'Trust' as a Condition of Stable Concerted Actions', in O.J. Harvey (ed.), *Motivation and Social Interaction*, New York: The Ronald Press Company, pp. 187–238.

Garfinkel, H. (1967), *Studies in Ethnomethodology*, Englewood Cliffs, NJ: Prentice Hall.

Giddens, A. (1984), *The Constitution of Society*, Berkeley: University of California Press.

Giddens, A. (1990), *The Consequences of Modernity*, Cambridge: Polity Press.

Giddens, A. (1991), *Modernity and Self-identity*, Cambridge: Polity Press.

Giddens, A. (1994), 'Risk, Trust, Reflexivity', in U. Beck, A. Giddens and S. Lash (eds), *Reflexive Modernization*, Cambridge: Polity Press, pp. 184–97.

Hann, M.S. (1968), 'Die Idee des Vertrauens bei Konfuzius', in J. Schwartländer (ed.), *Verstehen und Vertrauen*, Stuttgart: Kohlhammer, pp. 27–38.

Hardin, R. (1993), 'The street-level epistemology of trust', *Politics & Society*, **21** (4), 505–29.

Hardy, C., N. Phillips and T. Lawrence, T. (1998), 'Distinguishing Trust and Power in Interorganizational Relations: Forms and Façades of Trust', in C. Lane and R. Bachmann (eds), *Trust Within and Between Organizations*, Oxford: Oxford University Press, pp. 64–87.

Hollis, M. (1998), *Trust Within Reason*, Cambridge: Cambridge University Press.

James Jr., H.S. (2002), 'The trust paradox: a survey of economic inquiries into the nature of trust and trustworthiness', *Journal of Economic Behavior & Organization*, **47** (3), 291–307.

Jensen, M.C. and W.H. Meckling (1976), 'Theory of the firm: managerial behavior, agency costs, and ownership structure', *Journal of Financial Economics*, **3** (4), 305–60.

Jepperson, R.L. (1991), 'Institutions, Institutional Effects, and Institutionalism', in W.W. Powell and P.J. DiMaggio (eds), *The New Institutionalism in Organizational Analysis*, Chicago: University of Chicago Press, pp. 143–63.

Kee, H.W. and R.E. Knox (1970), 'Conceptual and methodological considerations in the study of trust and suspicion', *Journal of Conflict Resolution*, **14** (3), 357–66.

Kierkegaard, S. ([1843] 1985), *Fear and Trembling*, London: Penguin Books.

Lane, C. and R. Bachmann (1996), 'The social constitution of trust: supplier relations in Britain and Germany', *Organization Studies*, **17** (3), 365–95.

Levinthal, D. (1988), 'A survey of agency models of organization', *Journal of Economic Behavior & Organization*, **9** (2), 153–86.

Lewis, J.D. and A. Weigert (1985), 'Trust as a social reality', *Social Forces*, **63** (4), 967–85.

Luce, R.D. and H. Raiffa (1957), *Games and Decisions*, New York: Wiley.

Luhmann, N. ([1968, 1975] 1979), *Trust and Power: Two Works by Niklas Luhmann*, Chichester: Wiley.

Luhmann, N. (1988), 'Familiarity, Confidence, Trust: Problems and Alternatives', in D. Gambetta (ed.), *Trust: Making and Breaking Co-operative Relations*, Oxford: Basil Blackwell, pp. 94–107.

Meyer, J.W. and B. Rowan (1977), 'Institutionalized organizations: formal structure as myth and ceremony', *American Journal of Sociology*, **83** (2), 340–63.

Meyerson, D., K.E. Weick and R.M. Kramer (1996), 'Swift Trust and Temporary Groups', in R.M. Kramer and T.R. Tyler (eds), *Trust in Organizations*, Thousand Oaks: Sage, pp. 166–95.

Möllering, G. (2001), 'The nature of trust: from Georg Simmel to a theory of expectation, interpretation and suspension', *Sociology*, **35** (2), 403–20.

Möllering, G. (2003), *Trust: Social Science Theories and their Application to Organisations*, Unpublished PhD Thesis, University of Cambridge, UK, Judge Institute of Management.

Powell, W.W. and P.J. DiMaggio (eds) (1991), *The New Institutionalism in Organizational Analysis*, Chicago: University of Chicago Press.

Rousseau, D.M., S.B. Sitkin, R.S. Burt and C. Camerer (1998), 'Not so different after all: a cross-discipline view of trust', *Academy of Management Review*, **23** (3), 393–404.

Schütz, A. ([1932] 1967), *The Phenomenology of the Social World*, Evanston, IL: Northwestern University Press.

Seligman, A. (1997), *The Problem of Trust*, Princeton, NJ: Princeton University Press.

Shapiro, S.P. (1987), 'The social control of impersonal trust', *American Journal of Sociology*, **93** (3), 623–58.

Simmel, G. ([1908] 1950), *The Sociology of Georg Simmel*, New York: Free Press.

Simmel, G. ([1900] 1990), *The Philosophy of Money*, 2nd edition, London: Routledge.

Simon, H.A. ([1947] 1997), *Administrative Behavior*, 4th edition, New York: Free Press.

Sydow, J. (1998), 'Understanding the Constitution of Inter-organizational Trust', in C. Lane and R. Bachmann (eds), *Trust Within and Between Organizations*, Oxford: Oxford University Press, pp. 31–63.

Sztompka, P. (1999), *Trust: A Sociological Theory*, Cambridge: Cambridge University Press.

Walgenbach, P. (2001), 'The production of distrust by means of producing trust', *Organization Studies*, **22** (4), 693–714.

Williamson, O.E. (1993), 'Calculativeness, trust, and economic organization', *Journal of Law and Economics*, **36** (2), 453–86.

Zaheer, A., B. McEvily and V. Perrone (1998), 'Does trust matter? Exploring the effects of interorganizational and interpersonal trust on performance', *Organization Science*, **9** (2), 141–59.

Zucker, L.G. (1986), 'Production of Trust: Institutional Sources of Economic Structure, 1840–1920', in B.M. Staw and L.L. Cummings (eds), *Research in Organizational Behavior*, Vol. 8, Greenwich, CT: JAI Press, pp. 53–111.

3. Formation of trust in German–Mexican business relations[1]

Torsten M. Kühlmann

INTRODUCTION

Since the 1980s, cross-border business cooperation has gained momentum as a third form of internationalization besides direct exports and the acquisition or foundation of foreign subsidiaries (Contractor and Lorange 1988). Over the years different forms of international cooperative arrangements have been established, such as strategic alliance, joint venture, contractual production, licensing or marketing partnership. In particular this trend is sustained by small and medium-sized companies (SMEs) that try to compensate for their disadvantage of scarce resources (for example finance, know-how, management capacity) by employing cooperation strategies in their efforts for internationalization (Weber and Kabst 2000).

Yet cooperative interfirm relationships which cross national borders are difficult to manage and tend to show high failure rates. In order to explain the widespread break-up of international business cooperation, management scholars have repeatedly argued that mutual trust is of paramount importance for cross-border collaboration to be successful (Aulakh et al. 1996; Ariño et al. 2001; Child 2001; Currall and Inkpen 2002; Sako 1998).

The importance of trust stems from the interdependence of cooperating partners and the behavioural uncertainty inherent in any cooperation (Seifert 2001). *Interdependence* is characteristic for a cooperation because the goals of one partner can only be obtained depending on the cooperating partner's choice of means, which takes the interests of both parties into consideration. Cooperating partners depend on the longstanding existence of the collaboration, because they make transaction-specific investments that only pay off in the long run, share valuable know-how, or refrain from competition with each other. *Behavioural uncertainty* in cooperation is due to the freedom of action that both partners have kept back. Therefore, there is no perfect guarantee whether the partner actually complies to the agreed-upon objectives of the cooperation. Opportunism proves to be a central risk. Opportunistic behaviour can be described as gaining a maximum of advantage for oneself regardless of the partner's costs (for example application of the newly acquired partner's know-how in order to strengthen one's own market position).

Trust is a social mechanism that enables people to act in situations of interdependence and behavioural uncertainty (Luhmann 2000). Although many definitions of trust from different disciplines have been offered, previous conceptualizations have emphasized two major components of trust (Rousseau et al. 1998; Currall and Inkpen 2002). First, trust reflects subjective expectations about the partner's competence and benevolence. The trustor assumes that the trustee is able and willing to acknowledge and respect the interests of the trustor as well as his own interests. A trusting partner expects from his cooperating counterpart professional competence as well as goodwill (Barber 1983; Shaw 1997; Sako 1992; Seifert 2001). These anticipations can be described as the cognitive component of trust (see Table 3.1).

Table 3.1   Components of trust

The trustor's cognitive component	• Dual expectation • based on imperfect information • about the trustee's ability (competence expectation) and • willingness (benevolence expectation) • to consider and respect the cooperation partner's interest in his actions
The trustor's behavioural component	• Disposition to make risky contributions (tangibles/intangibles)

Second, trust is signified by the decision to rely on the trustee, that is to engage in action that allows its outcomes to be determined by the trustee. Thus, trust is also made up of a behavioural component. Even though the trustor possesses only incomplete information about the competencies and intentions of the trustee, he voluntarily neglects the risk of a possible incorrect judgement. Trust needs not necessarily be granted in every respect. One can trust a person regarding timely payments, but not regarding his ability to develop a market. Depending on the area of trust, expectations regarding competence or motivation become more important (Hardin 1991; Mayer et al. 1995).

According to his decision to trust, the trustor is willing to make contributions and to refrain from measures of governance and control against opportunistic behaviour. In other words: he acts as if the cooperating partner can only choose from a limited set of cooperation-friendly actions in the future (Luhmann 2000). Contributions can be of tangible or intangible nature: investments, transfer of know-how, granting of exclusive rights, provision of personnel, and so on. These trust-based contributions are risky because the dangers, which have been trustingly ignored, still exist (Dyer and Chu 2000). Risk describes the potential of negative outcomes the trustor will experience when he places his fate into the trustee's hands and the latter turns out to be untrustworthy. Risk not only nurtures the need for trust, but also results from trust. When trusting, external risks are merely substituted by internal security about the partner's future trustworthiness.

The proposed conceptualization of trust recognizes that the referent of trust may vary (Currall and Inkpen 2002; Dyer and Chu 2000). Trust can be placed in an individual or in another organization as a whole. Following this specification, person-oriented trust in a business relationship describes the extent to which a member of one firm trusts his counterpart in the cooperating company. In contrast, organization-oriented trust represent's the individual's trust toward the partner firm as an entity.

In international/intercultural business cooperation mutual trust is of particular importance. In an international context, explicit contractual agreements tend to lose efficiency as a functional equivalent of trust because different legal systems are involved. Contracts in cross-border business cooperation are more complicated and less exhaustive. It is also more time-consuming, more expensive, and riskier to assert contractual claims across borders than within a country. The great distance of the partners does not permit regular face-to-face contacts of company representatives and makes it difficult to detect opportunistic behaviours of the other party (Ripperger 1999).

As outlined above, the need for trusting collaboration increases in cross-border cooperation. At the same time, the trust creation process between representatives of different countries/cultures is more difficult because the main requirements for trust creation are met to a far smaller extent than in national cooperation (Ripperger 1999): as a foreigner, one is not familiar with the rules of social interaction and communication that the cooperating partner adheres to. Therefore it is more difficult to deduce signs of trustworthiness from the partner's actions. Also, there is quite often a deficiency of knowledge about the existence and effectiveness of an institutional framework that monitors compliance to the rules (laws, organizations, constitutions of the economy). In many cases, there is a lack of reliable information on the reputation of the cooperating partner. In addition, nations differ systematically regarding the level of trust that is generally granted. The evolution of trust becomes even more difficult in cooperation with companies from countries such as China and Mexico where people are comparatively hesitant to trust anyone outside of their own family (Centro de Estudios Educativos 1987; Fukuyama 1995; Doney et al. 1998).

We can summarize that the need for a high level of trust and the difficulty of its evolution in an international/intercultural context constitute a 'Dilemma of Trust'. Despite the attention given to it in the literature on international collaboration, 'trust remains an under-theorized, under-researched, and therefore poorly understood phenomenon' (Child 2001: 275). In particular, the antecedents, levels and benefits of trusting cross-border business relationships have received little empirical attention from the scholars in the field. Therefore, our study is directed at understanding the nature of trust in international cooperative arrangements between firms. Specifically, we investigate the following questions:

- To which degree do cross-cultural business partners attribute trustworthy characteristics to each other?
- Do discrepancies arise between trust on the personal and the organizational level?
- What generates and stabilizes trust between business partners from different nations?
- What measures of governance and control are used by the cooperating business partners?
- Which benefits of trustful cooperation can be noticed?

RESEARCH SETTING

German–Mexican business cooperation served as the setting for our explorative research. We selected this field of international collaboration for several reasons.

First, the economic relationships between Mexico and Germany have intensified significantly in the last decade. Germany represents the principal commercial partner for Mexico in the European Union. In 2000 sales of German products in Mexico rose to 5 billion euros. Besides Brazil, Mexico receives the second highest inflow of German foreign direct investment in Latin America. The Free Trade Agreement between Mexico and the European Union, which came into force in 2000, is expected to further improve business ties between Mexico and Germany.

Second, the forms of German–Mexican cooperative arrangements differ widely, thus providing insights from a broad range of cooperation.

Our sample comprises strategic alliances and joint ventures as well as distribution partnerships.

Third, societies vary substantially in the degree to which their members trust each other and the conditions for creating trust. Fukuyama (1995) as well as Knack and Keefer (1997) distinguish high-trust societies from low-trust ones. Germany can be regarded as a high-trust society. Based on widely shared values and moral standards, and enforced by an effective legal system, Germans are inclined to trust others, even when there is limited knowledge and experience about them. By contrast, Mexico is a low-trust society, where people cannot take protection by the legal system for granted. Under these circumstances, offering trust to other persons signifies a high risk. The threat of opportunistic behaviours inhibits the development of trust.

MEASUREMENTS

To examine the role of trust in cross-border business cooperation we used semi-structured interviews. The measure of trust at the personal and organizational level was based on statements from Mexican and German managers who were asked to describe trustworthy foreign persons/ organizations in a pilot study. In addition, we adopted items from trust measures already in use, such as the 'Conditions of Trust Inventory' by Butler (1991), the 'Organizational Trust Inventory' by Cummings and Bromiley (1996), the 'Measure of Boundary Role Persons Trust' by Currall and Judge (1995), as well as the 'Scales of Organizational and Interpersonal Trust' by Zaheer et al. (1998).

The scale of person-oriented trust refers to the degree of trust a boundary role person of one company has in his counterpart of the partner firm. The scale consists of ten items, describing the trustworthy traits and actions of the other firm's boundary role person. The agreement with these statements was assessed on a 3-point Likert scale from 'strongly agree' to 'strongly disagree'. The estimated reliability for the personal trust scale in our sample is 0.65 (Cronbach's α). Company-oriented trust corresponds to the degree of trust the boundary role person of one company shows towards the partner firm as an entity. We operationalized trust on that level using ten items, tapping the extent of the trustworthy partner firm's characteristics. Likewise, the answers were measured on a 3-point Likert scale. Cronbach's α for this scale was at 0.63. In addition, we used open-ended questions to determine the strategies of trust-building, governance and control mechanisms in the partnership as well as the effects of trusting collaboration.

DATA COLLECTION

We conducted interviews in Germany as well as in Mexico during 2001. The sample for this study consisted of German small and medium-sized companies which collaborate with Mexican partner firms as well as Mexican SMEs cooperating with German companies. Lists of relevant firms were made available to us by Chambers of Commerce from both countries. For each participating company we attempted to identify and to interview the manager who is directly involved in the cooperation. As the majority of companies are owner-managed we mostly chose the owner himself as our informant. All interviews lasted approximately one to two hours and were conducted in German or Spanish. Data collection always took place at the informant's workplace. The interviews were tape-recorded and transcribed in all but five instances (in these instances detailed notes were taken).

In total, we were able to conduct interviews with 30 Mexican and 30 German informants. The companies they represented are primarily from the following industry sectors: mechanical engineering, environmental engineering and tourism. The typical form of cooperative arrangement in our sample is the distribution partnership (46 per cent).

RESULTS

Trust in Boundary Role Persons and Partner Companies

When asked to judge their boundary role person from the respective partner company, the majority of respondents assert characteristics of trustworthiness that suggest/justify a trusting attitude and action toward that person. These perceptions of trustworthness comprise behavioural as well as personal characteristics (see Figure 3.1). Most frequently the respondents stress characteristics like competence, openness, discretion and comprehensibility.

Comparing the assessments of the boundary role persons, which are given by German and Mexican respondents, we discovered the higher tendency of Mexican managers to use characteristics of trustworthiness in the evaluation of their German partners unreservedly rather than vice versa. The judgment of the respective partner's company is also dominated by trust-promoting characteristics, such as competence, honesty, reputation or fairness. Again, Mexican respondents tend to describe the partner companies more explicitly as trustworthy than vice versa (see Figure 3.2).

This general answering pattern leads to the question whether it is due to different experiences or to a culturally determined tendency towards

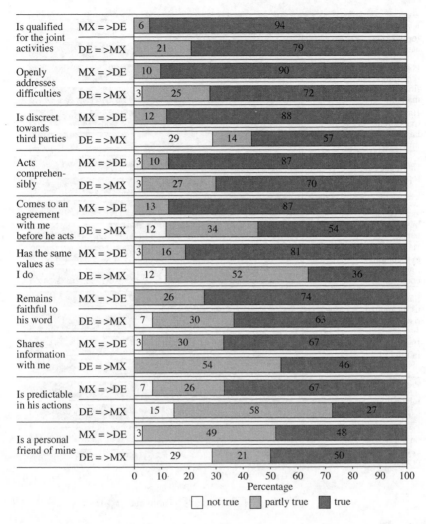

| | | not true | partly true | true |

Notes: MX = >DE: Mexican assessment of German partner; DE = >MX: German assessment of Mexican partner

Figure 3.1   Description of the boundary role person

cautious, social-harmony preserving answers. In a comparative study, Hui and Triandis (1989) demonstrated that respondents from Latin-American countries tended more often toward the extremes of a scale than Asian respondents. But the amount of detail that Mexican respondents give about their – positive – experiences with their German cooperation partners, as

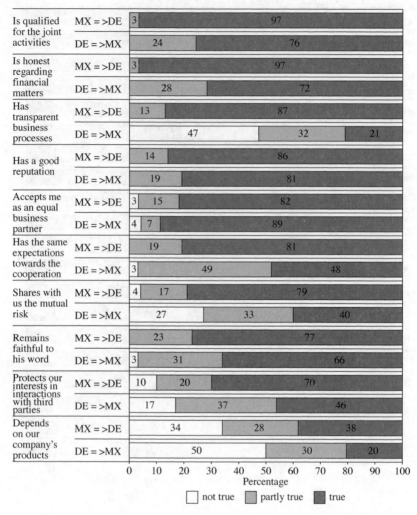

Notes: MX = > DE: Mexican assessment of German partner; DE = >MX: German assessment of Mexican partner

Figure 3.2   Description of the cooperating company

well as the comparable amount of conflict that is perceived by both the Mexican and German respondents, do not correspond with the hypothesis of a systematic response bias in the Mexican sample.

Since the positive assessment of the foreign boundary role person converges with that of the foreign cooperating company, one might assert that the respondents do not distinguish between person-oriented and company-oriented trust. In order to provide empirical evidence for this assertion, we combined both the person-oriented and the company-oriented attributes of trustworthiness in two indices of trust and correlated them. The correlation within the German sample turned out to be much smaller than the one within the Mexican sample (see Figure 3.3). Thus, Mexican respondents tend to trust a company if the boundary role persons of that company prove to be trustworthy and vice versa. Their German counterparts do not perceive any interdependence between these two types of trust.

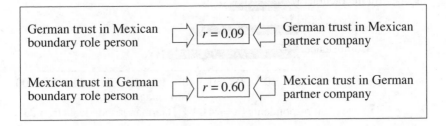

Figure 3.3 Relationship between person-oriented and company-oriented trust in the German and Mexican samples

Corresponding to this answering pattern, German respondents state more often than their Mexican counterparts that a replacement of the boundary role person would not affect their level of trust in the partner company. About one half of the German respondents expect no effect on company-oriented trust, whereas only one third of the Mexican respondents assume a lack of consequences.

Management of Trust

In the business cooperation studied, activities to manage trust take place. On average, German as well as Mexican respondents name two to three trust-building/trust-promoting measures. Considerable differences between the two samples can be recognized regarding the type of measures employed (see Figure 3.4).

About 70 per cent of the German respondents indicate building trust toward their Mexican counterparts by systematic nurturing of the personal relationship. These measures comprise phone calls, letters, visits, dinner invitations, sightseeing trips and presents. Only 30 per cent of the Mexican respondents intentionally employ these types of actions in order to create trust. Far more often than their German counterparts, Mexican respondents mention reliable business relationships and the demonstration of honesty

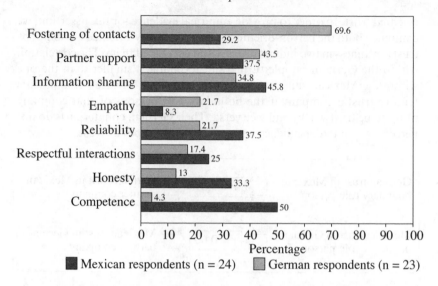

Figure 3.4   Trust-promoting measures employed by German and Mexican boundary role persons

and competence as intentionally taken measures to gain the foreign partner's trust. Apparently, both parties act as if they try to contradict the assumed heterostereotype of *the* typical German or *the* typical Mexican. German business partners attach great importance to close, friendly relationships, whereas their Mexican partners demonstrate competence, reliability and honesty.

Two additional groups of frequently used trust-building behaviours are the support of the boundary role person in the cooperating company beyond formal requirements as well as the sharing of company information. There is almost no difference between German and Mexican respondents regarding the frequency at which they report these activities.

Also a remarkable distinction in the management of trust can be observed at the organizational level. Whereas German respondents often point out their voluntary support of the partner company – for example through material contributions – as a trust-building measure, their Mexican counterparts emphasize their efforts to create transparent business processes. In other words, German companies try to contradict the heterostereotype of toughness, by generously offering assistance, whereas Mexicans try to rectify the impression of improvisation and corruption through openness. Another measure frequently used by companies from each country to develop trust is the demonstration of the company's competence (see Figure 3.5).

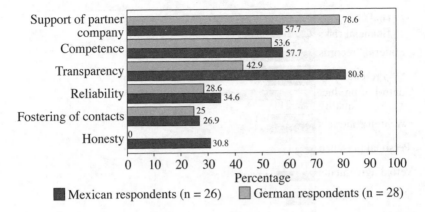

Figure 3.5   Trust-promoting measures employed by German and Mexican companies

The number of trust-building behaviours mentioned by the Mexican sample tends to be greater regarding both aspects of trust, person-oriented as well as company-oriented trust. The effective management of trust is of greater importance for Mexican partners because they are well aware of the heterostereotype of the typical Mexican ('unreliable', 'corrupt', 'improvising') and also because Mexican legislation cannot be considered an adequate substitute for trust.

Control Mechanisms in Business Cooperation

Even in trusting partnerships, companies do not stop monitoring the actions of their business partners. German respondents mentioned more often than their Mexican counterparts that they use control mechanisms (see Figure 3.6). Control measures applied by the German partners focus heavily upon a foresighted safeguarding of the financial aspect of the cooperation (for example advance payment; declaration of suretyship), whereas the Mexican partners concentrate their control activities on a retrospective analysis of the economic transaction (payments, delays, product quality) as documented in their own company's records.

From the majority of the respondents' point of view, control mechanisms have neither positive nor negative effects on their intensity of trust (see Figure 3.7). This attitude contrasts the results of numerous studies, which proved that control mechanisms sometimes have trust-destructive and sometimes trust-creating effects (Aulakh et al. 1996; Das and Teng 1998). Apparently, the respondents considered the control mechanisms as

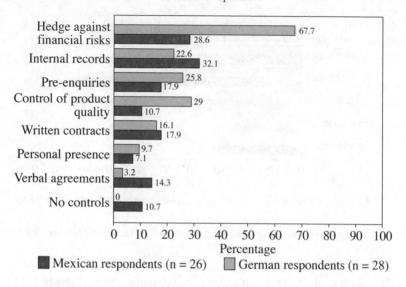

Figure 3.6   Control measures employed by German and Mexican companies

normal business routine rather than as measures based on distrust in the respective partner's competence or good faith. The majority of German respondents that state any influence at all, consider control mechanisms a sign of distrust, which subsequently reduces the level of trust. As opposed to their German counterparts, most Mexican respondents who suppose a relationship between trust and control presume control mechanisms to promote trust: control confirms the appropriateness of earlier offered trust and allows for the further development of trust.

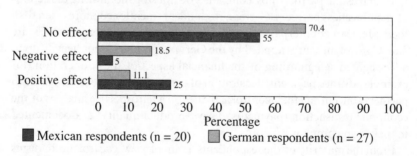

Figure 3.7   Effects of control mechanisms on trust from the German and the Mexican perspective

Effects of a Trustful Cooperation from the Boundary Role Person's Viewpoint

Mainly, German respondents attribute time-saving effects to a trustful relationship (see Figure 3.8). On the one hand, trust reduces the need for elaborate contracts and agreements. On the other hand, the trustor can manage without time-costly control mechanisms. About one half of the German respondents mention that trust helps to foster continuous cooperation. But, for the vast majority of the Mexican respondents, cooperation's stabilization is the main consequence of trust. From the Mexican point of view, trust leads to strong loyalty and faithfulness to the partner. Stability resulting from trust is so important in Mexico because of the traditionally unstable political and economic environment. Under these circumstances, long-lasting relationships between cooperating partners are especially appreciated. Furthermore about 45 per cent of the Mexican respondents attribute the reduction of behavioural uncertainty to trust.

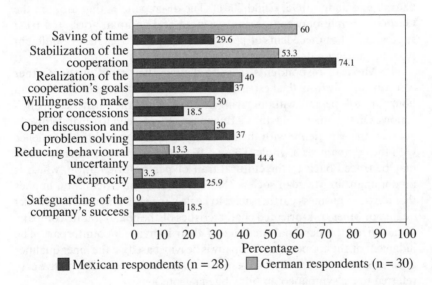

Figure 3.8   Effects of trust from the German and the Mexican perspective

DISCUSSION

Our research, concentrating on German–Mexican business cooperation, demonstrates that existing partnerships can be characterized to a great extent by characteristics that have been recognized as antecedents/correlates of person-oriented and company-oriented trust in the literature. There are considerable differences between German and Mexican partners regarding the intensity with which they attribute trust-promoting characteristics to the cooperating boundary role person/company. This finding challenges the generalizability of the often quoted rule 'I trust because you trust' (McAllister 1995) or 'trust begets trust' (Creed and Miles 1996). Contrary to this rule, the high trust Mexican partners show in their counterparts is not being reciprocated by the latter. The case of partnerships that show asymmetric trust needs to be integrated in the research on the evolution of trust (Inkpen and Currall 1998).

From the German respondents' point of view, the level of person-oriented trust is independent from the level of company-oriented trust. Yet, within the Mexican sample, we found a strong positive correlation between the two levels of trust. Thus, our empirical results only lend partial support to the importance the existing literature ascribes to the boundary role person in the development of interorganizational trust (Ring and van de Ven 1994; Currall and Judge 1995; Child 2001). The discrepancies that arose in the German sample between person-oriented and company-oriented trust suggest that the antecedents of person-oriented level trust may be different from the antecedents of company-oriented trust.

The Mexican respondents seem to deduce their trust in the partner company mainly from their experience of the trustworthiness of the German boundary role person, without giving much weight to the partner company's actions. On the other hand, the German respondents tend to separate strictly between the experience with the boundary role person and the experience with the company as a whole. These differences in the assessment process may be traced back to the cultural trait of person-orientation, which is predominant in Mexican society (Kras 1989). Person-orientation implies that Mexican business partners tend to neglect the performance, the product quality or other task-oriented characteristics of the collaborating company in favour of the personal qualities of their individual counterpart. The judgment of the cooperating company is heavily based on the inner qualities attributed to the boundary role person of that company (in the positive case referred to as 'sympatico' or 'muy buena gente').

Trust in a cooperative relationship is subjected to an active management of trust. In managing trust, both parties employ measures that are directed at contradicting the assumed heterostereotype of their respective culture. In other words, management of trust is not based on an in-depth analysis of possible areas of conflict in the cooperation, but on stereotypical assumptions about the characteristics of the typical German or the typical Mexican.

In order to reduce uncertainty about the partner company's operations, trust is coupled with continuous measures of control. The majority of respondents do not see any relationship between the level of trust and the extent of control. Nevertheless, there is a tendency for German respondents to consider control mechanisms as destructive to trust, whereas their Mexican counterparts tend to consider them trust-promoting. A possible reason for these differing opinions can be found in the differing degrees of generalized trust in German and Mexican societies. Those respondents originating from Mexico, a society with a generally low level of trust, might tend to view mechanisms of control as a guarantee for the goodwill of the partner and perceive this guarantee as the basis for the building of more trust. Members from a society with a greater propensity to trust each other, like Germany, might consider these mechanisms as substitutes for an insufficient level of trust in the partner.

The benefits of a trusting business cooperation can be found in the area of day-to-day interactions as well as in long-term business development. Whereas German respondents emphasize the operative aspect of time-saving, Mexican respondents stress the stability and security of the business relationship.

LIMITATIONS OF THIS STUDY AND IMPLICATIONS FOR FUTURE RESEARCH

There are several limitations to this study. Due to limited resources and the small size of the participating companies, we interviewed only one key person from each company. Therefore the subjectivity of their answers could not be controlled for and put into perspective by further interviews with additional company representatives. Further research projects should strive to interview several representatives from each company. Additionally, it would be desirable to supplement the respondents' perceptions with data from participant observations of the day-to-day interaction routines.

The small sample size prevented us from analysing the data separately according to different forms of cooperative arrangements. Thus, we cannot asses whether our results apply to German–Mexican cooperative relationships in general, or whether they vary according to the form of the cooperation. Furthermore, it remains unclear which forms, antecedents and consequences trust displays in cooperations that involve people from countries other than Mexico and Germany. A first insight into the question whether the results can be generalized beyond German–Mexican business cooperation will be given by ongoing research on cooperation between German and foreign SMEs in Africa and Asia.

Many authors argue that a high level of trust between cooperating companies is a central prerequisite for the cooperation's success. Although we can agree with this line of reasoning, based on the answers of our respondents, our study lacks 'hard' data about the economic success of business relationships with differing levels of trust. Therefore further research is needed to explore the influence of trust on the economic success of cross-border business cooperation.

NOTE

1. The author thanks Oliver Schumann for his assistance with the collection and analysis of the data. Funding for this research was provided by the Bavarian Research Network Area Studies (FORAREA).

REFERENCES

Ariño, A., J. de la Torre and P.S. Ring (2001), 'Relational quality: managing trust in corporate alliances', *California Management Review*, 44, 109–31.
Aulakh, P.S., M. Kotabe and A. Sahay (1996), 'Trust and performance in cross-border marketing partnerships: a behavioral approach', *Journal of International Business Studies*, 27, 1005–32.
Barber, B. (1983), *The Logic and Limits of Trust*, New Brunswick: Rutgers University Press.
Butler, J.K. (1991), 'Toward understanding and measuring conditions of trust: evolution of Conditions of Trust Inventory', *Journal of Management*, 17, 643–63.
Centro de Estudios Educativos (1987), *Cómo Somos los Mexicanos*, Mexico: Editorial CREA.
Child, J. (2001), 'Trust – the fundamental bond in global collaboration', *Organizational Dynamics*, 29, 274–88.
Contractor, F.J. and P. Lorange (eds) (1988), *Cooperative Strategies in International Business. Joint ventures and technology partnerships between firms*, Lexington: Lexington Books.
Creed, W.E.D. and R.E. Miles (1996), 'Trust in organizations. A conceptual framework linking organizational forms, managerial philosophies, and the opportunity costs of controls', in R.M. Kramer and T.R. Tyler (eds), *Trust in Organizations. Frontiers of theory and research*, Thousand Oaks: Sage, pp. 16–38.
Cummings, L.L. and P. Bromiley (1996), 'The Organizational Trust Inventory (OTI). Development and validation', in R.M. Kramer and T.R. Tyler (eds), *Trust in Organizations. Frontiers of theory and research*, Thousand Oaks: Sage, pp. 302–30.
Currall, S.C. and A.C. Inkpen (2002), 'A multilevel approach to trust in joint ventures', *Journal of International Business Studies*, 33, 479–95.
Currall, S.C. and T.A. Judge (1995), 'Measuring trust between organizational boundary role persons', *Organizational Behavior and Human Decision Processes*, 64, 151–70.
Das, T.K. and B.S. Teng (1998), 'Between trust and control: developing confidence in partner cooperation in alliances', *Academy of Management Review*, 23, 491–512.

Doney, P.M., J.P. Cannon and M.R. Mullen (1998), 'Understanding the influence of national culture on the development of trust', *Academy of Management Review*, 23, 601–20.

Dyer, J.H. and W. Chu (2000), 'The determinants of trust in supplier–automaker relationships in the U.S., Japan, and Korea', *Journal of International Business Studies*, 31, 259–86.

Fukuyama, F. (1995), *Trust. The social virtues and the creation of prosperity*, New York: Free Press.

Hardin, R. (1991), 'Trusting persons, trusting institutions', in R.J. Zeckhausen (ed.), *Strategy and Choice*, Cambridge: MIT Press, pp. 185–209.

Hui, C.H. and H.C. Triandis (1989), 'Effects of culture and response format on extreme response style', *Journal of Cross-Cultural Psychology*, 20, 296–309.

Inkpen, A.G. and S.C. Currall (1998), 'The nature, antecedents, and consequences of joint venture trust', *Journal of International Management*, 4, 1–20.

Knack, S. and P. Keefer (1997), 'Does social capital have an economic pay-off? A cross-country investigation', *Quarterly Journal of Economics*, 112, 1252–88.

Kras, E.S. (1989), *Management in Two Cultures. Bridging the gap between U.S. and Mexican managers*, Yarmouth: Intercultural Press.

Luhmann, N. (2000), *Vertrauen*, Wien: Lucius & Lucius.

Mayer, R.C., J.H. Davis and F.D. Schoorman (1995), 'An integrative model of organizational trust', *Academy of Management Review*, 20, 709–34.

McAllister, D.J. (1995), 'Affect and cognition-based trust as foundations for interpersonal cooperation in organizations', *Academy Management Journal*, 38, 24–59.

Rousseau, D.M., S. Sitkin, R.S. Burt and C. Camerer (1998), 'Not so different after all: a cross-discipline view of trust', *Academy of Management Review*, 23, 393–404.

Ring, P.S. and A.H. van de Ven (1994), 'Developmental processes of cooperative interorganizational relationships', *Academy of Management Review*, 19, 90–118.

Ripperger, T. (1999), 'Die Effizienz des Vertrauensmechanismus bei der Organisation internationaler Transaktionen', *Jahrbuch für Neue Politische Ökonomie*, 18, 257–301.

Sako, M. (1992), *Prices, quality and trust: Interfirm relations in Britain and Japan*, Cambridge: Cambridge University Press.

Sako, M. (1998), 'Does trust improve business performance?', in C. Lane and R. Bachmann (eds), *Trust Within and Between Organizations*, Oxford: Oxford University Press, pp. 88–117.

Seifert, M. (2001), 'Vertrauensmanagement in Unternehmen: eine empirische Studie über Vertrauen zwischen Angestellten und ihren Führungskräften', in R. Lang, C. Baitsch and P. Pawlowsky, *Arbeit, Organisation und Personal im Transformationsprozeß*, München: Hampp, S. 8–117.

Shaw, R.B. (1997), *Trust in Balance: Building successful organizations on results, integrity and concern*, San Francisco: Jossey-Bass.

Weber, W. and R. Kabst (2000), 'Industrialisierung mittelständischer Unternehmen: Organisationsform und Personalmanagement', in Gerhard and Lore Kienbaum Stiftung, J. Gutmann and R. Kabst (eds), *Internationalisierung im Mittelstand. Chancen – Risiken – Erfolgsfaktoren*, Wiesbaden: Gabler, S. 5–89.

Zaheer, A., B. McEvily and V. Perrone (1998), 'Does trust matter? Exploring the effects of interorganizational and interpersonal trust on performance', *Organization Science*, 9, 141–59.

4. Breaking out of distrust: preconditions for trust and cooperation between small businesses in Tanzania

Malin Tillmar

SMALL BUSINESSES AND TRUST IN TANZANIA

The importance of small businesses as catalysts for development as well as livelihoods in sub-Saharan Africa has been widely recognized (Olomi, 1999a). In Tanzania, small businesses have increasingly become important as sources of both employment and additional income, as the public sector has been shrinking (Tibandebade et al., 2001). Cooperation and networking between such small enterprises provide opportunities for them to overcome the liabilities of smallness, to survive and grow (Trulsson, 1997; K'obonyo, 1999). Through social and professional networks, they can access skills, market information, production networks and finance (McCormick, 1996).

Studies in Tanzania have strongly indicated that such cooperation is constrained by lack of trust (Ærøe, 1991, 1992; Trulsson, 1997; Bågens, 1998). Trulsson (1997) notes that building relations of trust is a deliberate strategy in handling the institutional environment, but few studies go further in elaborating on the issue of trust between businesses in the Tanzanian context (compare Ærøe, 1991; Bågens, 1993).

Within the expanding literature on trust, there is often a lack of conceptual clarity (compare Mayer et al. 1995; Huemer, 1998). Views differ regarding functions, reasons and the evolution of trust, as well as the appropriate level of analysis. Many argue that trust is influenced by culture (Fukuyama, 1996; Sztompka, 1999) and/or the institutional framework (Zucker, 1986; Sztompka, 1999). Bachmann (2000) has brought forward that cultural comparisons would be important for theoretical development on trust.[1] This chapter aims to contribute insights through studying cooperation and trust in a context seldom dealt with by western organizational researchers.

Various authors have discussed constraints of both formal and indigenous institutions on business operations in African contexts (Marris and Somerset, 1971; Hydén, 1983; Berry, 1993; Dia, 1996; Grettve, 1996; Mothander, 1996; Trulsson, 1997; K'obonyo, 1999; Rugumamu and Mutagawaba, 1999; Themba et al., 1999; and others). Only a few recognize the enabling aspects of indigenous institutions (compare Chamlee-Wright, 1997; Zakaria, 1999) or discuss how actors transform the institutional conditions (compare Tripp, 1997; Lyon, 2000). This chapter approaches small business cooperation from the perspective of the actors, while analysing both constraining and enabling elements of the formal and indigenous institutional structure.

Empirically, the study deals with businesses with fewer than ten employees[2] engaged in trade and retailing in a remotely situated town in central Tanzania. The cooperation studied between these businesses ranges from exchange of ideas and experiences to financial support. Yet the interest is not instant exchange, where immediate rewards are present. Reflecting this, cooperation is defined as when people act 'in the interest of the collectivity, and refrain from opportunistic actions even though immediate or short term rewards are not forthcoming' (Alvesson and Lindkvist, 1993, p. 433). This study will attempt to uncover 'the rules of the game' influencing small business cooperation and trust by looking more closely into indigenous practices. 'Rules of the game' is an expression used by North (1990) when referring to the formal and informal institutional framework. Here 'rules of the game' is used as an umbrella term for the various kinds of circumstances faced by business owners prescribing 'how to do things around here'.

The main objective of this study is to identify the rules of the game influencing cooperation and trust among small-business owners in urban Tanzania. In doing so the ambition is to contextualize the issue of trust. I will also tentatively, and inspired by empirical observations, elaborate on a typology of trust and give recommendations with regard to how cooperation and trust can be supported and developed.

SETTING THE SCENE

This study was conducted in Singida, which is a town with about 110,000 inhabitants.[3] It is the regional capital of Singida Region, situated in central Tanzania. Due to the defective infrastructure Singida is still a remote town, since it is about twelve hours by car from the largest town of Dar es Salaam and six hours from the town of Arusha. Apart from agriculture and livestock keeping, commerce and trade are important sources of income in the region. This study deals with micro businesses in the trade sector. Due to the widespread practise of diversification, each business owner is often involved in both buying and selling of cash crops, transport and retailing. This applies also to the informants of this study. Yet, all operate small shops in Singida town dealing with, for example, stationery, spare parts, women's clothing and food. The main problems faced concern the high costs of transportation and lack of capital for investments. As the business owners point out themselves, these problems could be minimized through cooperation.

Still, in the beginning of the longitudinal studies, practically all business owners interviewed expressed very pessimistic views on cooperation. For example, Henry Madaraka, one of the key informants, said in January 2000:

> It will just fail. If there is an economic group, then sooner or later the chairman who can take all the money will take it and disappear. It is better to do business on your own ... It is difficult to find someone trustworthy and to know whether people are actually trustworthy...

In the following sections, the reasons for this pessimism will be discussed as well as how and why the attitudes changed over time.

THEORETICAL FRAMEWORK

If there is any emerging consensus in the 'confusing potpourri' (Shapiro, 1987, p. 625) of definitions of trust in the literature, it would be that trust is closely linked to the issue of risk and vulnerability.[4] I, like the majority of authors, find it meaningful to relate trust to a situation of risk and view trust as important since it facilitates cooperation under conditions of risk. However, risk should be regarded in the broad sense of both various kinds of economic and social risks. The environment and the future are always uncertain, and thus we always need trust, although to varying degrees.

Trust is here broadly defined as 'a bet about the future contingent actions of others' (Sztompka, 1999, p. 25). This is close to Luhmann's (1979) view of trust as a 'gamble'. In Sztompka's (1999) terms, trust may be both primary, that is to say based on, for example, reputation and performance, or derived through mechanisms of accountability and/or pre-commitment. With this broad definition, I thus include both calculus-based (Lewicki and Bunker, 1996) trust, consistent with discussions within more economic approaches (compare Williamson, 1981; Hardin, 1991), and trust that goes beyond rational calculations and involves emotions (see Rousseau et al., 1998), morality (see Frank, 1988; Solomon, 1999,) and internalized social norms. I have found this combination rewarding for the understanding of various facets of trust identified in empirical studies.[5]

An overview of trust literature as well as an empirical study of small-business cooperation in an urban centre in rural Sweden (Pettersson, 1999) resulted in a typology of trust. Nine varieties of trust, illustrated in Table 4.1, were found relevant for small-business cooperation.[6]

Table 4.1   Nine varieties of trust

	Levels of trust		
Objects of trust	General	Category	Specific
Goodwill	I trust the good will of people	I trust the good will of category x	I trust the good will of person x
Commitment	I trust the commitment of people	I trust the commitment of category x	I trust the commitment of person x
Competence	I trust the competence of people	I trust the competence of category x	I trust the competence of person x

Starting with the levels of trust, one may trust people in a society generally, as in the 'culture of trust' of Sztompka (1998, 1999) and the institutionally-based trust of Zucker (1986). To Sztompka (1999) the 'culture of trust' is not only an aspect of cultural values, but it is also influenced by institutional and legal mechanisms. He argues that normative coherence (when morality, customs and law provide the basis of social interaction), stability of the social order, transparency of government agencies and mechanisms to ensure accountability are factors that need to be satisfactory in order for a society to develop general trust. Institutional mechanisms are thus not substitutes for trust in Sztompka's view (compare Fukuyama, 1996). Rather, like Zucker (1986) as well as Hagen and Choe (1998), Sztompka (1999) views institutional mechanisms as the safeguards enabling trust.[7] The view taken here follows that of Sztompka (1999) in the sense that both institutional and cultural aspects in a society may influence what is termed general trust in the typology above.

Trust may also refer to a specific relationship as in Sztompka's (1998, 1999) reflected trustworthiness and, for example, in Ring's (1996) fragile and resilient trust. There are numerous discussions and conceptualizations of this level of trust in the literature. Zucker's (1996) process-based trust as well as the calculus-, knowledge- and identity-based trust discussed by Lewicki and Bunker (1996) are examples.

My empirical study of small-business cooperation in a small Swedish town (Pettersson, 1999) highlighted the importance of another level of trust that was neither general in society, nor specific to a certain person or organization. It was found that trust was often automatically directed to different *categories* of people, such as indigenous or immigrant people, men or women and so on. It relates to the stereotyping discussed by McKnight et al. (1998) and is also similar to the characteristic-based trust of Zucker (1986), who focused on salient characteristics and kinship.

The vertical dimension in Table 4.1 concerns the object of trust, that is what kind of behaviour is trusted. Nooteboom (1996) discusses good will trust and competence trust (see also Sako, 1997). Good will trust can be related to Fukuyama (1996), who refers to loyalty, honesty and cooperative behaviour when defining trust. Ring's (1996) 'resilient trust' includes openness and discretion. By trust in '*good will*' I mean expectations of open, honest and moral behaviour. Expressed differently, trust in good will means that actors are not expected to act opportunistically.[8]

Ring also discusses 'fragile trust', where functional competence and consistent behavior is the target of trust. Sztompka (1998) notes that actors do not always expect high moral standards but rather instrumental effectiveness. Trust in good will is thus not the only relevant object of trust in business relations. An alternative object is a person's *competence*, which is here defined as the other party's possibility of performing according to the agreement, following Nooteboom (1996).

The importance of the third object of trust included in the typology, *commitment*, was suggested by an empirical study (Pettersson, 1999). Business owners were trusted for being open and honest (good will) as well as for having the possibilities to perform satisfactorily (competence). Still, cooperation did not occur since some business owners were not trusted to prioritize fulfilling their tasks, that is to commit themselves enough to joint interests and joint actions.[9] I thus suggest that our understanding of trust would be enriched by separating the three objects: good will, competence and commitment.[10]

These varieties of trust are by no means mutually exclusive and do not exist independently. The actual trust experienced by person Y regarding person X, may well be influenced by all nine varieties of trust.

METHODOLOGY

To mitigate the problem of studying a different cultural context, I designed the study to enable as broad and rich an understanding of the context and the indigenous institutions as possible. I lived for more than a year in the area studied. The total number of interviews with business owners was 55 and these were conducted in Kiswahili.[11] The research design included not only interviews with key informants and other business owners, but also participant observations and many general discussions with different people.

A model summarizing the design is presented in Appendix 4.1. It shows in which periods the different methodologies of empirical research took place. With regard to the more informal 'preparatory study' I have indicated the period of time in which it was conducted. In the rest of the appendix, each star signifies one occasion of participant observation, interview or discussion, respectively.

On Participant Observations and Action Research

The participant observations mainly concerned workshops and business training seminars, attended between November 1999 and 1 March 2000. Since important information came out of these observations, this part of the methodology in retrospect became more significant than planned. The participant observation can be related to 'action research' since I was employed as a consultant within the Sida funded 'Land Management Programme' (LAMP). My role was to build up and advise a business development team and business development training, mainly in the rural areas around Singida. This study concerns Singida Town, where some business training was also conducted. This training started in November 1999 with one session a week and continued until the beginning of March 2000. This study focuses on a few participants of that training. Participant observations from March until June concerned meetings and ceremonies within the TCCIA (Tanzanian Chamber of Commerce Industry and Agriculture).

The basis of action research is that it is not only about understanding or explaining a social reality, but also about developing a situation (van Beinum, 1998). It also involves recognizing and respecting the 'empirical object as a subject' (ibid., p. 4). This has characterized the study, which could also be described as clinically oriented (Normann, 1975). Both understanding the external circumstances faced by business owners, and their own perceptions and views, have been focused on. This has been done with the interest of facilitating their understanding of how to handle their external circumstances (ibid.).

I have sympathy with the view that both practical interests and research are important and that knowledge for both purposes can be developed in daily work (see Argyris and Schön, 1991). When conducting the Tanzanian study one ambition was to generate knowledge relevant for both practical and theoretical purposes through conscious reflection in daily work. I used Molander's (1993) discussion of knowledge in action to make my reflections more conscious. Developing knowledge in action requires an alternation between pools in four spectra, Molander argues. The spectra concern: part and whole, closeness and distance, criticisms and confidence, action and reflection.

In my view, the first two spectra are linked to each other. When a researcher reflects over a part, for example the behaviour of a business owner, closeness is important.[12] Yet, to see patterns and understand the conditions as a whole, it is necessary to distance oneself from the specific situation. Alvesson and Deetz (2000) capture the idea when they say that reflective social research is about being familiar with a situation, without getting stuck in that familiarity. It has been my ambition to achieve this balance. The balance between criticism and confidence was also important. When I acted as Business Development Advisor I naturally had confidence in what I did. At the same time, a critical perspective is needed to achieve conscious reflection. It was my ambition to succeed in this alternation through continuously evaluating my work, with the purpose of improving it. During these periods the critical perspective was in focus. In the same way, some periods were characterized by action and other periods by reflection. The alternation between reflection and action took place over the hours of the day as well as the days of the week. During autumn 2000 and February–May 2001, reflection was the only focus. I terminated my assignment as Business Development Advisor in June 2000 and returned as a consultant during January 2001, when I also conducted interviews.

Some of the trainers who worked with business development were singled out over time as 'dialogue partners'. These trainers interacted frequently with business owners in their daily work, through education, advisory services or information meetings. As a researcher I had regular dialogues with them in order to get background information and to confirm or contrast views expressed by business owners. I established what Jonsson (2001) calls an 'interactive system of dialogue', that is, a forum for discussions which does not belong either in the world of the practitioner or in the world of the researcher. Such a system of dialogue is rather a link between these worlds. The most important dialogue partners have been Mr Mechack at the Tazanian Chamber of Commerce Industry and Agriculture (TCCIA), Mr Tawaga and two other business trainers. My relationships to them have to a high degree been characterized by joint action and joint learning (compare van Beinum, 1998). The dialogues have been significant and are presented separately in the model, since they have not been counted as interviews. The 'general discussions' (see Appendix 4.1) were held continuously in informal settings of everyday life and are difficult to quantify.

On Interviews

The 55 interviews were unstructured and often driven by examples brought up by the informants. Topics covered were: social and cultural rules of the game, ways of relating to other business owners, experiences and attitudes concerning cooperation, issues constraining and enabling cooperation and so on. The duration of the interviews varied between one and two hours. The model shows when they were conducted. I have first listed the four selected key informants and noted when I talked to them. These are two male and two female business owners that participated in the training. Then, I have specified interviews with the actors who served as 'substitute key informants' during the second period of empirical studies in January 2001, when two of the key informants unfortunately were not available. Interviews with others, who during the process became important sources of empirical information, are then specified. Other interviewed business owners such as chairmen within the TCCIA, successful business owners in town and other actors described in the empirical section, are grouped together under the title 'others'.

Combining the Methods

The risk that I experienced with combining action research with interviews was that interviewees would have difficulty separating my role as a development worker and my role as a researcher. When I conducted interviews, I therefore regarded it as important to clarify my role. Many actors in the area recognized me as a development worker. I saw a potential risk that business owners could try to influence my view of their operations, hoping to obtain credits or other benefits from me and/or the project. I carefully explained that discussions and interviews were not linked to the development project and that information I was given about specific businesses and specific cooperation would not affect decisions within my development work. My impression was that the selected informants and key interviewees understood this distinction. Furthermore, the risk of bias related to my role as a development worker was minimized by the fact that the development project was focused on rural areas and the interviews were conducted with actors in the urban area.

THE CASE OF SINGIDA IN TANZANIA

This section aims at giving an overview of 'the rules of the game' as well as changes observed through the empirical study. These issues will then be elaborated on further in the next section.

The Rules of the Game

It is obvious that the low capacity of the formal institutional framework in Tanzania constrains business cooperation and contributes to the negative attitudes expressed. None of the business owners interviewed trust the police or the courts. These institutions are referred to as corrupt and not of any help in case of fraud. An interviewee for example said the following:

> The police disturb completely! They move around in circles. He will favour one if he gets money, than he will receive money from the other and he will favour him. He will accept from the one who complains and from the other part as well. Ah ... they can not help anyone. Many people do not go to the police. Almost ... even if they did not exist we would just continue to live our lives.

Several indigenous institutions also affect the degree of trust and cooperation. Tribalism, witchcraft and gender have been identified as major indigenous and informal institutions that obviously influence levels of trust and cooperation.

There are prejudices against people of different tribes. The Chagas are, for example, regarded as being unreliable, but competent in business. People of the indigenous tribe, the Nyaturu, are not viewed as competent in business. Due to 'legal' mechanisms of sanctions and safeguarding of rights within the tribal communities, members of, for example, the Chaga tribe are able to cooperate. In case of fraud or cheating, the Chaga turn to the elected leaders in their local tribal organization, or the elders in their home region, for arbitration.[13] This facilitates cooperation among Chagas. They explain:

> It is a very normal thing. It helps a lot due to the problems with the courts. Chagas will be afraid of running away with money because of this. It is easy to cooperate because he/she knows that this is a possibility.

Interviewees said that when people of a tribe meet in a distant region, they care more about each other and help each other in business. Other tribes have started similar organizations in Singida, inspired by seeing the function of the 'Chaga-society'. Yet, these organizations are not active and are not claimed to fill any major function for business purposes. For business conflicts involving 'non-Chagas' it is much more complicated to find a mechanism of arbitration:

> If you are of the same tribe, you go to the tribal organization. If it is the neighbour you go to the cell leader. There is a leader for every ten houses. If it is not a neighbour or someone related you need to find another friend whom both can trust. Or one can go to a friend of the other or someone who knows the one he has problems with.

Due to the lack of institutions for resolution of business conflicts, the TCCIA in Singida has recently started to take on such issues. Business owners have started to turn to the executive officer for advisory services in case of conflict.

Belief in witchcraft is widespread in all spheres of life in the Tanzanian society. Witchcraft is also regarded as a way for some business people to earn their money. It is an indigenous institution that breeds uncertainty, suspicion and distrust. Rumours are widespread about for example some bus-operators and a shop owner who are said to have practised witchcraft in order to get rid of competitors. As expressed by Mama Vicky, this creates a situation where people feel that: 'You have no faith, you never know.'

Also gender influences cooperation in several ways. One is that men and women, due to cultural norms, seldom talk to each other about business issues or socialize on a collegial level. This was expressed by both male and female interviewees as well as observed during the training sessions. A second aspect of gender is that women are said to cooperate more than men. It is said that women have some kind of solidarity and that they need each other more than men. Mrs Baraka narrates how two younger women, who had come into conflict with each other, consulted her. She was rather annoyed with the situations that had occurred and told them that 'if you will not trust each other, you will not develop'. However, neither women nor men trust the business competence of women. On the other hand, several actors argue that women in other ways are more reliable, committed and trustworthy than men. This is because they cannot disappear or cheat anyone, since they have to stay around and take care of their children. A typical statement is:

> Women are more trustworthy than men. They are not courageous, they are afraid. … They are afraid even to borrow and they try harder than man (to pay back). They have children. Where would they run away to? Also if they cooperated with a man they would be afraid of him that he would do something bad with her.

Another businesswoman said:

> Women cooperate because we see that we are behind, we need to like each other, to help each other. Later you will also be helped yourself. If someone cannot help you with money she will help you in other ways, with advice.

Not only women are said to cooperate because they need each other. At the end of the empirical study Mr Mziwa, who operates a small shop, compares his situation with owners of larger businesses and says that small business owners would not be able to develop without helping each other. Another rule of the game important for the small-business owners is that of reciprocity. Business owners expressed a perceived obligation to reciprocate when others had acted cooperatively. If one did not reciprocate the relationship would turn bad and then one would not be helped when in need, Mr Moshi explains. Mr Mziwa said:

> The cooperation of helping each other to lend money, is important. But if you have decided to help each other you have to do that. If he has already helped you and he needs help you can not refuse. But you have not written anything, it is to trust each other. No one has ever refused so far. (That is, in the cooperation where he is involved.)

In the constrained economic situation and with the inadequate formal institutions, people had to fend for themselves. Cooperation was at times necessary and business owners strove to gain knowledge of each other's character. It was regarded as important:

> To understand a person and his weaknesses, commitment and habits. If his interest is to put money in his pockets or if he will take more wives and spend money at bars if he gets hold of money...

Changing Attitudes and Practices

Changes in attitudes as well as practices actually took place during the period of empirical study. Cooperation was to a larger extent regarded as possible and new cooperation was established. This could be observed at the closing session of the training on 1 March 2000, where the business owners had lively and open discussions and exchanged ideas. It is also clearly illustrated by the fact that 16 business owners in Singida town during 2000 started up their own Savings and Credit Cooperative Society, named the UHURU.[14] This change is experienced by not only the business owners interviewed, but also by business trainers and Mr Mechack at the TCCIA.

A typical response after the end of the training came from Henry, who in January 2000 said that cooperation was impossible.

> After the end of the training and after thinking about the things we learnt there I think that cooperation is possible if you write a contract and everything to make sure that every member has his/her rights and he/she can withdraw if he/she thinks things are not good.

It thus seems as if the business training had significant impact on this change, although this was not the purpose of the training. One reason for this was the content of the training. That is, learning accounting and writing of contracts facilitates cooperation. Many emphasized the importance of learning to practise book-keeping and argue that it facilitates control over the money and thus lowers the problem of trust (see the following section). Learning to write contracts enabled the establishment of the UHURU Savings and Credit Cooperative Society and some participants after the training said: 'There is no problem at all with trust here, since we have written everything down.' Owners of Singida Warehouse said:

> People have started to practice bookkeeping. If you write down things you will know who is responsible, you will have a bank account and you will know what expenses you have and everything. People will not be able to take money. Accounts really lower the problem of trust. If you do not look very carefully, you can not do business with people.

An equally important impact of the training is the fact that business people got the opportunity to meet and get to know each other, which enabled building of relationships and trust. As an illustrative example, Mama Mmari said:

> I was familiar with Tarimo before the training, but just enough to say hi, not enough to discuss business issues with him. Now we have a reason to discuss. We started to know each other better after being together there at the seminars. Tarimo was in my discussion group. So, it was easy to start discussions with him.

The training enabled men and women to meet and interact without causing any strange suspicions. This enabled men and women to get to know each other and when some participants started the UHURU Savings and Credit Cooperative Society, both men and women were included. Mama Oliva was very happy about that:

> We have joined together different sexes. It is better. We can get some good and important advice. Men have a different understanding and knowledge than women. They know more about ways to look for money. They know people, they have talked to people and they know where the opportunities are. From this cooperation we are expecting to get ideas from men.

The training was not the only reason for change. The improved capacity of the TCCIA in Singida also had an impact. Having an organization that takes care of one's interests seemed to strengthen the feeling of unity among the studied business owners.

Analysis: Trust in the Tanzanian Context

To discuss the overall problems of trust found between business owners in Singida the typology of trust is presented in Table 4.2, with quotes from Singida placed inside. The 'varieties' of trust in the model will be discussed seriatim below. Thus, although this was doubted at the outset, the model was found useful for understanding the complexity of trust in the Tanzanian context. I found the significance of trust in the category level particularly obvious. The objects of trust (*good will, commitment* and *competence*) differ, however, in immediate importance. The capabilities and financial strength of the business are important, but many only see the problem of trusting someone's good will when it comes to money. It is without doubt the most central and problematic object of trust in the Tanzanian context. As a colleague said: 'Concerning money you can not trust anyone.'

Table 4.2   The typology of trust in Tanzania

Objects of trust	Levels of trust		
	General	Category	Specific
Good will	'Here you have no faith, you never know.' 'Concerning money you can not trust anyone.'	'Nyaturus are often not open. You can agree and then later he/she goes behind your back. He/she will refuse and break the agreement.' 'Women have a spirit of sympathy.'	'There are some, like x,y and z, I try to be close to them. We talk about business issues and help each other.'
Commitment	'The problem with us Africans is that we have many things, family, farm and other problems. We cannot commit ourselves fully to one thing.' 'You can not know if someone will work with effort and if he/she will care.'	'Women commit themselves more than men.'	'Regarding to commit oneself. ... it depends on private things. Maybe four people (out of eight) can show up, but many do not come.'
Competence	'Generally I think it fails due to lack of education.' '...the problem of this place is lack of education.'	'To find someone from here is not easy if you are looking for knowledge.'	'X can do a lot of things.' 'We asked G for advice.'

General trust

We can see from the quotes in the first column of the typology that there is a lack of general trust in good will as well as commitment and competence. Mama Vicky maintained that due to the suspicions of witchcraft you never know who has evil designs on you. The multitude of commitments and diversification of activities, contribute to difficulties of general trust in commitment. General trust in competence is limited by the lack of education.

The Tanzanian society seems to have difficulties with almost all the factors which according to Sztompka's (1999) theory contribute to general trust, that is normative coherence, stability of the social order, transparency of government agencies and mechanisms to ensure accountability.

Concerning normative coherence this study found that the security and predictability that existed largely stemmed from indigenous customs and norms of reciprocity. With regard to stability of the social order, the frequent changes in laws, regulations and government structure in Tanzania[15] leads to the opposite of stability. There is no tradition of transparency. Some businessmen even expressed beliefs that the authorities do not want people to know and understand the law. Under such circumstances of secrecy, suspicion, rumours and conspiracy theories are likely to thrive (see Sztompka, 1999). The rumours of witchcraft discussed in the previous section are an example. This is clearly a part of a vicious circle of distrust in the context. People are restrictive with their interaction and thus do not know each other, which again adds to suspicion and rumours.

The accountability of other people and institutions refers to the existence of back-up systems such as the law, the police, courts, consumer protection agencies and so on. As discussed above, such systems are not functioning properly in Tanzania and they were not trusted by people. The widespread use of corruption is common knowledge in Singida. The accountability existing is derived from social pressure among family, friends and neighbours. The fact that women can be trusted due to their commitment to home and children is an example of accountability, so are the mechanisms of arbitration within the Chaga community. Henry Madaraka and the other early members of the UHURU Savings and Credit Cooperative Society consciously used accountability when they chose new members. These should have fixed assets and family in Singida, to make sure they did not run away with money. Disappearing with money, going 'underground', is otherwise easy in a society where the police (besides not being trustworthy) have limited cooperation between regions and limited resources.

Category trust

The most commonly used principles for categorizing business owners as trustworthy or untrustworthy are gender and ethnicity (tribal affiliation). As can be understood from the quotes in the second column in the typology in Table 4.2, people are being trusted and distrusted depending on whether they fall into the category of being Chaga or Nyaturu, men or women. The overall pattern is that Nyaturus are distrusted by some people in terms of good will. However, the same applies to the Chaga and some people even gossip about a Chaga-mafia. Chagas are said to be clever and like cheating. Nyaturus may say that they agree to do something but then violate the agreement, according to the rumours. Women, on the other hand, tend to be trusted for both good will and commitment. As far as competence is concerned, Nyaturus and women tend to be distrusted whereas Chagas are said to be competent in business.

As illustrated by quotes in the previous section, it was found in this study that trust in women's competence was low ('a woman can not know things'). On the other hand, women were more trusted for good will and commitment (see Table 4.2). The norm of reciprocity was expressed more strongly among women.

The propensity for Chagas to trust other Chagas and women to trust other women relates not only to primary trustworthiness, but also to trustworthiness derived through accountability. The indigenous institutions to ask elders within the tribal community for advice provide accountability and thus possibilities for derived trustworthiness. In the urban centres of modernity it has not been possible for many tribes to maintain this custom. Many of the Chagas have moved out of their traditional area and they are active in business in most towns. In Singida, as in many other towns, they have been most successful in building up a local Chaga hierarchy with heads representing each sub-area in their home region. In case of business conflicts, these heads or the general chairman are contacted for arbitration (see quotes in the previous section).

Another indigenous institution is that women stay at home taking care of children. This adversely affects the possibilities of women to operate businesses. It also provides certainty and accountability, since women are unlikely to steal money, disappear and leave children behind. Neither will they fail to commit themselves, since they are eager to support their children. Since women's financial and social position due to indigenous institutions is lower than that of men, they are forced to work harder. This is another potential reason for the widespread perception that women are more committed than men. Being more vulnerable they are also more scared of what might happen to them if they fail.

Specific trust

Long-term relationships with strong specific trust were few in the urban area with a migrant population from different regions. The model in Table 4.2 shows the quotes indicating existence of specific trust.

Specific relations of trust with various actors were built up deliberately,[16] but very carefully. Since everyone lives under severe resource constraints and the institutional framework for safeguarding property rights is not effective, risks of fraud are high. Everyone has negative experiences of having trusted someone and lost money. Strategies for building (primary) trust involve testing others, gradually entrusting them with more and more money while closely monitoring their actions.

Among business owners in Singida, common norms of reciprocity were also used to build relations of trust. In relation to employees, it is common that business owners provide education and support for their employees, in return for loyal and committed work in the future. If one actor helps another, this creates an obligation to reciprocate when the first actor is in need, according to the business owners (compare quote in the section on general trust). I suggest that this provides predictability and facilitates trust.

The considerations within the UHURU Savings and Credit Cooperative Society when choosing additional members were examples of using trustworthiness derived through accountability. To be accepted, members should have not only a family but also a house and a capable business, in order to eliminate the incentives to run away with money.

CONCLUSIONS OF THE STUDY

Trust and Need

This study suggests that trust largely derives from the *need* to cooperate. Cooperative action was necessary and in absence of general trust, trust was largely personalized or related to indigenous mechanisms of accountability. Despite contextual constraints to trust and cooperation, the mutual need to cooperate, the common interest, is the single most important determinant of whether cooperation will arise or not. As Mr Mechack simply expressed it: 'Common interest brings people together'. A similar conclusion is drawn in a study of international strategic alliances with China, which is also a difficult situation without common social and institutional frameworks (Child, 2000).

It is a common view in Singida that women cooperate more than men. Although female networks give limited access to market information and capital, many women would have difficulty sustaining themselves and their businesses without female cooperation and solidarity. Women at the 'upper end' and those who could get support from their husbands were not as interested in the female networks, according to the study of Chamlee-Wright (1997). I would suggest that the solidarity expressed to a significant extent stems from mutual need.

Small business owners in Singida are also known to cooperate more than 'big' businessmen. Reasons are the same. Small business owners lack capital and thus need each other. The cooperation and organization between the Chagas in Singida can also be understood on the same lines. People of the same tribe, not living in their home area, also need each other more than they do in their home region. There is no specific Chaga organization or solidarity among Chagas in the home region of Kilimanjaro, according to Mr Moshi.

Elaborating on the Typology of Trust

The explicit distinction between primary trustworthiness based on characteristics and derived trustworthiness based on accountability, are main features in the refined typology of trust, presented in Appendix 4.2. In this sense, the typology has similar traits with Sztompka's (1999) theory, since this distinction is also important in his view. The view of category trust as a specific and equally important kind of trust, in between specific trust and general trust, is an important difference between the view of trust taken here and Sztompka's view. Furthermore, the focus here is more on the role of indigenous institutions. Quotations from the empirical description have been placed inside the elaborated typology, in order to exemplify expressions of the different kinds of trust.[17] Some quotes refer to trust and others to distrust.

This study shows that specific, category and general trust can all be built up using mechanisms of accountability. Category trust was especially salient in the Tanzanian context. All three objects of trust were relevant, but good will trust is the most problematic object in the context. Trust was important not only in the competence of business owners themselves, but also in the 'capabilities' of the business, that is its potential and financial strength. The third object of trust could thus be termed capability trust, in order to encompass also such capabilities. Furthermore, I suggest that our understanding of both *general* and *category* levels of trust would be enriched by the introduction of 'indigenous institutions' into our analysis.

General trust refers to norms and values contributing to trust among citizens of a society, as well as the structural context[18] providing prerequisites for trust. In this study, we have also seen how indigenous institutions can create both accountability and norms on which to base some degree of trust. Such indigenous institutions can affect the whole population, as in the case of norms of reciprocity. They can also apply only to a specific category of business owners, such as the case of the Chaga organization and women's opportunities.

In order to highlight the influence of indigenous institutions on trust, the concept has been included in the typology as influencing trust on the various levels. This study showed that trust in *category accountability* was especially influenced by indigenous institutions. Mechanisms of accountability within tribes as well as female accountability due to domestic responsibilities have been highlighted. Indigenous institutions also influence trust related to *category characteristics*, through for example conceptions of some tribes not being reliable and women being more inclined to solidarity. The institution of reciprocity facilitates normative coherence and thus affects the whole society through influencing trust linked *to general norms/values* in a positive direction. Beliefs in and tales of witchcraft, constitute an indigenous institution that creates suspicion and thus decreases trust related to general norms/values.

Breaking out of Distrust

Authors have discussed the clash between formal and indigenous institutions (North, 1990; Berry, 1993; Seppälä, 1998; Havnevik, 2000; and so on). From this study, I would agree with Zakaria (1999) that development will be hindered as long as indigenous values are neglected by donor institutions. Naturally, there might be problems with 'lock-in' effects due to people being more used to the indigenous institutions (Havnevik and Hårsmar, 1999). However, I would still like to give an optimistic view of the possibilities for change. If business owners were convinced that the police system functioned well, and if they trusted the police to the same extent as they trust their tribal leader, they would be likely to turn to the police. Among business owners in urban areas, indigenous mechanisms of accountability are used because of an experienced *need* for them. This applies to both traditional institutions such as arbitration by tribal elders and very recently created mechanisms such as counselling by the Tanzanian Chamber of Commerce Industry and Agriculture (TCCIA). It would be in line with these findings to expect that faced with changes in the formal institutional framework, 'indigenous' institutions will also be changed.

However, existence of formal institutions and markets is obviously not enough. Actors will not change their behaviour until they trust formal institutions better than their present system.[19] That is, when formal institutions are objects of the population's trust (see Giddens, 1996), they can also serve as sources of trust in society (Sztompka, 1999). The present situation with, for example, corruption and mismanagement (World Bank, 2001) indicates that trust would be difficult to achieve only from the macro level.

Is there then a way to approach indigenous institutions without either disposing of them, or accepting them fully?

The practices and norms referred to above as indigenous institutions relate to cognitive conceptions of 'the rules of the game' which depend on earlier experiences and knowledge. It is common that business owners have been pushed into their activities (Olomi, 1999b) due to unemployment and they are often not well educated. Their perceptions of the rules of the game at their disposal are limited. This study has shown that providing business education and training contributes to widening frames of reference of the business owners regarding the rules of the game. Through training, business people attain knowledge of business principles, book-keeping, marketing, contract writing, tax systems and so on. It gives them the possibility to make informed choices on which institutions to act on and which institutions provide the best opportunities.

The first result that could be seen from the training was that people had started to practise book-keeping and had a feeling of control over their operations. Recall that owners of Singida Warehouse said: 'Accounts really lower the problem of trust. If you do not look very carefully, you can not do business with people.'

There was an increased understanding that writing contracts was not as difficult as thought earlier. Obviously, starting to write contracts and constitutions facilitated cooperation. What may seem to be a paradox is that there was still no effective formal institutional framework to enforce the contract. My interpretation is that the contract still created a feeling of security and weightiness of the agreement. With a contract, it is also easier to use indigenous mechanisms of arbitration and sanctions.

Discussion groups were a central part of the training. These groups remained the same from September 1999 until March 2000 and were mixed, with both male and female participants of different tribes. Men and women thus started to exchange business ideas, without risking any rumours. Within the Savings and Credit Cooperative Society that started there are now both men and women of various tribes.

Through being an arena where business owners could meet and get to know each other, the training enabled creation of trust in specific characteristics, as illustrated by quotes in the empirical section. Even people who had known each other earlier, such as Mama Oliva, Eliwaza, Mariamu and others, now had a reason to discuss business issues.

To provide arenas where business people could meet and get to know each other contributes to decreasing suspicion and enables building of specific trust. Training is a particularly suitable arena, since principles of control, such as book-keeping and contract writing can be taught. Furthermore, the encounters can also be managed strategically, for example through mixing men and women as well as different tribes within discussion groups.

NOTES

1. In my dissertation (Tillmar, 2002), I compare the expressions of trust in the Swedish and the Tanzanian context. A typology of trust that will be used as a tool of analysis in this chapter was generated from a study which I conducted in the Swedish context. Here the focus is on issues specific to the Tanzanian context, but for a further elaboration on the typology and its applicability, I refer to my dissertation.
2. Since the term 'micro businesses' sometimes refers only to 'one-man firms' in NUTEK (2001), I have chosen to use the term 'small businesses' when referring also to the really small, that is businesses with fewer than ten employees.
3. Estimations from *Taarifa ya hali ya maendeleo ya mkoa wa Singida* (Singida, Regional Commissioner's Office, 1999).
4. Busacca and Castaldo (2001) made a quantitative analysis of words used in definitions of trust, and found risk, action, individual and beliefs to be key terms. Bigley and Pearce (1998) found that actor vulnerability was the common theme of trust research. Lane (2000) similarly notes the common assumption that trust relates to coping with risk and to situations when one's activities depend on the actions of another person. Rousseau et al. (1998) find not only risk and vulnerability but also interdependence being focused on by researchers from various disciplines.
5. A further theoretical elaboration on various reasons for trust is outside the scope of this chapter, and I refer to Tillmar (2002).
6. Note that I refer to 'good will' rather than 'goodwill'. This is since a person's good will relates to acting in an honest and morally correct way, and should not be confused with the term 'goodwill', which within business administration and accounting theory implies something totally different.
7. Note that the role of legal institutions was also recognized by Luhmann (1979).
8. Opportunism is used in the sense of Williamson's definition, meaning '*self-interest seeking with guile*' (Williamson, 1981, p. 554).
9. Note that commitment is thus here interpreted as an object which needs to be trusted, rather than as an outcome of trust (see Morgan and Hunt, 1994).
10. I refer to Tillmar (2002) for a further elaboration on the issue of commitment as an object of trust.
11. In order to protect the integrity of individuals I have chosen to use fictitious names in this study.
12. The analytical tool used was developed through my earlier studies in the Swedish context. This should not be interpreted as a methodology starting from a distanced western perspective. Being open to the empirical reality, with as 'inductive' an approach as possible, has been important in order to assess the applicability as well as to develop and refine the typology.
13. I refer to Tillmar (2001 or 2002) for further descriptions and discussions of the function of these tribal organizations.
14. UHURU is a fictitious name.
15. See also, for example, Havnevik and Hårsmar (1999) for a further elaboration on the issue of changes in the social order in Tanzania.
16. Having a wide network provides not only access to information and inputs but also serves as an insurance mechanism in case of problems. Similar patterns have been found by

numerous authors (Berry, 1993; McCormick, 1996; Seppälä, 1998; Zakaria, 1999; and Lyon, 2000).
17. For further explanations I refer to Tillmar (2001), and for a further elaboration of the typology of trust, I refer to my dissertation (Tillmar, 2002).
18. That is, normative coherence, stability of the social order, transparency, accountability and so on.
19. It should, however, be noted that traditional power structures are likely to be stronger and more constraining to entrepreneurial action in the village context of Seppälä's (1998) study than in the urban context of this study.

REFERENCES

Ærøe, A. (1991), *Rethinking Industrialization: From a National to a Local Perspective*, Ph.D. serie 7.91, Handelshøjskolen i København.
Ærøe, A. (1992), 'New Pathways to Industrialisation in Tanzania: Theoretical and Strategic Considerations', *IDS Bulletin*, **23** (3).
Alvesson, M. and S. Deetz (2000), *Kritisk samhällsvetenskaplig metod*, Lund: Studentlitteratur.
Alvesson, M.L. and Lindkvist L. (1993), 'Transaction Cost, Clans and Corporate Culture', *Journal of Management Studies*, **30** (3), 427–52.
Argyris, C. and D. Schön (1991), 'Participatory Action Research and Action Science Compared, A Commentary', in W. Whyte (ed.), *Participatory Action Research*, Thousand Oaks: Sage.
Bachmann, R. (2000), 'Conclusion: Trust – Conceptual Aspects of a Complex Phenomenon', in C. Lane and R. Bachmann (eds), *Trust Within and Between Organizations: Conceptual and Empirical Applications*, Oxford: Oxford University Press.
Bågens, L. (1993), *A Network Approach to Third World Industrialization: Capability Accumulation through Technological Exchange*, Göteborg: Department of Industrial Marketing, Chalmers University of Technology.
Bågens, L. (1998), *Inter-firm Linkages and Learning: An Empirical Exploration of Firms in the Third World*, Göteborg: Department of Industrial Marketing, Chalmers University of Technology.
Beinum, van H. (1998), 'On the Practice of Action Research', *International Journal of Action Research and Organizational Renewal*, **3** (1–2), 1–29.
Berry, S. (1993), *No Condition is Permanent: The Social Dynamic of Agrarian Change in Sub-Saharan Africa*, Wisconsin: The University of Wisconsin Press.
Bigley, G.A. and J.L. Pearce (1998), 'Straining for Shared Meaning in Organization Science: Problems of Trust and Distrust', *Academy of Management Review*, **23** (3), 405–21.
Busacca, G. and S. Castaldo (2001), *Trust in Market Relationships: An Interpretative Model*, paper presented at the EISAM Workshop on 'Trust Within and Between organizations', Vrije Universiteit Amsterdam, The Netherlands, 29–30 November.
Chamlee-Wright, E. (1997), *The Cultural Foundations of Economic Development: Urban Female Entrepreneurship in Ghana*, New York: Routledge.
Child, J. (2000), 'Trust and International Strategic Alliances: The case of Sino-Foreign Joint Ventures', in C. Lane and R. Bachman (eds), *Trust Within and*

Between Organizations: Conceptual Issues and Empirical Applications, Oxford: Oxford University Press.

Dia, M. (1996), *Africa's Management in the 1990s and Beyond – Reconciling Indigenous and Transplanted Institutions*, Washington, DC: The World Bank.

Frank, R.H. (1988), *Passions Within Reason: The Strategic Role of the emotions*, New York: W.W. Norton.

Fukuyama, F. (1996), *Trust: Social Virtues and the Creation of Prosperity*, London: Penguin Books.

Giddens, A. (1984), *The Constitution of Society*, Cambridge: Polity Press.

Giddens, A. (1996), *Modernitetens Följder*, Lund: Studentlitteratur.

Grettve, A.I.E. (1996), 'Entreprenörskap och afrikanska företag', in L. Wohlgemuth and J. Carlsson (eds), *Förvaltning Ledarskap Institutionsutveckling: På Afrikas Villkor*, Uppsala: Nordiska Afrikainstitutet.

Hagen, J.M. and S. Choe (1998), 'Trust in Japanese Interfirm Relations: Institutional Sanctions Matter', *Academy of Management Review*, **23** (3), 589–600.

Hardin, R. (1991), 'Trusting Persons, Trusting Institutions', in R.J. Zeckhauser (ed.), *Strategy and Choice*, Cambridge, MA: The MIT Press.

Havnevik, K. (2000), 'The Institutional Heart of Rural Africa: An Issue Overlooked?' in K. Havnevik (ed.), *The Institutional Context of Poverty Eradication in Rural Africa*, Uppsala: Nordiska Afrikainstitutet.

Havnevik, K. and M. Hårsmar (1999), *The Diversified Future – An Institutional Approach to Rural Development in Tanzania*, Stockholm: Almqvist & Wiksell International.

Huemer, L. (1998), *Trust in Business Relations: Economic logic or social interaction?*, Umeå: Boréa bokförlag.

Hydén, G. (1983), *No Shortcuts to Progress: African Development Management in Perspective*, Los Angeles: University of California Press.

Jonsson, L. (2001), *Kunskapsbildning i samverkan mellan forskning och praktik: En studie av interaktiv kunskapsbildning avseende kommunchefers chefskap*, Linköping: Linköpings Universitet.

K'obonyo, P.O. (1999), 'Flexible Specialisation and Small Enterprise Development in Kenya', in L.K. Rutashobya and D.R. Olomi (eds), *African Entrepreneurship and Small Business Development*, Dar es Salaam: DUP, University of Dar es Salaam.

Lane, C. (2000), 'Introduction:Theories and Issues in the Study of Trust', in C. Lane and R. Bachmann (eds), *Trust Within and Between Organizations: Conceptual Issues and Empirical Applications*, Oxford: Oxford University Press.

Lewicki, R.J. and B.B. Bunker (1996), 'Developing and Maintaining Trust in Work Relationships,' in R.M. Kramer and T.R. Tyler (eds), *Trust in Organizations: Frontiers of Theory and Research*, London: Sage Publications.

Luhmann, N. (1979), *Trust and Power*, New York: John Wiley & Sons Ltd.

Lyon, F. (2000), 'Trust, Networks and Norms: The Creation of Social Capital in Agricultural Economies in Ghana', *World Development*, **28** (4), 663–81.

Marris, P. and A. Somerset (1971), *African Businessmen*, London: Routledge & Kegan Paul.

Mayer, R.C., J.H. Davis and F.D. Schoorman (1995), 'An Integrative Model of Organizational Trust', *Academy of Management Review*, **20** (3), 709–34.

McCormick, D. (1996), 'Small Enterprise Development: A Network Approach', in D. McCormick and P.-O. Pedersen (eds), *Small Enterprises: Flexibility and Networking in an African Context*, Nairobi: Longhorn Kenya Ltd.

McKnight, D.H., L.L. Cummings and L. Chervany (1998), 'Initial Trust Formation in New Organizational Relationships', *Academy of Management Review*, **23** (3), 473–90.
Molander, B. (1993), *Kunskap i handling*, Göteborg: Daidalos.
Morgan, R.M. and S.D. Hunt (1994), 'The Commitment–Trust Theory of Relationship Marketing', *Journal of Marketing*, **58**, 20–38.
Mothander, B. (1996), 'Management och privat företagsamhet', in L. Wohlgemuth and J. Carlsson (eds), *Förvaltning Ledarskap Institutionsutveckling: På Afrikas Villkor*, Uppsala: Nordiska Afrikainstitutet.
Nooteboom, B. (1996), 'Trust, Opportunism and Governance, A Process and Control Model', *Organization Studies*, **17** (6), 985–1010.
Normann, R. (1975), *Skapande företagsledning*, Lund: Aldus.
North, D.C. (1990), *Institutions, Institutional Change and Economic Performance*, Cambridge: Cambridge University Press.
NUTEK Swedish Business Development Agency (2001), *SMEs in Sweden: Structural Change and Policy Development*, Infonr 20–2001.
Olomi, D.R. (1999a), 'Scope and Role of Research on Entrepreneurship and Small Business Development', in L.K. Rutashobya and D.R. Olomi (eds), *African Entrepreneurship and Small Business Development*, Dar es Salaam: DUP, University of Dar es Salaam.
Olomi, D.R. (1999b), 'Entrepreneur Characteristics and Small Firm Performance', in L.K. Rutashobya and D.R. Olomi (eds), *African Entrepreneurship and Small Business Development*, Dar es Salaam: DUP, University of Dar es Salaam.
Pettersson, M. (1999), *Förtroende i samverkan: en studie av småföretagare i ett regionalt utvecklingsprojekt*, Department of Management and Economics, Linköpings Universitet, Linköping.
Ring, P.S. (1996), 'Fragile and Resilient Trust and their Roles in Economic Exchange', *Business and Society*, **35** (2), 148–75.
Rousseau, D.M., S.B. Sitkin, R.S. Burnt and C. Camerer (1998), 'Introduction to Special Topic Forum – Not so Different After All: A Cross Discipline View of Trust', *Academy of Management Review*, **23** (3), 393–404.
Rugumamu, S.M. and B.B. Mutagawaba (1999), 'Entrepreneurship Development in Africa: Some Reflections From Tanzania', in L.K. Rutashobya and D.R. Olomi (eds), *African Entrepreneurship and Small Business Development*, Dar es Salaam: DUP, University of Dar es Salaam.
Sako, M. (1997), 'Does Trust Improve Business Performance?' in C. Lane and R. Bachmann (eds), *Trust Within and Between Organizations*, Oxford: Oxford University Press.
Seppälä, P. (1998), *Diversification and Accumulation in Rural Tanzania*, Uppsala: Nordiska Afrikainstitutet.
Shapiro, S.P. (1987), 'The Social Control of Impersonal Trust', *American Journal of Sociology*, **93** (3), 623–58.
Singida, Regional Commissioner's Office (1999), *Taarifa ya hali ya maendeleo ya mkoa wa Singida*, 2–6 February.
Solomon, R.C. (1999), *A Better Way to Think About Business: How Personal Integrity Leads to Corporate Success*, New York: Oxford University Press.
Sztompka, P. (1998), 'Trust, Distrust and Two Paradoxes of Democracy', *European Journal of Social Theory*, **1** (1), 19–32.
Sztompka, P. (1999), *Trust: A Sociological Theory*, Cambridge: Cambridge University Press.

The Planning Commission Dar es Salaam and Regional Commissioner's Office, Singida (1997), *Singida Region Socio-Economic Profile.*

Themba, G., M. Chamme, C.A. Phambuka and R. Makgosa (1999), 'Impact of Macro-Environmental Factors on Entrepreneurship Development in Developing Countries', in L.K. Rutashobya and D.R. Olomi (eds), *African Entrepreneurship and Small Business Development*, Dar es Salaam: DUP, University of Dar es Salaam.

Tibandebade, P., S. Wangwe, M. Msuya and D. Mutalemwa (2001), *Do Decent Jobs Require Good Policies? A Case Study of MSEs in Tanzania*, Country Report, ILO In Focus Programme Boosting Employment through Small Enterprise Development, Economic and Social Research Foundation.

Tillmar, M. (2001), *Breaking out of Distrust: A Case Study of Small-Business Cooperation in Tanzania*, Research in Management, Economics, and Law, Department of Management and Economics, Linköping University, Report no 0101.

Tillmar, M. (2002), *Swedish Tribalism and Tanzanian Agency: Predonditions for Trust and Cooperation in a Small-Business Context*, Department of Management and Economics/Business Administration, 58, Linköping University, Linköping.

Tripp, A.-M. (1997), *Changing the Rules: The Politics of Liberalization and the Urban Informal Economy in Tanzania*, Los Angeles: University of Califonia Press.

Trulsson, P. (1997), *Strategies of Entrepreneurship – Understanding Industrial Entrepreneurship and Structural Change in Northwest Tanzania*, Tema Teknik och Social Förändring, Linköpings Universitet, Linköping.

Willamson, O.E. (1981), 'The Economics of Organization: The Transaction Cost Approach', *American Journal of Sociology*, **87**, 448–577.

World Bank (2001), *Aid and Reforms in Africa: Lessons from Ten Case Studies*, Washington, DC: Online Media Briefing Center.

Zakaria, Y. (1999), *Entrepreneurial Ethics and Trust: Cultural Foundations and Networks in the Nigerian Plastic Industry*, Aldesho: Ashgate Publishing Ltd.

Zucker, L.G. (1986), 'Production of Trust, Institutional Sources of Economic Structure 1840–1920', *Research in Organizational Behavior*, 8, 53–111.

APPENDIX 4.1   SUMMARIZING THE RESEARCH DESIGN

	April 1999	Nov 1999	Jan 2000	Feb 2000	March 2000	April 2000	May 2000	June 2000	Jan 2001
Prep. study	------	------							
Participant observation		**	*****	****	***	**	**	*	**
Interviews									
Key informants									
Henry			**		**	***	*	**	*
Mrs Mmari			**	**	***	***	**	**	**
Vicky			*	*	*	***	**	*	
Mr Baraka							*		
Substitute informants									
Mama Oliva			*		*		*		
Mrs Baraka					**				
Other actors									
Eliwaza			**		**				
Fancy					*				
Others			**	***	**	**	**		*******
Dialogues									
Tawaga		**	**	**	**	**	**		*
Mechack		**	**	**	**	**	**	**	**
Continuous general discussions	*	*******	********	*********	*********	********	********	********	******

78

APPENDIX 4.2   A REFINED TYPOLOGY OF TRUST

Objects of trust	Formal institutions	Indigenous institutions			Individual action	
	General structure	General norms/values (reciprocity, witchcraft)	Category accountability (tribalism, gender)	Category characteristics (solidarity, gender, tribalism)	Specific accountability	Specific characteristics
Good will (Reg. money, witchcraft)	Concerning money you cannot trust anyone.	Here you have no faith, you never know. Witches are many here in Singida.	Chagas will be afraid of running away with money because of this.	Nyaturus are often not open. Men do not cooperate, they are not open. Women have the spirit of sympathy.	But if it was people who already had some assets ... in order to reduce the reason to disappear.	To trust each other we are 5–10 people who know that we have a good relationship and if I explain my problem ... he will give me.
Commitment (Hard-working)	The problem is that we have many things, family, farm, and other problems. We cannot commit ourselves fully to one thing.	But if you have decided to help each other you have to do that. If he has already helped you and he needs help you cannot refuse.	Women commit themselves more than men. They do not disappear in the forest, where would they go?	We in TCCIA need to have unity and to plan meetings, but the attendance is very low ... in Moshi, it is not like here.	To provide education in order to ensure loyalty and hard work. To supervise in order to assure work effort.	... he has the habit of committing himself ...
Capabilities (Competence and financial strength)	Generally I think it fails due to lack of education.	People do not plan on a long-term basis.		To find someone from here is not easy if you are looking for knowledge. A woman cannot know things.	It is necessary to make sure that the others have income, if the organization is going to develop.	... capability of his business is good ... ... those that we have joined with definitely know things.

5. Trust and performance: institutional, interpersonal and network trust

Andrej Rus

INTRODUCTION

A revival of interest in trust marks a stage in a long journey ideas have traveled in the past 150 years. About 100 years ago the key concern for incipient social sciences had been the rise of industrial society and the break-up of traditional bases of social solidarity. Their major concern was how social solidarity could be preserved in the face of an emerging capitalism and chaotic urbanization that uprooted people from their small rural communities and brought them to the amoral wilderness of alienated urban areas. The critics claimed that industrial society had broken up traditional bonds that had served as a basis of trust, 'one of the most important synthetic forces within society' (Simmel 1950: 318). The modernists represented by Durkheim countered that a new industrial order was creating a new basis for social solidarity through an organic division of labor which required closer cooperation, thus creating stronger than ever moral bonds between the people.

In just 100 years the question has been reversed. We are no longer concerned with how economic development affects the quality of social relationships and social solidarity. Instead, we are concerned for the health of the industrial order, seeking ways in which 'moral order', social capital and trust in a society could help promote its economic development. To paraphrase, we have stopped asking the economy what it can do for trust and society, and are now asking society what it can do for the economy. Economic growth that was once perceived as a villain bringing destruction to the moral foundation of society is today being nursed to health with extra doses of trust and social capital. Thus social solidarity, moral order, trust and social capital have in the past 100 years changed their place in a structural equation from dependent variables to a set of powerful predictors of economic growth. Trust is no longer viewed as an endangered species but rather as a stimulant of economic growth and a significant factor in the production equation. It should therefore come as a shock to the classics to realize that the key concern of this chapter is how trust affects company performance.

Trust has been studied at three very different levels. Macro approaches to trust try to determine the link between the level of trust in a given society and its level and pace of development. Fukuyama's influential book (1995) has set the agenda by proposing that trust determines the economic performance of a society. This debate is usually cast in terms of social capital where social capital is almost invariably operationalized as trust (Fukuyama 1995). Political scientists have been deeply concerned about the effect of trust and the effectiveness of political and economic institutions (Putnam 1993; Norris 2002). The general idea present in macro approaches is that the average level of trust in a society can be viewed as a public good and as such it affects individual behavior in the population. In Luhmann's (1988) formulation sytemic trust reduces complexity and makes communal life better and easier by inspiring confidence in people who do not have to question the functioning of technical and social systems.

In contrast to the macro level analysis there is a micro approach to trust which sees interpersonal trust as important attribute of social relationships. Interpersonal trust was defined in terms of expectations between two or more actors. In Simmel's view, trust (which he calls confidence) is a 'hypothesis about future behavior' (1950: 318). It is a state in which actors expect benevolent behavior from others. Trust is viewed as a part of social relationships which give those relationships such as friendship a defining character. This micro approach to trust has been extended to organizational and societal levels without much critical thought.

On the mezzo level, research has focused on interorganizational relations examining trust between organizations. This research has examined trust as an alternative governance mechanism to hierarchy and market in various interorganizational contexts (Bradach and Eccles 1989). Trust has been most vividly brought up in the studies of industrial districts (Brusco 1982, 1992; Pyke et al. 1992; Dei Ottati 1994; Bagnasco and Sabel 1995; Staber 1998) and remains to be treated as the key force keeping industrial districts economically viable and competitive. It has been examined in buyer–supplier networks (Lorenz 1988; Sako 1992; Lane and Bachmann 1997; Lazerson 1995). And it was identified as the mechanism for diffusion of innovation among organizations (Haunschild 1993; Haveman 1993; Davis and Greve 1997) and the spread of interorganizational collaboration such as strategic alliances (Gulati 1995).

The purpose of this chapter is to look at the effect of trust on company performance. The idea that trust leads to improved economic performance has been widely theorized but there is surprisingly little empirical evidence that would support it (Deakin and Wilkinson 1998; Kern 1998; Sako 1998). Much less has been done to identify mechanisms through which trust defined at three different levels affects the behavior and performance of companies. The purpose of this chapter is to fill this gap and examine the mechanisms through which different types of trust affect performance. The chapter begins by proposing a typology of trust based on the distinction between micro, macro and mezzo level, and proceeds by examining the ways in which each type of trust affects performance. In an empirical section the chapter examines evidence of the three types of trust on company growth of small and medium enterprises in three countries. The chapter concludes with a discussion of the implications of the three types of trust and the three ways in which it affects performance.

THREE BASES OF TRUST

Trust is a dimension of interpersonal relations that is associated with three elements: interdependence among actors, uncertainty or risk regarding the behavior of the other party to a transaction, and expectations that the other party will not abuse the trusting actor's vulnerability (Lane 1998). Trust is usually defined as an expectation by an actor that the other party will fulfill its obligations in spite of uncertainty and opportunities for defection and self-serving behavior (Gambetta 1988; Creed and Miles 1996). Instead of converting uncertainty into risk by employing impersonal governance mechanisms such as contract or hierarchy (Williamson 1996), trusting parties go on living with uncertainty. They do not simply bracket off uncertainty (Mollering 2002) but embed it in a trusting personal relationship. Thus, in trusting relationships uncertainty is never operationalized in terms of risk as suggested by Luhmann (1988). Risk requires information, calculation, assessment, monitoring, management and governance. Trust, on the other hand, avoids all those steps required for rational management of a transaction. Actors accept uncertainty in a given transaction and do not manage it directly. Instead they manage the social relationship that is underlying the implicit or explicit contract. When actors base transactions on trust they actually shift governance from a transaction to a relationship. They convert transactional uncertainty into relational certainty. When transactions with the same actor are frequent, governance based on trust can result in a significant reduction of transaction costs. If transaction frequency with the same actor is low, trust can lead to excessive transaction costs because it would require that actors maintain close relationships with many individuals.

The defining characteristic of trust is that uncertainty is not operationalized as a set of objectives, conditions and processes that control the level of risk involved in a given transaction. Actors do not know what the outcome will be and they do not design governance mechanisms that would enforce the terms of the contract. Because trusting parties do not try to rationalize the uncertainty in a transaction 'all trust is in a certain sense blind trust' Giddens (1990: 33). This makes trust both a virtue of the present and a relic of the past. Trust was one of the three medieval virtues of chivalry complementing friendship and loyalty, which is why today's references to trust still invoke an echo of heroism and noble behavior.

While trust is blind, the choice of a partner whom we trust is not blind but is highly informed. We place trust with only those people that we know are trustworthy. Thus, a leap of faith involved in a single transaction based on trust is preceded by an intensive cultivation, monitoring and management of a personal relationship with a view to reconfirming the trustworthiness of a business partner. Thus trust may be blind but the decision of who to trust is taken with care. Trustworthiness of partners is determined based on extensive information gathered by trusting parties. The importance of information for trust has been strongly emphasized by Simmel, who viewed it as a key element in defining trust: 'confidence is intermediate between knowledge and ignorance about man. The person who knows completely need not trust; while the person who knows nothing can, on no rational grounds, afford even confidence' (1950: 318).

Trust requires that actors collect information on the trustworthiness of their partners in a transaction. This information is graded on a nuanced nominal scale. Since trust resides in a personal relationship it is rarely manifested alone. More often it features as one of the elements of a broader relational package such as friendship (best friend, good friend, just friend), kin, acquaintance, coworker, neighbor and so on. While trust is a necessary component of many of these relational packages, it is not a sufficient element that would define a distinctive relationship. In fact, phenomenology of trust does not yield trust as a type of relationship but only as one of several dimensions of many types of relation. This means that trust can not appear alone: trust is always embedded in a particular type of relationship.

Trust therefore requires information. Actors can obtain information about their partners from very different sources. Information about the trustworthiness of a partner in a transaction comes from three fundamentally different sources. Information can come from macro sources such as public information provided by institutions, from a mezzo level such as interorganizational networks and from a micro level that is defined by personal experience with a given partner. Based on the source of information, we distinguish three different types of trust: interpersonal trust, network trust and institutional trust.

Interpersonal trust depends on information that comes from personal experience of an actor with particular others. This process-based trust (Zucker 1986) relies on a personal relationship between two actors and is therefore highly particularistic. Trust does not arise from a history of repeated transactions but from a history of a given relationship with an exchange partner and reflects the quality of this relationship: friends trust each other while adversaries do not. Trust is therefore embedded in a particular personal relationship. Disentangling trust from a multiplex social relationship can be difficult. Burt and Knez (1996) show that trust is strongly correlated with closeness between actors. The more intensive the relationship the harder it is to distinguish trust from other properties of this relationship. Moreover, there is a question how much trust there is in intensive relationships marked by high intimacy and closeness. A close relationship between two actors who know each other well and who go back a long way may need no trust because they know almost everything about one another. This is the situation of Luhmann's familiarity which involves no risk but also no trust because 'the person who knows completely need not trust' (Simmel 1950: 318).

Network trust is based on information about transaction partners that comes from social networks in a form of referrals or gossip (Burt 1992; Burt and Knez 1996). This source of trust is based on indirect ties between an actor and the exchange partner with a mediator playing a key role in linking the two parties. What distinguishes network trust from a dyadic trust is that the relevance of information regarding the trustworthiness of an exchange partner depends on a triad rather than a dyad (Simmel 1950). An actor who has trust in a mediator accepts the third party as trustworthy based on the recommendations of a mediator. An actor may know nothing about the third party from direct experience but trusts the information about the third party obtained from a trustworthy mediator. The mediator extends trust to the third party not only by passing available information to an actor. The mediator also guarantees the trustworthiness of the exchange partner by mortgaging his relationship with an actor. Such a guarantee is meaningful only when the mediator places a high value on his collateral which makes him vigilant about the accuracy of his recommendation. This implies that network trust can function only when ties between an actor and the mediator are strong and embedded in an intensive relationship.

Although there have been many studies of industrial districts that pointed out the role of trust for interorganizational relations, the discussions were mostly limited to dyadic trust, that is, actors learning from the experience from one another. It seems that with neglect of indirect ties the studies overlooked the fact that networks represent an important source of information regarding the trustworthiness of exchange partners. Information from networks is crucial because it extends the reach of interpersonal trust. If personal experience can confirm the trustworthiness of only a small number of people whose qualities are reaffirmed in frequent association and extensive socializing, the reliance on referrals can extend the reach of trust from a small world to a much wider group of people. Since 'the personal network supplies the entrepreneur with a universal resource kit' (Johannisson 2000: 371) the implications of a broader network for the performance of a firm can be easily appreciated. Network trust enables actors to multiply their reach within the limits of their time budget constraints and thus broaden their access to resources and opportunities.

Institutional trust 'generalizes beyond a given transaction and beyond specific sets of exchange partners' (Zucker 1986: 63). Actors base their expectations regarding the behavior of others based on the reliability, impartiality and efficiency of the institutional system (Rothstein and Stolle 2001). Efficient, fair and reliable institutions make individual behavior predictable by spelling out the alternatives and placing price in the form of sanctions on non-desirable behavior. Institutional trust is therefore trust by inference: since all actors in a given system face the same incentives and constraints, they are expected to behave in a uniform way. Institutional trust is therefore highly universalistic. It is often called systemic trust (Lane 1998).

The defining characteristic of institutional or systemic trust is its generalizability beyond the immediate context in which an actor operates. It does not involve trust in people but rather trust in institutions. This is what Luhmann (1988) calls confidence. Confidence means that actors enter into economic transactions believing that their expectations will not be disappointed. Although breach of contract and scams are possible, actors enter into economic transactions confident that most of the people will not breach their contracts. Confidence leads actors to neglect the possibilities of opportunism or outright danger and act as if there is complete certainty that people or systems will function as expected. They do not question a particular transaction or exchange partner, because they do not base their trust on their relationship with a person but on their relationship with an institution. They extend their trust to all individuals and transactions that are located within a trustworthy institutional framework.

Confidence thus determines the degree to which actors trust strangers. The more confidence there is in the political, economic, legal and social system, the more actors will decide to extend trust to people they do not know. Confidence in an institutional system leads actors to derive their knowledge about actors not from private experience with particular individuals but from public information about the reliability, impartiality and efficiency of an institutional system.

> The traditions and institutions, the power of public opinion and the definition of the position which inescapably stamps the individual, have become so solid and reliable that one has to know only certain external facts about the other person in order to have the confidence required for the common action. ... motivation and regulation of this behavior have become so objectified that confidence no longer needs any properly personal knowledge. (Simmel 1950: 319)

Because it encourages trust in strangers, confidence has a positive effect on the degree of participation in the economy. This vastly expands opportunity space not only because it increases the number of available transaction partners but also because those transaction partners are willing to approach the people whom they do not know with the same positive expectations of trust.

What differentiates the three types of trust is therefore the origin of information about the trustworthiness of a partner. It is useful to draw a parallel to the concept of the strength of a tie from network analysis (Granovetter 1973, 1982). Interpersonal trust depends on information that travels through strong ties. Network trust depends on information that is passed through weak ties, and institutional trust depends on public information that requires no ties. It is interesting to note that of the three different types of trust it is network trust that comes closest to the original definition of trust. Interpersonal trust grows out of close personal relationships between actors, thus eliminating uncertainty and the need for trust. Institutional trust arises from actors' confidence in the proper functioning of institutions which serves to diminish uncertainty regarding the behavior of all actors within a given institutional domain. With vanishing uncertainty the need for trust also vanishes because actors can be confident of the effectiveness of the institutional environment in maintaining minimal standards of behavior. Network trust is different from the other two types of trust because uncertainty is never diminished; it is sustained throughout the exchange. Actors do not know how the exchange partner will perform his duties because they only know the mediator who brought them together. While uncertainty is sustained, actors are able to suspended it not by minimizing or eliminating it, but by employing the leverage of a relationship with the mediator. We should therefore rethink definitions of trust that are currently based on a dyadic model. According to Simmel (1950) expectations that are purely dyadic are fully private and have no social dimension. Only expectations that involve at least three parties become socially relevant and represent a social constraint that has significance for an actor's behavior that extends beyond his or her private world.

TRUST AND PERFORMANCE

'The idea that high-trust relations might improve economic performance has been widely theorized, but relatively little empirical evidence has been produced in its favor' (Deakin and Wilkinson 1998). Trust is believed to raise the economic performance of individual transactions (Arrow 1974), organizations (Gulati 1995; Sako 1998), industrial regions (Pyke et al. 1992) or even societies (Fukuyama 1995). While literature is almost unanimous in stating that trust creates economic advantages, there is much less debate about the mechanisms through which trust would generate such favorable results. The usual argument is that trust facilitates cooperation and that cooperation is what leads to increased efficiency and performance (for example Sako 1992). Cooperation is a potent concept that has captured the imagination of sociologists and economists alike. In the analysis of industrial districts cooperation is often named as the key competitive advantage that has led to the success of small firms in the face of intense competition from giants in consolidating and globalizing industries (Pyke 1992). By fostering cooperation, trust lowers transaction costs, encourages investment in cooperative ventures and encourages the development of customer-specific assets without the risk of inflexibility (Dei Otatti 1994). Trust is seen as 'the central mechanism to allow for an efficient solution of the problem of co-ordinating expectations and interaction between economic actors' (Bachmann 2001: 338). Trust fosters mutual learning between customer and supplier which is the source of flexibility in face of high specialization (Powell 1996). Trust is a situation where opportunism has been minimized and economic actors can therefore focus on work rather than on erecting safeguards against cheating or betrayal. Trust is therefore assumed to 'contribute ... to a significant reduction of transaction costs; and open up opportunities for strategic action, enhance system stability and yet support organizational change' (Sydow 1998: 32).

The centerpiece of the argument linking trust and performance is therefore a close association between trust and cooperation. In the literature trust is closely associated with cooperation to the point that they seem synonymous with one another (Lane and Bachmann 1997). Trust leads to cooperation which in turn reduces transaction costs (Arrow 1974), reduces the need for monitoring (Granovetter 1985; Sako 1992) and increases flexibility (Ring and van de Ven 1992) because actors are more willing to share knowledge (Sako 1998) and other resources (Pyke 1992; Bagnasco and Sabel 1995; Dei Ottati 1996) which helps them to resolve their differences before they grow into disputes (Arrigheti et al. 1997). Thus, cooperation supposedly allows the parties to substitute costly governance mechanisms with a cheaper ongoing communication which enables them to do more (core business) with less (overheads) thus improving business performance.

Identification of trust and cooperation creates serious problems for explaining performance (see Gambetta 1988 for a critique). First, it is implied that cooperation depends on high levels of trust. This could mean that moderate levels of trust have no effect on performance. That would be inconsistent with evidence from classic studies of social structure from Durkheim's suicide, to Banfield's amoral familialism in an Italian village to Fukuyama's depiction of cohesive Chinese families, all of which demonstrated that high levels of trust and solidarity within a group can result in negative if not tragic consequences such as suicide. High social solidarity within the group can lead to isolation of a group from a society and that leads to deterioration rather than improvement of economic performance (Fukuyama 1995). More recently, studies of social networks showed that situations that give rise to a high level of trust often inhibit actors from exploiting opportunities and prevent them from maximizing their potential performance (Granovetter 1973; Burt 1992; Uzzi 1996). Second, if cooperation really requires high levels of trust that leads to isolation, the actors in cooperative situations may be deprived of resources available in a broader business community (Johannisson 2000). While Zucker (1986) only expressed concern over the excessive costs associated with building a fragile trust through intensive relationships, Kern (1998) has warned that high levels of trust may provoke close cooperation among companies in an industrial district to such a degree that they become locked in the existing relationships causing them to lose their key strategic asset, that is their flexibility. That can be detrimental to highly specialized small companies because they do not control sufficient resources for their survival but instead depend on the ad hoc pooling of resources from a wide variety of firms in an industrial district to complete any given order (Dei Ottati 1994). Third, high levels of trust and cooperation may not only cut off a company from resources but also from business opportunities (Burt 1992). Close cooperation with a few partners may turn advantage into liability because of the sunk costs that such cooperation has required. High levels of trust and cooperation may build barriers to communication with a wider business community thus distorting or diverting information about business performance and opportunities.

Above we have argued that trust does not only vary in intensity but also in kind. By distinguishing different types of trust it is possible to look at different ways in which trust affects performance. Interpersonal, institutional and network trust do not affect performance in the same way, that is, via cooperation. Interpersonal trust can generate sufficient intensity for cooperation to arise spontaneously because it is based on close ties and a high level of intimacy. Institutional and network trust, in contrast, link strangers rather than old friends and rely on weak if not only symbolic ties. It is hard to imagine how either of these two types of trust could generate cooperation and lead to increased performance. It is clear that there is more than one way through which trust affects performance. We propose that each type of trust has an effect on performance through a different mechanism.

Interpersonal trust affects performance by giving rise to *cooperation*. Cooperation requires that all parties refrain from opportunism and depends on strong social control that can be provided only by cohesive social groups. Interpersonal trust is good at just that because it is based on relationships that arise from continuing interaction and is supported by a broader network of personal relations. Uncertainty is externalized to a network of interpersonal relationships which has a normative potential through a system of informal sanctions. In case something goes wrong, the enforcement of *implicit* contracts is provided by means of social pressures and a threat of informal sanctions carried out by individuals in a network. Social control is a suitable governance mechanism in a closed social world characterized by a high density of relationships and few structural holes (Coleman 1988). Such social structures encourage cooperation among actors who belong to the same community and know each other well. Interpersonal trust is therefore a bonding mechanism which integrates a community, produces a strong normative order enforced by a system of informal sanctions and thus enables cooperation.

Social control is less effective in a more open network with diversified contacts, non-overlapping relationships and disconnected by structural holes which is the case in network trust. While dense social structures provide strong normative support that increases the chances of fulfillment of implicit contracts, that is accepted formal and informal obligations, a sparse social network loses its normative potential. It may lead to cooperation but cannot enforce it because social sanctions have little effect on actors embedded in a sparse network characterized by multiple structural holes (Burt 1992). However, the reliance on interpersonal ties provides a stable channel of communication which in turn creates ample opportunities for informal coordination. Trust acts not as a bonding mechanism but as a governance mechanism. For Williamson 'governance is the means by which order is accomplished in a relation in which potential conflict threatens to undo or upset opportunities to realize mutual gains' (1996: 12). Network trust works through the third parties which creates commitments to the mediator and not to the contracting party. Actors do not feel pressured to subdue their individual preferences for the sake of the collective good of cooperation but fulfill their obligation to the third parties by openly communicating their interests to one another and seeking pragmatic solutions to their divergent interests. While this may eventually lead to cooperation, the key effect of network trust on performance is through the coordination of actors in a market which allows them to better exploit opportunities.

Institutional trust inspires confidence which encourages both friends and strangers to enter into business transactions. Institutional trust has a positive impact on performance by means of opening up access to potential business partners. Uncertainty is externalized to an institutional environment with the expectation that if something goes wrong the institutional environment will enforce the terms of the contract. Institutional trust is therefore a linking mechanism which encourages parties to participate in the market but leaves it up to the parties to negotiate the standards of behavior among themselves. Unlike interpersonal trust it does not produce order among economic actors but rather provides confidence among actors that the terms of the contract will be observed. Institutional trust thus provides assurance akin to pre-contractual solidarity. Performance increases due to higher rates of participation in the economy which multiplies opportunities and resources, essential for growth and improved performance.

Different types of trust may all have a positive effect on performance. However, the mechanisms through which trust affects company performance may be very different. Undifferentiated approach to trust may lead to disappointing findings because empirical effects may be confounded. For example, we know that interpersonal trust is associated with both close ties and close cooperation, and is basically the source of goodwill trust (Sako 1992). As such it is expected to reduce transaction costs and lead to the sharing of scarce resources. However, a high level of interpersonal trust is necessarily limited to a narrow circle of family and close friends who may offer strong social support that may help a company to survive the fluctuations of the market. This buffer against market shocks may actually lead to disastrous results as the company may ignore market signals for too long and persist in a wrong line of business, wasting its resources in the process. Even if it remains successful, it may hit the limits of growth by getting stuck in a local niche without the possibility of gaining the support of a broader network of weak ties that allow the company to grow and reach out of its small resource pool. Network trust may enable a company to reach beyond a narrow range of market opportunities and help it to coordinate resources with other firms and thus outwit the liability of smallness. Network trust may link the company into a wider system of production and mobilize resources that are scattered in a much wider inter-organizational space. Working through referrals, companies may not develop close relationships with their partners that would guarantee goodwill trust, but they could benefit from competence trust essential for coordination, by means of reputation and referrals that are the domains of the third party gossip available in networks. Performance could be enhanced in spite of the lower level of interpersonal trust. Institutional trust vastly extends the potential range of customers and suppliers and facilitates access to resources throughout the system. Confidence in the system means that actors have a high level of contractual trust and will enter into transactions with strangers that are based in that system. Institutional trust provides a stable framework for the performance of contracts that are negotiated between actors by facilitating access. Institutional trust does not improve company performance by reducing transaction costs. Contracts are still needed to specify particular obligations of each partner. However, since all actors in the system are expected to adhere to the terms of their contracts, companies have a much wider choice of partners, customers, resources and opportunities. Access to this broad variety contributes to improved allocative efficiency and thus the increased performance of companies.

The key argument of this discussion is summarized in Table 5.1. Interpersonal trust is based on the goodwill of all exchange partners and encourages cooperation among them. Economic performance benefits from improved execution among cooperative partners. Network trust is based on referrals by the third parties about the competences of exchange partners. Network trust encourages coordination of resources among actors based on the recognized complementarities in competences. Economic performance benefits from improved resource mobilization that reaches beyond the narrow circle of a focal actor to encompass a wider circle of actors and resources. Institutional trust persuades actors to participate in transactions thus opening up mutual access to each other irrespective of their histories and knowledge of one another. Actors base their exchange on contracts which compensate for the lack of personal contact among parties of the exchange. Improved performance comes from improvements in resource allocation that are traded and evaluated on universalistic rather than particularistic metrics.

The key implication of this argument is that different types of trust open the path for different types of behavior. That means that different types of trust can have independent effects on performance. It is possible that interpersonal trust may have a negative effect on performance due to excessive embeddedness in the local group while moderate levels of institutional and network trust offset the negative effect on performance. In the empirical part of the chapter we look at the types of trust and their effect on performance.

Table 5.1   Three ways in which trust affects performance

Type of trust	Interpersonal trust	Network trust	Institutional trust
Behavioral basis	Goodwill	Competence	Contract
Mechanism	Cooperation	Coordination	Access
Performance is result of improved:	Resource implementation (execution)	Resource mobilization	Resource allocation (opportunity)

Note: the second line in this table refers to Sako's (1992) typology of goodwill, competence and contract trust

TRUST AND SME DEVELOPMENT IN THREE COUNTRIES

The data come from a survey of SMEs in Bosnia, Macedonia and Slovenia (Bartlett and Bukvič 2001; Bukvič et al. 2001). The survey covered 794 small and medium-sized firms in the three countries in all sectors except agriculture. It was based on an earlier survey carried out in 1993, which collected information about small firms in Slovenia and Bulgaria at an earlier stage of transition (Bartlett and Prašnikar, 1995). A representative sample was drawn from each of the three countries. These were random stratified samples drawn from a population of firms that had at least 2 and not more than 250 employees. The exclusion of the firms with one or zero employees was necessary to make sure that the samples would include only companies with at least minimal motivation for growth. This was also done to avoid swamping the sample with a large number of micro firms, and to capture medium-sized firms as well as smaller firms in the sampling frame. The strata were defined for firm sector and firm location. We restricted the trade sector to 30 per cent of the sample and firms located in the area of the national capital to 40 per cent of the sample. The data were collected by personal interviews with owners and managers of the selected firms in the autumn of 2000.

Dependent Variable

The key performance measure for small and medium enterprises is growth in sales. There are many other measures that would be more desirable indicators of performance. But many of the measures in the SME sector are notoriously unreliable because of the widespread practice of working the books in order to minimize the declared taxes. Entrepreneurs are much more aggressive in their accounting than managers in larger companies. They go to great lengths to hide revenue, exchange favors, and dream up imaginative business expenses to draw untaxed cash out of their firm. In addition, there were many non-response items especially in Macedonia, which made the use of quantitative measures of performance unusable. Given that in the period 1997–1999 the tax regimes have been very loose in Bosnia and Macedonia, it was impossible to complement the survey data from official statistics. The discrepancy between what entrepreneurs declare to tax authorities and what they actually make is high also in Slovenia. We asked entrepreneurs whether the sales in his or her company increased, decreased or stayed the same in 1999. This was a subjective, self-reported performance measure but it turned out that it was quite reliable. It did not correlate with sales, added value or profit measures. However, when we correlated it with the growth in company employment or the growth of the value of assets over the period of three years, correlation was significant. We chose to use it as a dependent variable because it had the fewest missing cases and it validly represented the substantive growth of the firms.

Types of Trust

The three types of trust that were discussed above should be discernable not only analytically but also empirically. The data reduction technique of factor analysis lets us determine the underlying structure of the 15 questions that refer to behavioral and attitudinal dimensions of trust (see Table 5.2). We expected three factors: one representing institutional trust; the second, network trust; and the third, interpersonal trust. The results of factor analysis reported in Table 5.2 produced four rather than the expected three factors. While interpersonal and network trust emerged as coherent factors, it was institutional trust that was split into two components: political and economic. Trust in political institutions and trust in economic institutions are quite different not only in their levels but also in the nature of their relationship to an entrepreneur. Entrepreneurs can choose their business partners; when dealing with the state and its agencies such choice disappears. While the empirical split of institutional trust makes a lot of sense, we will consider both dimensions as analytically representing institutional trust. We take these results as confirming our analytical threefold typology of trust.

Based on the results of factor analysis, we constructed four synthetic variables to represent trust in political institutions, trust in economic institutions, network trust and interpersonal trust in further analysis. We treated each factor as a separate measurement model and obtained regression-based factor scores. This yielded four continuous trust variables that have no

Table 5.2 Loading of items on four factors

In general…	Institutional trust		Network trust	Interpersonal trust
	Political	Economic		
Do you have TRUST in the state government	+			
Do you have TRUST in state administration	+			
Do you have TRUST in banks	+			
Do you have TRUST in chamber	+			
Do you have TRUST in local government	+			
What is the level of corruption of state officials	−			
Do you have TRUST in business partners		+		
Do you have TRUST in large firms		+		
Do you have TRUST in small firms		+		
Do you have TRUST in customers		+		
Employed people based on recommendations			+	
Gave or received business based on recommendations			+	
How important are informal ties for doing business?			+	
Do you trust your current partners?				+
How close are your ties with those partners?				+

natural scale. In addition to trust variables we were also looking at control variables. Two variables controling for organizational contingencies were: age of the firm and firm size. Age of the firm was measured as the number of years from the beginning of its operations. The age of a firm is important because of the effect of corporate lifecycles (Adizes 1999). At their invitation companies experience the liability of newness which slows down their growth as they struggle for legitimacy (Stinchcombe 1965; Hannan and Freeman 1989). After the initial few years the survivors experience steep growth before it gradually levels off as the companies gain their market share and meet barriers to growth. Since our sampling framework focused on companies that had at least two employees, there were very few newly founded firms in our sample. The median and average age was 8 and 12 years respectively, indicating the fact that we sampled the firms that were beyond the initial stage of their lifecycle. We can thus expect that the effect of firm age on performance will be negative. Controlling for firm age will make performance independent of company lifecycles.

The second control variable is company size, which refers to the number of employees. Since the variable was so far from normal distribution we recoded it into a normal variable with four standard modalities from micro firms to medium-sized enterprises. The expected effect of this variable on performance is positive because size gives companies market power and access to capital to fuel their growth. Note that our sample had an administrative cut-off point of 250 employees, so our sample is right censored and includes no large companies where the relationship between size and growth could be reversed. Controlling for the effect of company size will render performance independent of this structural effect.

The second set of controls was intended to capture a substantive part of the variation between countries. This is a three-country study and requires controls for countries. But country dummies are usually black box variables that invite interesting speculations that are mostly untestable. We tried to model the country effect in a more meaningful way by distinguishing two substantive characteristics of market regime. One was the perceived fairness of competition on the market and the other was the severity of late payments for a firm. Perceived fairness of competition on the market was measured on a five-point scale. The problem of late payments was measured as the number of weeks companies on average waited for their overdue receivables. Fairness and late payments are substantively linked and together characterize the level of institutional performance, that is, the level of order and discipline in economic life. These can be very low in transitional economies where the administrative capacity of the state is severely curtailed. Since our aim was to establish the effect of institutional trust on performance it was essential to control for institutional performance in the economy in order to avoid the risk of confounding the effects of institutional trust on company performance.

Trust and Performance: Results

Table 5.3 presents the results of multiple regression on performance. Models I and II are baseline models that include no effects of trust variables. All effects are significant and in the expected direction. The perceived sales performance is positively affected by fair competition and larger firm size and is negatively affected by the financial indiscipline of business partners and the higher age of the firm. Model II also includes country variables which reduce the effect of country characteristics but do not wipe out the effects. Both late payments and fairness are lower but significant. The largest drop is in the beta coefficient for delayed payments which seems to be absorbed most by the country variable. All three countries differ significantly from one another in the level of perceived sales performance. The baseline country was Macedonia where the level of perceived sales performance was in the middle between Slovenia (the highest) and Bosnia (the lowest), a result which was expected in the light of the recent history. The R2 in Model II increased almost twofold, indicating the amount of additional variance explained by country effects.

Models III and IV estimate the effects of three different types of trust on perceived sales performance. Institutional trust – both economic and political – has a significant effect on perceived sales performance. Network trust has a significant effect too. It is interpersonal trust which is insignificant as a factor predicting perceived sales performance. Trust variables add a significant amount of explanatory power over model I increasing explained variance from 7 per cent to 12.7 per cent. The effect of trust on performance is significant net of organizational and market regime variables. After controlling for the context variables of fairness of competition and severity of delayed payments, and the organizational variables of firm age and firm size, trust maintains a significant effect on company performance.

The fact that institutional trust has an independent effect on controls is very important. Often, institutional trust is associated with the effectiveness of the institutional environment (Rothstein and Stolle 2001). Our results indicate that trust in economic and political institutions increases performance net of institutional effectiveness measured by the two context variables. One explanation of this result is that there might be different underlying causal mechanisms at work. While trust in political and economic institutions encourages economic actors to participate in economic exchange, creating multiple avenues of access to each other in the process, the perceived fairness of competition refers to the actual experience after access to the market

Table 5.3   The effects of institutional, interpersonal and network trust on perceived sales performance (OLS)

	Model I	Model II	Model III	Model IV	Model V	Model VI
Institutional trust						
Political institutions			0.154***	0.125**	0.156***	0.128***
Economic institutions			0.103**	0.113**	0.102**	0.113**
Network trust			0.124***	0.093**	0.125**	0.094**
Interpersonal trust						
Closeness			0.060*	0.035	0.098*	0.063
Trust net of closeness (residuals)					−0.037	−0.040
Background						
Fairness of competition	0.155***	0.110***	0.126***	0.094**	0.126***	0.095**
Delayed payment	−0.152***	−0.075**	−0.127***	−0.070	−0.123***	−0.068
Firm age	−0.102 **	−0.124***	−0.111**	−0.128**	−0.113**	−0.129**
Firm size	0.111***	0.133***	0.090*	0.114**	0.086	0.111**
Context						
Slovenia		0.187***		0.168***		0.170***
Bosnia and Herzegovina		−0.101**		−0.072		−0.063
Macedonia		base		base		base
R^2	0.070	0.124	0.127	0.163	0.132	0.167
N	640	640	415	415	415	415

Notes: * sig. <0.10 ** sig. <0.05 ***sig. <0.01

has been gained. Thus institutional trust influences behavior *before* actors can learn from experience, while the sense of fairness of competition comes *after* experience has been gained and analysed.

The second important point refers to network trust. Network trust has a significant positive effect on performance net of interpersonal and institutional trust. This is a significant finding which proves the validity of the argument behind the proposed typology. Not only are there good theoretical reasons for distinguishing among the three forms of trust, there is also empirical evidence that network trust has an independent effect on company performance. This was the core idea of typology. We suggested that each type of trust affects performance through a different mechanism: network trust by facilitating coordination among economic actors, institutional trust by means of opening up access to market opportunities, and interpersonal trust by encouraging cooperation. The results give support to these ideas.

Model IV includes dummies for countries. Perceived sales performance in Slovenia is significantly more favorable. What is important is the fact that even after controlling for country effects the network and institutional trust remain significant. Explained variance increases significantly from 12.7 per cent to 16.3 per cent. All trust effects are positive as predicted except for interpersonal trust. Its significance is wiped away by country effects. This is somewhat of a mystery because the theory would predict that interpersonal trust has a positive effect on performance on the individual level. This means that, controlling for systemic factors, interpersonal trust should be gaining rather than losing in its importance.

To examine this question we need to disaggregate the factor of interpersonal trust. The factor consists of two variables pertaining to respondents' actual business partners: 'trust your partners' and 'close with your partners' (see Table 5.2 for details on factor composition). While trust and closeness correlate with one another there is important asymmetry in the association. Of those who have very strong ties with their partners 81 per cent also completely trust their partners. However, of those who completely trust their partners there are just 37 per cent who also have a very close relationship with their partner. The correlation is obviously the result of an inherent asymmetry between closeness and trust. Those who have a very close relationship almost always trust their partners. However, of those who trust their partners not all actually have a high degree of intimacy or closeness. If you are close, you also trust. But to trust, you need not have close relationship with a partner.

Since trust and closeness correlate at the level of 0.5 they can be entered into the linear regression model only after taking out their interaction. The results presented in Models V and VI shed some light as to what may be going on in this puzzle. Model V shows that only closeness has a significant effect on performance while trust (net of closeness) has no significant effect. Interestingly, the effects are in the opposite direction. While closeness has a positive effect on performance, trust has an insignificant but negative impact. This puzzling result is actually consistent with the argument presented above. We argued that interpersonal trust affects performance by encouraging cooperation. Cooperation requires such a high level of mutual understanding and adjustment that it is possible only in relationships with high intimacy, that is in close personal relationships. We also argued that trust appears under conditions of uncertainty which tends to be eliminated in close personal relations. What these results seem to suggest is that closeness to partners slightly improves company performance through cooperation. However, trust itself, net of closeness, actually indicates a failure to establish a close enough relationship between two actors to overcome uncertainty from a transaction, thus leading to reduced rather than increased performance. In short, the failure of interpersonal trust to have a significant effect on performance can be explained by the failure of trust and success of closeness to produce cooperation.

CONCLUSION AND DISCUSSION

This chapter analysed the relationship between company performance and trust. While prior research has concentrated on the problem of *whether* trust affects performance, the emphasis of this chapter was on *how* trust improves the economic performance of the firm. To establish the causal mechanism behind the positive effect of trust we proposed to distinguish among three types of trust: interpersonal, institutional and network trust. We argued that each type of trust was associated with a different causal mechanism: institutional trust leads to improved access to business partners, network trust to improved coordination among loosely linked actors, and interpersonal trust to their close cooperation. Improvement in performance comes from the optimization of different costs: improved access reduces opportunity costs, improved coordination reduces information acquisition costs and cooperation reduces transaction costs, narrowly defined.

One of the key implications of this was that each type of trust could have an independent effect on performance. In the analysis of three national samples of entrepreneurs in Slovenia, Bosnia and Macedonia we found supporting evidence that different types of trust have independent effects on performance. Institutional trust had a strong and consistent positive effect net of other types of trust, organizational characteristics and the country-specific nature of economic affairs. By having trust in economic and political institutions, economic actors experienced improved sales over the year prior to the time of interviews. This result raises an important question that has been overlooked by the institutional school (Powell and DiMaggio 1991; Scott 2001). The central tenet of institutional theory is that there is little or no variation left after the institutional environment is taken into account. How is it possible that trust in political and economic institutions would have a significant effect after controlling for the institutional environment itself? The explanation offered in this chapter complements institutional theory by arguing that actors who trust political and economic institutions derive their advantages over distrustful actors by virtue of improved access to business partners. They are simply more willing to enter into transactions with a wider array of actors which expands their choices, reduces dependence, minimizes their opportunity costs and improves their performance. Institutional trust therefore does not only have an effect on a system level affecting all actors within a system, but also influences micro behavior within a particular institutional context.

The second important finding was an independent effect of network trust on performance that received scant attention in previous studies. This effect was also strongly positive and consistent net of organizational and context variables. It is remarkable that network trust has an independent effect from institutional trust. While both indicate that actors do business with strangers, the way the strangers are approached is different. Network trust means that economic actors can benefit from doing business with strangers whom they contact based on referrals by the people they know. The benefit of trusting the strangers based on trust in institutions is thus complemented with the trust in strangers that are known to our friends and acquaintances. The independence of institutional and network trust effects proves that there is not a common underlying factor explaining the effectiveness of both. While institutional trust encourages access to new business partners, thus lowering opportunity costs, referrals provide cheap but reliable information on potential partners, thus cutting the cost of information gathering and processing.

One of the surprises came from the fact that interpersonal trust had an insignificant effect on performance. Measured as trust in particular business partners net of closeness, it even had a negative effect. Further investigation of this phenomenon revealed that intimacy (closeness) between partners and trust in partners are actually at odds. Trust seems to complement the lack of closeness in a business relationship. Interpersonal trust therefore reveals a weakness rather than the strength in a business relationship based on interpersonal trust. Closeness is the key to close cooperation while trust as a weak supplement for intimacy leaves too many doubts to allow fully fledged cooperation to yield tangible benefits. It is remarkable that interpersonal trust does not lead to improved performance net of other types of trust and organizational and context controls. This suggests an interesting hypothesis, namely, that reduced transaction costs do not, by themselves, translate into economic advantage. If true this hypothesis could lead to serious rethinking of transaction cost economics. If transaction costs are insignificant for the overall performance of the firm, then the transaction cost theory may be mistakenly explaining organizational phenomena that are in fact driven by other factors.

The findings could also lead to the rethinking of the cooperative phenomenon. The literature from various disciplines from sociology to economics takes cooperation as an undisputed ideal of economic behavior. Not only does it lead to lower transaction costs, it also produces superior results because partners to a collaborative project invest effort, skills and identities into the product or service. The identity part means that they really care that their part is fulfilled to the standards of their partners regardless of formal obligations. To the economists cooperation holds a promise of flexibility as small units can pool their resources to achieve global competitiveness while staying small and nimble. To sociologists, cooperation is the hallmark of social existence, the ultimate realization of interdependence and self-discipline which makes it possible for a society to be held together without the brutal force of a sovereign. However, these results suggest that cooperation depends on close ties which are few and expensive to maintain in terms of time. Moreover, they usually come packed in triads and larger packets which often indicates closure of close ties in isolated islands of cooperation. Such cooperation holds all the promise of flexibility and solidarity but it fails to produce significant results because it tends to be locked in small closed networks that have trouble reaching beyond their narrow clique. Cooperation may reduce transaction costs but at the expense of higher opportunity and information search costs.

These ideas have important consequences for the academic exploration of trust and policy implementation. First, research on trust should free itself from the image of strong ties and cooperation and should look at the role of weak ties that are abundantly available in social networks. This is not an original idea (Granovetter 1973), however, it could fruitfully redefine the current research agenda. Second, policies that try to promote economic growth through formation of various local partnerships too often emphasize cohesion among various actors in the hope that something good would come out of this. However, results are usually disappointing. Building cohesive networks of diverse actors blocks rather than promotes action. The result is not a failed attempt but a failure to attempt anything. As a policy recommendation one should begin by promoting loose but overlapping associations that would leave enough freedom to actors and yet provide ample opportunities to join resources with others. The ideal is to build a trustworthy institutional environment and to create loose business associations that would help the formation of network trust. These two forms of trust have been shown to be more effective in promoting the economic performance of the firm than a classic interpersonal trust, which relies on intensive intimate relationships that may limit the scale and scope of business opportunities and information.

REFERENCES

Adizes, Ichak (1999), *Managing Corporate Lifecycles*, Paramus, NJ: Prentice Hall Press.

Arrighetti, Alessandro, Reinhard Bachmann and Simon Deakin (1997), 'Contract law, social norms and inter-firm cooperation', *Cambridge Journal of Economics*, 21, 171–95.

Arrow, K.J. (1974), *The Limits of Organization*, New York: Norton.

Bachmann, Reinhard (2001), 'Trust, power and control in trans-organizational relations', *Organization Studies*, 22(2), 337–65.

Bagnasco, Arnaldo and Charles F. Sabel (1995), *Small- and Medium-size Enterprises*, London: Pinter.

Bartlett, W. and Janez Prašnikar (1995), 'Small firms and economic transformation in Slovenia', *Communist Economies and Economic Transformation,* 7(1), 81–101.

Bartlett, Will and Vladimir Bukvič (2001), 'Barriers to SME growth in Slovenia', *MOST*, 11, 177–95.

Bradach, Jeffrey J. and Robert G. Eccles (1989), 'Price, authority, and trust: from ideal types to plural forms', *Annual Review of Sociology*, 15, 97–118.

Brusco, Sebastiano (1982), 'The Emilian model: productive decentralisation and social integration', *Cambridge Journal of Economics*, 6, 167–84.

Brusco, Sebastiano (1992), 'The idea of the industrial district: its genesis', in F. Pyke, G. Becattini and W. Sengenberger (eds), *Industrial Districts and Inter-firm Co-operation in Italy*, Geneva: International Institute for Labour Studies, pp. 10–19.

Bukvič, Vladimir, W. Bartlett, Andrej Rus, D. Sehič, and V. Stojanova (2001), *Barriers to SME Development in Bosnia, Macedonia, and Slovenia (Phare-ACE Project P97 8089-R Final Report)*, Ljubljana: GEA College.

Burt, Ronald S. (1992), *Structural Holes: The social structure of competition*, Cambridge, MA: Harvard University Press.

Burt, Ronald, S. and Marc Knez (1996), 'Trust and third-party gossip', in Roderick Moreland Kramer and Tom R. Tyler (eds), *Trust in Organizations: Frontiers of theory and research*, Thousand Oaks, CA: Sage Publications, pp. 68–89.

Coleman, James (1988), 'Social capital in the creation of human capital', *American Journal of Sociology Supplement*, 94, S95–S120.

Creed, W.E.D. and R.E. Miles (1996), 'Trust in organizations: a conceptual framework linking organizational forms, managerial philosophies, and the opportunity costs of controls', in Roderick Moreland Kramer and Tom R. Tyler (eds), *Trust in Organizations*, London: Sage, pp. 16–38.

Davis, Gerald F. and Henrich R. Greve (1997), 'Corporate elite networks and governance changes in the 1980s', *American Journal of Sociology*, 103(1), 1–37.

Deakin, Simon and Frank Wilkinson (1998), 'Contract law and the economics of interorganizational trust', in Christel Lane and Reinhard Bachmann (eds), *Trust Within and Between Organizations: Conceptual issues and empirical applications*, New York: Oxford University Press, pp. 146–72.

Dei Ottati, Gabi (1994), 'Cooperation and competition in the industrial district as an organization model', *European Planning Studies*, 2, 463–83.

Fukuyama, Francis (1995), *Trust: The social virtues and the creation of prosperity*, New York: Free Press.

Gambetta, Diego (1988), *Trust: Making and breaking cooperative relations*, Oxford, UK; Cambridge, MA: Basil Blackwell.

Giddens, Anthony (1990), *Central Problems in Social Theory: Action, structure, and contradiction in social analysis*, Berkeley: University of California Press.

Granovetter, Mark (1973), 'The strength of weak ties', *American Journal of Sociology*, 78(6), 1360–80.

Granovetter, Mark (1982), 'The strength of weak ties: a network theory revisited', in Peter V. Marsden and Nan Lin (eds), *Social Structure and Network Analysis*, Beverly Hills: Sage, pp. 105–30.

Granovetter, Mark (1985), 'Economic action and social structure: the problem of embeddedness', *American Journal of Sociology*, 91, 481–510.

Gulati, Ranjay (1995), 'Familiarity breeds trust? The implications of repeated ties for contractual choice in alliances', *Academy of Management Journal*, 38, 85–112.

Hannan, Michael T. and John Freeman (1989), *Organizational Ecology*, Cambridge, MA: Harvard University Press.

Haunschild, Pamela R. (1993), 'Interorganizational imitation: the impact of interlocks on corporate acquisition activity', *Administrative Science Quarterly*, 38, 564–92.

Haveman, Heather A. (1993), 'Follow the leader: mimetic isomorphism and entry into new markets', *Administrative Science Quarterly*, 38, 593–627.

Johannisson, Bengt (2000), 'Networking and entrepreneurial growth', in Donald L. Sexton and Hans Landstrom (eds), *The Blackwell Handbook of Entrepreneurship*, London: Blackwell, pp. 368–86.

Kern, Horst (1998), 'Lack of trust, surfeit of trust: some causes of the innovation crisis in German industry', in Christel Lane and Reinhard Bachmann (eds), *Trust Within and Between Organizations: Conceptual issues and empirical applications*, New York: Oxford University Press, pp. 203–213.

Lane, Christel (1998), 'Introduction: theories and issues in the study of trust', in Christel Lane and Reinhard Bachmann (eds), *Trust Within and Between Organizations: Conceptual issues and empirical applications*, New York: Oxford University Press, pp. 1–30.

Lane, Christel and Bachmann, Reinhard (1997), 'Cooperation in inter-firm relations in Britain and Germany: the role of social institutions', *British Journal of Sociology*, 48, 226–54.

Lazerson, Mark (1995), 'A new Phoenix? Modern putting out in the Modena knitwear industry', *Administrative Science Quarterly*, 40, 34–59.

Lorenz, Edward H. (1988), 'Neither friends nor strangers: informal networks of subcontracting in French industry', in Diego Gambetta (ed.), *Trust: Making and breaking of cooperative relations*, Oxford: Blackwell, pp. 194–210.

Luhmann, Niklas (1988), 'Familiarity, confidence, trust: problems and alternatives', in Diego Gambetta (ed.), *Trust: making and breaking cooperative relations*, Oxford, UK; Cambridge, MA: Basil Blackwell, pp. 94–107.

Möllering, Guido (2002), 'Rational, institutional and active trust: just do it!?', Chapter 2, this volume.

Norris, Pippa (2002), *Democratic Phoenix: reinventing political activism*, Cambridge, UK; New York, NY: Cambridge University Press.

Powell, Walter W. (1996), 'Trust-based forms of governance', in Roderick Moreland Kramer and Tom R. Tyler (eds), *Trust in Organizations. Frontiers of Theory and Research*, Thousand Oaks: Sage, pp. 51–67.

Powell, Walter W. and Paul DiMaggio (1991), *The New Institutionalism in Organizational Analysis*, Chicago: University of Chicago Press.

Putnam, Robert D. (1993), *Making Democracy Work: Civic traditions in modern Italy*, Princeton, NJ: Princeton University Press.

Pyke, Frank (1992), *Industrial Development Through Small-Firm Cooperation*, Geneva: ILO.

Pyke, Frank, G. Becattini and Werner Sengenberger (1992), *Industrial Districts and Inter-firm Cooperation in Italy*, Geneva: ILO.

Ring, P.S. and Andrew H. van de Ven (1992), 'Structuring corporative relationships between organizations', *Strategic Management Journal*, 13, 483–98.

Rothstein, B. and D. Stolle (2001), 'Social capital and street level bureaucracy: an institutional theory of generalised trust', ESF Conference Social Capital: Interdisciplinary Perspectives, UK, 15–20 September.

Sako, Mari (1992), *Prices, Quality, and Trust: Inter-firm relations in Britain and Japan*, Cambridge; New York, NY: Cambridge University Press.

Sako, Mari (1998), 'Does trust improve business performance?' in Christel Lane and Reinhard Bachmann (eds), *Trust Within and Between Organizations: Conceptual issues and empirical applications*, New York: Oxford University Press, pp. 88–117.

Scott, W. Richard (2001), *Institutions and Organizations*, Thousand Oaks, CA: Sage Publications.

Simmel, Georg (1950), *The Sociology of Georg Simmel*, trans. and ed. K.H. Wolff, Glencoe, Ill.: Free Press.

Staber, Udo (1998), 'Inter-firm cooperation and competition in industrial districts', *Organization Studies*, 19(4), 701–25.

Stinchcombe, Arthur L. (1965), 'Social structure and organizations', in James G. March (ed.), *Handbook of Organizations*, Chicago: Rand McNally & Co., pp. 142–93.

Sydow, Jorg (1998), 'Understanding the constitution of interorganizational trust', in Christel Lane and Reinhard Bachmann (eds), *Trust Within and Between Organizations: Conceptual issues and empirical applications*, New York: Oxford University Press, pp. 31–63.

Uzzi, Brian (1996), 'The sources and consequences of embeddedness for the economic performance of organizations: the network effect', *American Sociological Review*, 61, 674–98.

Williamson, Oliver E. (1996), *The Mechanisms of Governance*, New York: Oxford University Press.

Zucker, Lynne G. (1986), 'Production of trust: institutional sources of economic structure', *Research in Organizational behavior*, 8, 53–111.

6. Managing trust and the risk of information leakage in collaborative research and technology development: results from a case study in a specialist chemicals industry

Andreas Hoecht

INTRODUCTION

Nowadays it is hardly surprising that the strategic management and the knowledge management literature broadly agree in that companies operating in research-intensive industries should pursue 'outward-looking' research and technology development strategies. The optimistic view that competitive advantages can be gained from strategic alliances and collaborative technology development that permeates the strategic management literature (Porter, 1987; Bleeke and Ernst, 1992; Doz and Hamel, 1997) is supported by a wealth of detailed studies on collaborative research, in particular on research networks in technology intensive industries (Newell and Clark, 1990; Powell et al., 1996). Looking inward is no longer a viable option. Even the most resourceful firms appear no longer able to rely exclusively on internal R&D and explorative knowledge creation in particular relies on participation in research networks (Powell, 1990). Participation in collaborative research and research networks, however, requires 'openness' and relatively free information exchange as a vital precondition for successful organizational learning. And it is this openness and free information exchange that makes companies vulnerable to the risk of information leakage (McMillan et al., 1995). In an earlier paper, Hoecht and Trott (1999) developed a conceptual framework linking different technology development strategies with their associated risk of information leakage and the control mechanisms that can be used to deal with this risk. We found that trust and 'social control' become more important, the more outward-looking the technology development strategy pursued.

THE INDUSTRY CASE STUDY

This chapter explores the relationship between trust and the risk of information leakage in the management of collaborative technology development in more detail, and draws on the results of a small-scale empirical study the author undertook in the flavour and fragrance industry in order to explore the validity of a conceptual framework developed in Hoecht and Trott (1999). The research was designed around the need to understand more fully the process of building and managing trust in collaborative research and the role of managerial and social control in containing the risk of information leakage. The conceptual framework predicted that social control, such as individual researchers' concern for their reputation, internalized professional ethics and also the relationship commitment derived from the process of building trust, replaces increasingly ineffective bureaucratic control in outward-looking technology development strategies. The research objective was to expose the predicted relationship between the degree of 'openness' in research and technology development and the effectiveness of different types of 'control' to a first empirical test. The initial investigation set out to uncover information from a wide variety of people who had been involved in collaborative research and technology development. Table 6.1 illustrates the range of roles covered. Because of the exploratory nature of the research, this initial investigation used a semi-structured interview approach. The aim was to get the participants to talk freely and to discuss their ideas in their own terms. The key areas listed for discussion were:

- The selection of research collaborators
- The assessment of the risk of information leakage
- The instruments to control information leakage
- The effectiveness of these instruments
- The extent of control of contacts with other organizations

The organization's research is conducted in two different divisions, the ingredients research and the applied research division. Both divisions are headed by senior R&D managers who oversee the research carried out in the constituent research groups of their division and who are part of and accountable to the directorate level of the organization. Interviewing began with senior R&D managers and further interviews were conducted with people from a variety of research-related backgrounds including research scientists in different research groups. The interviews commonly lasted one to two hours and the interviewer usually spent a full day on site. To validate the interview material, summary feedback was provided to some of the key interview partners and their responses used to refine the findings of the original interviews. Table 6.1 lists typical key interviewees and their position and role in the organization.

Table 6.1   Typical key interviewees and their position and role in the organization

Role	Typical department or unit
Head of division, senior R&D manager	Ingredients research division
Head of division, senior R&D manager	Applied research division
Head of research group, R&D manager	Novel ingredients research group
Head of process R&D, R&D manager	Ingredients research
Senior research scientist	Analytical chemistry research group
Senior research scientist	Biochemistry research group
Research scientist	Novel ingredients group
Research scientist	Analytical chemistry research group

The fragrance and flavour research industry is highly suitable for a first explorative study into the conceptual framework as it is relatively small and specialized and, as a consequence, the active pool of researchers relatively small. The organization investigated is part of one of the biggest multinational firms in the chemical industry. It is also engaged in the production of fragrances, in flavours and in food technology research. Fragrance research is undertaken in a small number of international locations, the UK being host to the European research centre. The major competitors in terms of new product development and research in the fragrance sector are based in the European Union and the United States, with only very few organizations active in the field worldwide. Very limited applied research is, however, undertaken by the firm's clients themselves, but this research is essentially limited to fine-tuning of ingredients to the particular needs of the clients. The market-leading role in the UK is evident in that even clients that are closely allied with competitors of the parent organization frequently draw on the services of the company in question. The research is therefore not exclusive to the parent organization.

THE CONCEPT OF TRUST

Companies which cannot internalize their research needs, or which would have to pay high opportunity costs for doing so, need to trust their outside partners not to misuse their privileged access to information. Innovative applied research often develops out of the cooperation of firms and research institutions, where the collaboration is initiated with the help of previous academic contacts of key players in firms and universities. In this case the selection of and decision to trust a partner is typically made on the basis of prior professional and or social knowledge (Zucker et al.,1996; Liebeskind and Oliver, 1998). Personal knowledge and the desire to protect one's professional reputation are deemed sufficient safeguards to justify a limited scale disclosure of sensitive information. If the initial co-operation is successful, the scale of cooperation can be increased incrementally and higher levels of mutual trust will be reached (Lewicki and Bunker, 1996).

At this point it will be useful to introduce some definitions. Trust is not the same as confidence. Investors are confident that the value of their shares will rise over time and that the stock market will not collapse, but they trust that the broker will not run away with their money. Both confidence and trust are based on expectations about the future, but trust entails the exposure to the risk of opportunistic behaviour by others. One can say that an agent exhibits trust when he/she has no reason to believe that the trusted other will exploit this opportunity (Giddens, 1990; Humphrey and Schmitz, 1998). Prominent researchers of trust distinguish between different levels, qualities and sources of trust. Sako (1992) distinguishes between competence trust (confidence in the other's ability to perform properly), contractual trust (honouring the accepted rules of exchange) and goodwill trust (mutual expectations of open commitment to each other beyond contractual obligations). According to Zucker (1986: 53) trust can be produced in three different ways:

> Trust can be (1) process-based, where trust is tied to past or expected exchange, such as reputation or gift exchange; (2) characteristic-based, where trust is tied to a person, depending on characteristics such as family background or ethnicity; and (3) institutional-based, where trust is tied to formal structures, depending on individual or firm-specific attributes.

The sources of trust production are not mutually exclusive and often work in conjunction. For instance, while membership in an ethnic group (characteristic-based or ascribed trust) can be a vital initial advantage for setting up a business or having studied at a particular university for finding 'open doors', this will not be enough to sustain trust over time. Trust can be initiated as ascribed trust, but it will have to be 'earned' before long (Humphrey and Schmitz, 1998). Similarly, bestowing trust onto a person or an institution does not mean that methods of limiting the damage from potential 'betrayal' cannot be used. Contractual safeguards, access to legal redress and institutional assurances can have a very positive effect on cooperative business relations as Lane and Bachmann (1996) have shown in their comparison of the role of trust in UK and German supplier relations. The context of supplier relations, however, is quite different from collaborative advanced scientific research as will be discussed below.

It is important to keep in mind that trust is practised and exercised between individuals, even if they 'stand for' an organization. Trust is a personal judgement and carries an emotional as well as cognitive dimension, even if its object is a system (money, the market) or an institution (the legal profession, the health service). While trust at the system level is close to confidence – as there is no choice but to trust the currency to store value – trust in an institution or organization depends on the personal experience with individuals representing the organization at its 'access points' (Giddens, 1990). This does not mean that the institutional dimension should be underestimated. We trust a solicitor (if we do) not only because we feel that the person in question comes across as 'sincere' and professional, but also because we know and rely on the professional body's ability and willingness to strike dishonest solicitors 'off the list' and to compensate financial losses in cases of gross misconduct (Brewis et al., 1998).

In the context of collaborative R&D, institutional sources of trust production will, however, be of limited use only. It is clearly not possible to rely solely on institutional-based trust and legal safeguards for the protection of intangible, pre-competitive knowledge against misuse (Sitkin and Roth, 1993). Even if such safeguards were workable, the necessity to incorporate each little step along the development path of a collaborative research project into a contractual arrangement would cause enormous delays and hence endanger its very success. The level of trust needed here is the one labelled 'goodwill trust' by Sako (1992), where the mutual commitment goes beyond honouring what is explicitly agreed and the trustee can be trusted to exercise the highest level of discretion, to take beneficial initiatives and to refrain from taking unfair advantage even if such opportunities arise.

TRUST AND THE RISK OF INFORMATION LEAKAGE

There is a substantial body of literature on risk in the social sciences. Lupton (1999) traces the changes in the understanding of risk in the social sciences and classifies them according to their respective epistemological position. From a realist perspective, risk can be understood as variances in outcomes that are important to the risk-taking subjects. Das and Teng (2001) distinguish between actual risk and perceived risk in the management of strategic alliances and suggest that the perceived risk in inter-firm alliances is determined by both trust and control. For Das and Teng, both trust and control are able to reduce the perceived probability and impact of undesirable outcomes happening. While control aims at directly influencing the behaviour of others in a desired way, trust is based on a positive expectation about the others' behaviour, leading to a lowered risk perception in a relationship and making it possible for the trustor to ignore some of the 'objective' risk of the trustee behaving opportunistically. In this sense, trust and control together allow for a reduction of the perceived risks but not necessarily actual risk inherent in inter-firm relationships. Das and Teng (2001) further suggest that a distinction should be made between relational risk – the probability and consequences of unsatisfactory cooperation – and performance risk – the probability and consequences that alliance objectives are not achieved for reasons other than lack of cooperation between partner firms. They suggest that different types and combinations of trust and control are needed to manage theses types of risks, and recommend that relational risks should be addressed by building 'goodwill' trust among the partners.

The risk of information leakage is mainly a relational risk as the likelihood of valuable scientific information being known to third parties before ownership claims have been established[1] is greatly increased once organizational boundaries acting as 'efficient information envelopes' are transgressed (Zucker et al., 1996). Commercial science such as biotechnology research faces an information dilemma. Academic scientific research is based on the principle of open dialogue and sharing information as a common good and claims to new discoveries are made and recognized by publication and peer review of results. For commercial scientific research, on the other hand, the value of new discoveries is determined by the ability to keep them exclusive to the firm until ownership rights through patents have been firmly secured (Mansfield,1986; Eisenberg,1987). This has major implications in terms of the trustworthiness required from the scientists involved in such research. Within academic research communities, trust in the professional competence and in the personal integrity of a researcher are very closely interwoven. The credibility of researchers, the scientific community's trust in the validity of their research and, closely linked, their personal integrity or trustworthiness, tends to be directly related to their accumulated social capital in the research community: accumulated direct interpersonal experiences with other researchers (process-based trust), reputation (intermediated trust), academic peer review and recognition by research organizations (institutional trust) all contribute to the professional standing of established researchers (Liebeskind and Oliver, 1998).

The dimensions of trust are mutually reinforcing. From a certain level in a professional career, reputation or intermediated trust facilitates or may even predetermine the outcome of peer reviews for publications and research awards (institutional trust), and will lay the foundations for further opportunities to build process-based trust in selected research circles and networks. As peer assessment is the key to academic and scientific careers, reputation becomes the most precious career asset and needs to be zealously guarded.

The character assessment criteria to be eligible for commercial research participation, however, are substantially different from the values underpinning traditional academic credibility. Academic scientific credibility requires unreserved participation in social exchanges through peer review and the sharing of information as well as gaining a reputation for competence and fairness, whereas commercial credibility requires a commitment to secrecy so as to protect the commercial value of research results (Eisenberg, 1987). Because of the greatly increased risk of opportunistic behaviour associated with information that has to be kept exclusive to keep its value, the essence of trustworthiness shifts from being cooperative within the research community to being loyal to a commercial organization. As a consequence, initial expectations of others' trustworthiness tend to be reduced (the interpersonal trust stake is raised), intermediated trust is more difficult to establish and institutional trust created through the university system becomes relatively ineffectual (Liebeskind and Oliver, 1998).

Hence the intrusion of commercial interests into academic research can be expected to raise the demand for and the level of trust required for research collaborations while at the same time making it more difficult for new entrants to join research networks and leading to their eventual 'ossification'. One solution for overcoming the problem of network ossification is for high profile scientists working for commercial research firms to take on the role of 'boundary spanners' between the world of academic and commercial research. It is their task to make sure that academic scientists whose work is of interest to a commercial firm pass the tests of academic as well as commercial credibility. The important role of boundary spanners in overcoming network ossification is supported by the research of Burt (1999) on structural holes in networks and the brokerage opportunities of network entrepreneurs who are able to bridge information flows between otherwise disconnected groups of people (structural holes).[2] The trust/distrust judgements of boundary spanners regarding new relationship contacts are significantly improved by their privileged network positions which provide them with more varied information flows and help them to avoid the cohesive network clique dynamics of distrust amplified by uniform negative third party gossip.

TRUST, RISK AND CONTROL IN THE MANAGEMENT OF COLLABORATIVE TECHNOLOGY DEVELOPMENT

Firms have a constrained choice between a number of technology development strategies. Dependent on their resource and market position as well as their 'innovation environment', they may be able to rely on internal R&D and technology literature scanning with their own manpower (we define this as an *introspective strategy*); they may opt for a complementary *acquisitive* strategy and purchase technology or hire expert staff, they may concentrate on a dyadic *cooperative* strategy (joint venture, cooperative projects) or they may choose research networks (*extrovert strategy*) and the associated risks. Hoecht and Trott (1999) argued that the reliance on predominantly inward-looking strategies is often only suitable for firms operating in mature industries with incremental technology development, while 'knowledge-intensive' industries will call for a considerable degree of openness with a higher exposure to the risk of information leakage. In their model, the amount of risk is likely to increase along the vertical axis (introspective–acquisitive–cooperative–extrovert) simply because the effectiveness and reach of direct control mechanisms diminish. The principle 'hard' control mechanisms at a firm's disposal are direct monitoring and control through 'internalisation', and legal instruments such as employment contracts (including secrecy clauses) and legally binding agreements between firms such as cooperation contracts, patents and intellectual property rights (Creed and Miles, 1996). Internalization and bureaucratization may be very inflexible, but they do offer a significant amount of control over risks such as information leakage (Williamson, 1993). The risk of information leakage, however, needs to be weighed up against the risk of failing to have access to cutting-edge information and know-how.

Fortunately, firms do not have to rely on hard control instruments only. 'Social' control mechanisms are particularly important for firms that need to be outward-looking by nature of their industry. As a general rule, the more 'outward-looking' a firm's technology development strategy, the more emphasis is placed on 'social' control mechanisms. Legal remedies tend to be too slow and too costly for regulating complex and fast-moving technological developments and their associated intellectual property and ownership rights (Deakin et al., 1994; Liebeskind and Oliver, 1998). At the same time, as far as social control mechanisms are concerned, reputational concerns are one of the most important 'self-disciplining' mechanisms for individual professionals and 'knowledge workers' (Garsten and Grey, 1998) and they are particularly effective in the operation of research networks. The relationship between social and direct control is more complex than simple intersubstitutability and firms would be unwise to rely on one form entirely. Nevertheless, the higher degree of employee autonomy, which comes with outward-looking strategies, the more that some degree of substitution of direct monitoring for social control and trust will be necessary. Table 6.2 (adapted from Hoecht and Trott, 1999) gives an overview over the technology development strategies identified and their respective level of the risk of

Table 6.2 *Trust risk and control associated with different perspectives on technology development*

Technology development strategy	Technology development activity	Loci of knowledge base	Main source of risk (information leakage)	Level and type of trust required	Type and effectiveness of legal means
Introspective	Technology scanning (literature searching)	Individuals and research department	None, public knowledge	Minimal/competence	Not needed (knowledge in public domain)
Acquisitive	Internal R&D	Individuals and research department	Employee turnover related	Competence and contractual, moderate	Employment contract, high
	Purchase of technology	Other organization	Employee turnover related	Competence and contractual, moderate	Contract law, high
	Wholesale purchase of firm	Other organization	Employee turnover related	Competence and contractual, moderate	Contract law, high
Cooperative	Joint venture	Own and other organization's individuals and research department	Other firm's research staff and management	Competence, contractual and goodwill, high	Contract law and employment contracts, medium
	Joint technology project	Own and other organization's individuals and research department	Other firm's research staff and management	Competence, contractual and goodwill, high	Contract law and employment contracts, medium-low
Extrovert (aquisitive)	Hiring of independent experts	Individuals	Breach of secrecy	Competence, contractual and goodwill, very high	Contract law, secrecy agreement medium to low*
Extrovert (participative)	Research network participation	Primarily boundary spanners	Breach of secrecy; changing employer	Competence, contractual and goodwill, very high	Secrecy agreement, employment contract, low**

Notes:
* reputational concerns very effective
** reputational concerns very effective (network sanctions)

information leakage together with the associated demands in terms of type and level of trust and the effectiveness of legal remedies.

Table 6.2 identifies the location of the knowledge base and the associated risk of information leakage for each technology development strategy. It also predicts the types and levels of trust required and the effectiveness of legal means for each technology development strategy. In line with the arguments made by Zucker at al. (1996) and the design principles for inter-firm alliances established by Nooteboom (1999), the introspective strategy carries the lowest risk of information leakage and unwanted competence spill-over. Monitoring and control is relatively effective within organizational boundaries, employment contracts can be detailed and employees will only be employed if a minimum of trust exists in their professional abilities (competence trust) and their character as well as their willingness to behave within the rules of their employment contract (contractual trust). When a company pursues an acquisitive technology development strategy, in particular if it decides to acquire another firm, the risk of information leakage increases because it takes time to establish a new organizational boundary or 'information envelope' (Zucker et al., 1996) around the knowledge base of the firm to be acquired. Once the acquisition is successfully completed, the same internalization advantages identified for the introspective technology strategy should apply, but experience shows that acquisitions often face significant problems arising from clashes between organizational cultures, and that motivation and loyalty of the new employees can be problematic (Cartwright and Cooper, 1996). The risk of information leakage further increases with cooperative technology strategies because an organizational information envelope no longer exists and each participating organization needs to trust the management and research staff of the partner organization not to behave opportunistically. Employment contracts do not cover employees from another organization, contract law is of limited effectiveness only (see above), monitoring opportunities are limited and hence goodwill trust is needed. It is not enough to have trust in the other party honouring the agreed rules of exchange (contractual trust) because opportunities for opportunistic behaviour exist beyond what any contractual agreement could foresee. What is needed is goodwill trust, a mutual expectation of an open commitment to each other beyond contractual obligations (Sako, 1992).

The risk of information leakage is at its highest level when extrovert technology development strategies are pursued. With extrovert technology strategies, direct monitoring, supervision and managerial control becomes largely inoperable, contract law and secrecy agreements are put in place but transgressions are difficult to prove and hence, goodwill trust and social control, in particular reputational concerns, play a key role in handling this risk. Table 6.2 distinguishes between the hiring of independent experts (external consultants) and research network participation. I believe that professional network sanctioning abilities can be even more effective for boundary spanners than for independent professionals not rooted in a particular organization.

INSIGHTS FROM THE CASE STUDY

The company case study of the fine fragrance industry was conducted with the purpose to begin to explore the validity of the conceptual model capturing the relationship between trust, risk and control in (collaborative) research and technology development. The conceptual model distinguishes between four different technology development strategies subdivided into eight different technology development activities. The scope of the empirical study and the time and resources available did not allow for a full exploration of the model. It was therefore decided to explore the issues of trust, risk and cooperative behaviour between research scientists within the organization (internal R&D); the relationship between the organization and some of its key contractors involved in pre-market optimization of the production of new products (co-operative technology development); and the issues of trust, control and risk of information leakage in the relationship with external consultants/independent professional experts (extrovert technology development strategy). Unfortunately, there was no opportunity to gain insight into trust and the risk of information leakage in acquisitive technology development strategies as the organization on which the research was centred had only itself been acquired by a multinational company in the chemical industry in the not too distant past and had not pursued acquisitive technology development itself in its specialist field.

Research Activities

Research in the organization is conducted in two different divisions, the ingredient research and the applied research division. Both divisions are headed by senior R&D managers who oversee the research carried in the constituent research groups of their division and who are part of and accountable to the directorate level of the organization. The organization itself is part of a multinational company and is judged by its contribution to the overall concern. This results in an increasing pressure to deliver tangible research output and to be financially viable. The organization offers its services to strategic business units within the parent company and to outside clients. The corporate parent encourages information exchanges and research networking among its strategic business units, but the organization increasingly needs to rely on 'outsiders' for its collaborative research and technology development. The organization prefers to restrict its collaboration with other commercial organizations to non-applied, foundational research, but it draws on the expertise of external consultants for its new product development. The external consultants are distinguished academic scientists who either are still employed by or have been linked to highly regarded university research departments. External consultants are chosen for their high level of expertise and their standing in the research community. They are independent in the sense that they are either university-based, the university not being perceived as a commercial competitor, or have no 'live links' with current commercial competitors. The organization also uses outside commercial contractors for some new product development-related activities, mainly pilot production of new products in the pre-production stage.

Research Scientists within the Organization

All research scientists interviewed were fully aware of the confidentiality clauses in their contracts of employment and did not see them as problematic. The interviewees did not feel that these clauses were unreasonable. The dominant view was that they considered this to be normal for the type of work they were involved in. It was also mentioned that fragrance research was a very small industry and that 'no one in their right mind would want to risk their job with careless talk'. Furthermore, the researchers interviewed did not feel that there were many opportunities to betray the trust of their organization even if they wanted to, apart from, perhaps, conference attendances. Conference presentations, however, are usually made by senior scientists and research managers and the contributions of junior scientists, if put forward, are thoroughly checked by their superiors. Research managers, therefore, did not perceive this as a significant source for information leakage risks. The researcher scientists work in small groups headed by research group managers who are able to monitor their day-to day activities. The research scientists work on agreed projects, some of which can be pursued individually, while others require a joint effort. There was, however, very limited evidence of cooperation across research groups and divisions. A sizeable number of research scientists had been recruited as graduates from universities where the organization had existing research links. In some cases the research scientists had even spent an industrial placement year in the organization and had then later returned to be employed as junior researchers. Staff turnover was regarded as low by the research managers interviewed, which they saw as an indication of researchers being reasonably happy with their jobs. This judgement needs to be qualified, however, in so far as some of the research scientists said that due to the specialist nature of their work, employment opportunities outside the fragrance industry were very limited. The research managers interviewed were not able to pinpoint any particular case where they were convinced that the organization had been betrayed by a research scientist leaking commercially sensitive information. It was interesting to note that some of the research managers interviewed made a distinction between purposeful betrayal and accidental disclosure of sensitive information. They seemed to accept that accidental disclosure can never be totally controlled, but were very keen to do their best to 'combat' purposeful betrayal for private gain.

From the interviews conducted with research scientists, it appears to me that there are few opportunities for information leakage, partly because of the effectiveness of the organizational information envelope and the monitoring and management control exercised within the organization, and partly because of the specific nature of the industry itself. Legal control instruments such as employment contracts and secrecy clauses appear to be working well. Another factor that appears to help in containing the risk of information leakage is the professional identity developed by research scientists at university and later at work and the close links between the universities from where many graduates come and the organization they later work for. Their employer's trust in their competence and their character is likely to be facilitated by the social links that exist between the organization and the universities concerned.

During the interviews it became apparent that there was a lack of trust between the researchers and the research groups within the organization that affected the research productivity of the organization. I was told by a junior research scientist that there was a culture of withholding information from other scientists, in particular scientists from different groups. The respective group research manager admitted that there was a problem with information exchange across research groups and divisions and emphasized that the organization had launched a programme aiming at creating trust among research staff. I found that the programme was deemed to have very limited effect in the eyes of research staff I interviewed. According to my interviews, the main factor hindering free information exchange and full cooperation among research staff was that research careers depended on discoveries and these discoveries were attributed to individuals rather than groups when it came to promotion decisions.

This seems to be an example that information envelopes can exist at the sub-organizational level and have a negative impact on research success of an organization overall.

External Contractors

Most research managers accepted the need for collaboration with external researchers, in particular consultants, for the success of their research efforts. Research managers were less willing to accept the need to contract out some of the new product development-related activities, mainly pilot production of new products in the pre-production stage as they considered this technology development strategy less driven by the need for outside expertise and more dictated by the logic of corporate accountants. Most of the research managers felt that they would prefer to keep things in-house at such a critical stage. Asked about their confidence in legal contracts, there was a general belief that they were indispensable and effective, but further questioning revealed that the contractual trust bestowed on contractors by research managers was closely linked to their judgement that their parent company had sufficient economic muscle and sanctioning power to deter contractors from leaking any commercial secrets to competitors. They also emphasized that they made sure that the work of the contractors was closely supervised at all stages. Asked about the selection of external contractors, research managers expressed a preference for contractors who had worked for them before and who had proven to be trustworthy and 'had not caused trouble'.

The choice of contractors, however, was limited and I was left with the general feeling that the relationship with external contractors was not an easy one. Unfortunately my discussions about trust and the risk of information leakage with respect to external contractors did not go beyond the inter-organizational level and I am unable to comment in any detail on the development of interpersonal trust in these relationships. From the way research managers and the operations manager referred to external contractors in the interviews, however, it can be concluded that interpersonal trust judgements play a key role in the establishment of inter-organizational trust.

It is interesting to compare the organization's approach to cooperative technology development with external contractors in new product development close to marketization with its approach pursued in foundational research cooperation.

The organization is involved in a small number of cross-national prestigious research programmes. This was presented to be partly to keep a high profile in the industry, and partly to gain access to the eventual results of this research. Research managers maintained that both the input commitments and the rights to potential outcomes were very well controlled by detailed legal arrangements. They saw their participation as much as a matter of prestige and status in the research community as connected to the potential benefits of the research itself. They did not feel that information leakage was an issue that they should be worried about, predominantly because of the distance of the research from marketable outcomes.

External Consultants

The trust-building process was most clearly visible in relation to external consultants. All research managers interviewed expressed a preference for researchers with whom they had worked before. A consensus view emerged that they would normally rely on existing contacts when deciding about names of researchers for external consultancy input.[3] Asked how they would find new researchers if a particular expertise was not covered by their existing contacts, I was told that there were ways of 'sussing out' new individuals, such as checking database information on consultants and research scientists as formal sources of information and 'listening around' as a more informal way. The informal sources of information were judged to be more important for external consultants than for research scientists.

Although this point was not discussed in detail, the informal information gathering appears to be facilitated in that most consultants originally come from or are still linked to university departments and the network character of the academic research community. If key research managers from the organization keep their links to the academic community, they have access to the shared knowledge on the competence and character (trustworthiness) of individual members of this community (see Hagstrom, 1965; Liebeskind and Oliver, 1998). The research managers interviewed maintained that participation at workshops and conferences was also used to get to know and gently check on individuals who might be of interest to the organization. Newcomers were only considered if they were not filtered out by this process of informal and formal screening.

Almost all research managers emphasised in the interviews the importance of the 'character' impression individuals made upon them.[4] The majority emphasized that they did not want to employ someone who was too talkative about their work for previous employers as they felt that this indiscretion could hit back onto themselves. They perceived integrity, defined as being discreet about previous work, as at least as important as professional competence, which most of the research managers took for granted with someone who would be willing to work for them. Nevertheless, when asked about relationships and trust-building, I was told that even individuals who passed the initial tests would have to prove their reliability with smaller and then increasingly more important work for the organization. This would allow them to get to know the individuals both professionally and with regard to their trustworthiness.[5] Important contracts would only follow after trust had been built. As a further precaution the organization would not want to work with any external consultant who maintained 'live links' with any of their competitors.[6] This rule was considered to be of very high importance and generally recognized as such.

The rule was certainly applied to direct competitors, but upon further questioning I was told that there was a weakness in that it may not always be easy to determine which organizations would pose a potential threat of information leakage. Moving on to secrecy agreements, I was told that detailed secrecy agreements and indemnity clauses would be incorporated into contracts of employment as a matter of course. These, however, were seen by most interviewees more as a necessity than offering absolute real protection against the risk of betrayal. In the course of the interviews, a distinction emerged between information leakage risks stemming from purposeful betrayal and from accidental disclosure of sensitive information. The research managers felt that the risk of betrayal was much more prominent for applied research than foundational research, and a majority also felt that accidental disclosure could be harmful at all stages of research. Accidental disclosure was somehow accepted as 'accidents waiting to happen', but real resentment was aired for anyone betraying their organization deliberately.

I was told that the organization was seeking ways to further ensure the loyalty of the most important external consultants. One of these ways was to pay these consultants even when their services were not strictly needed to ensure permanent access to their expertise but also 'to keep them away from the competition'.[7] This was seen as a supplementary measure, however, as research managers were generally very convinced about the integrity of their external consultants.

In my interviews, the importance of social capital and trust for research collaboration was broadly confirmed. The reputation of key researchers, in particular external consultants, was judged to be their key asset, which they could not afford to lose. Most interviewees confirmed that in their opinion external consultants would lose the basis of their whole professional career if they were found to be untrustworthy.

Despite this belief, some of the research managers pointed out that it may not always be easy to detect information leakage and that involuntary information leakage was an inherent risk of all research collaboration. Some managers maintained that even deliberate betrayal might be difficult to detect in non-applied research ventures.

Although reputational concerns have been identified as powerful sanctioning mechanisms for distinguished researchers (see Liebeskind and Oliver, 1998), by far not all research managers were confident that their research networks would be effective enforcers in practice. I was told that this would very much depend on the skill/'criminal talent' of the individual and the coherence of the research network concerned.[8] While no research manager said that he would employ a consultant whom he wouldn't trust, the supplementary measures such as loyalty payments discussed above and legal means were used alongside social control mechanisms. Nevertheless, even if some degree of direct supervision and dependency was considered the best choice for keeping contractors 'on the path of virtue', research managers ultimately will have to trust their external consultants to have a paramount interest in safeguarding their own reputation.

DISCUSSION

I argued above that 'social control' and trust will become the more important the more outward-looking the research and technology development strategy an organization decides to pursue. The interviews broadly confirmed the predictions of the conceptual model. It is particularly interesting to compare the difference in the combinations of trust and control measures used in the relationships with external consultants and external contractors. External contractors appear to be treated much more in a traditional managerial–supervisory way with detailed contracts and close monitoring at all stages of the relationship. Interpersonal trust clearly plays an important part, but the emphasis is on qualified trust with visible control. This observation is in line with the research by van der Meer-Kooistra and Vosselman (2000) who distinguish between bureaucracy-based and trust-based management control approaches to inter-firm relations. The main difference is that while both rely on a significant level of trust, in bureaucracy-based inter-firm relations, activities and outputs are relatively easy to define and monitor, contingencies can be foreseen and hands-on supervision and control of the other party's behaviour is therefore possible. Bureaucracy-based inter-firm relationships need competence and contractual trust, but because the relationships are less open-ended and more defined than trust-based inter-firm relationships, goodwill trust is not as quintessential. According to van der Meer-Kooistra and Vosselman (2000), companies that have the upper hand in asymmetric relationships in terms of their bargaining power may feel attracted to bureaucracy-based control as the instrumentalization of economic power and dependence can be one of the most effective means to achieve compliance, even if this will undermine the development of higher levels of trust, in particular goodwill trust.

I am unable to judge all the relationships of the organization with its external contractors as they need careful case-by-case consideration and I have not been able to collect all the data (from both sides) needed to do so. However, from the interviews with research managers and the operations manager I conducted, I get the impression that the relationships of the company I investigated with its external contractors fits van der Meer-Kooistra and Vosselman's classification of bureaucracy-based management control in inter-firm relationships rather well. There is clearly no evidence of goodwill trust in the relationship between the organization and its external contractors, and the potential of using economic dependence and the sanctioning power of the multinational parent were specifically mentioned as reassuring control means of a last resort.

When comparing external consultants with external contractors, however, one has to bear in mind that the relationship with external consultants is significantly more inter-personal than inter-firm as the consultants act as individuals hired for their expertise and individual trustworthiness rather than as representatives of an organization. This helps to explain why their concern for their own professional reputation becomes of such paramount importance. Their standing in the research community is their accumulated social capital. It is particularly interesting to note that the research managers strongly believed that external consultants could not afford to lose their reputation for trustworthiness and would guard it zealously but were rather sceptical about the actual 'malfeasance detection' capability of research networks. In section 3, I emphasized the importance of boundary spanners in overcoming the tensions between academic credibility (based on open exchange of information) and commercial credibility (based on keeping commercial secrets) arising from the intrusion of commercial interests in academic research. I argued that their privileged network position would allow them to vet the academic as well as the commercial credibility of hired scientific experts with a high degree of certainty. This network theory-based reasoning does not appear to be entirely supported by the network sanctioning scepticism of some of the research managers. There are several possible explanations for this disagreement: The fragrance industry may not have a mature, developed and coherent research network structure compared with other industries where comparable research was undertaken. These research managers themselves may not have achieved the full status of boundary spanners and hence either lack the knowledge base to judge individual trustworthiness with such certainty or are not well connected enough to be sure to always be informed should a transgression occur. It is also possible that commercial research and academic research do not interlock with the same intensity as for instance in the biotechnology industry.

This does not mean that reputational concerns are ineffective, however. All research managers I interviewed did believe that reputational concerns have a powerful self-disciplining effect on the behaviour of external consultants (at the level of the individual's psyche) even if some were sceptical about the role of research networks as sanctioning bodies.

CONCLUSION

The principal aim of the small-scale case study was to explore the validity of the conceptual framework developed in Hoecht and Trott (1999), in particular the contention that trust and social control become the more important for research organizations, the more outward-looking they have to be. The investigation into the trust-building process with external consultants showed this quite clearly. It also shed more light on the incremental and highly inter-personal nature of the trust-building process, from initial screening and information-gathering about potential research partners to loyalty-enhancing measures taken beyond the duration of individual research projects. Important, commercially sensitive research will only be undertaken when trust has reached the 'goodwill trust' stage, but even then, control mechanisms, while clearly of limited use by themselves, are never quite absent. The 'no live-links with competitors' rule, lock-out clauses and secrecy agreements are not waived even at the most advanced stages of trust-based research collaboration. It appears that all parties accept this, partially as a matter of accepting the 'rules of the game' and partially in acknowledgement of a mutual understanding of professionalism. The presence of 'controls' therefore does not undermine the mutual trust developed between the parties involved, particularly as there is an awareness of their very limited effectiveness.

In the relationship with external contractors, on the other hand, controls play a much stronger and more explicit role. Trust is also an issue here, but it seems to be backed up by elements of power. In the last resort, the company, in its collaboration with external contractors, would not refrain from using its economic resources to complement the legal safeguards at its disposal in order to make the contractors comply with their demands. The emphasis here is on trust with visible control.

Finally, during the course of the interviews conducted, it became apparent that organizational information boundaries are indeed very effective in containing the risk of information leakage. It also emerged that trust within research-oriented organizations can be equally important as trust in external research collaboration. Without internal trust between in-house researchers even the best external research collaboration relationships will be of limited effect.

NOTES

1. The best-known instrument to protect valuable scientific knowledge is patenting. According to an empirical investigation undertaken by Mansfield (1986) based on 100 US manufacturing firms from different industries, the desire to protect commercially valuable information

through patenting is particularly strong in the chemical and pharmaceutical industry. Mansfield (1986) also found that R&D-intensive firms were more prone to use patenting than less R&D-intensive firms and that firms in general prefer patent protection over trade secret protection to safeguard their patentable innovations. Patenting, however, is not always possible, either because the speed of technological progress is making patenting too slow or because of the inability of the patent system to police transgressions effectively.

2. Burt (1999) shows that third party gossip amplifies the probability of trust in strong relationships and of distrust in weak relationships. At any given strength of relationship, ego's opinion of alter becomes more certain when embedded in strong third-party ties. As a result of ego being more certain of alter, he/she is more likely to trust or distrust alter. This means that managers operating in clique networks – without many structural hole opportunities – are exposed to more consistent third party gossip about relationships and are less experienced than network entrepreneurs in making sense of inconsistent interpretations of events. They rely on fewer sources of information, are accustomed to relying on third party interpretation of events and are subject to the amplified trust/distrust dynamics associated with third party gossip. Network entrepreneurs, on the other hand, are more likely to make more accurate trust/distrust judgements as they are less exposed to the inconsistencies of third party gossip and more experienced in making their own judgements based on a wider and more varied information base.

3. Following Coleman's (1990) classification, research managers expressed a preference for interpersonal over intermediated trust. Intermediated trust relies on a positive assessment of the trustworthiness of the individual upon whose recommendation the decision to trust another individual is being made.

4. In research communities, assessments of character, competence and credibility of individuals tend to be deeply interconnected. Latour and Woolgar (1979: 202), in the context of the likelihood of success of research grant applicants by individual scientists observe that 'the credibility of the proposer and the proposal are identical'.

5. This means that the trust relationship would then progress from intermediated and largely calculative trust to interpersonal, knowledge-based trust.

6. This rule was portrayed to us as an 'industry rule'. However, the specific position of the company as market leader in the UK without direct competition in basic research may allow the company to be more selective than companies operating in other fields of the chemical industry.

7. This could be interpreted as a sign that the 'goodwill' level of the trust relationship has not been reached in the cases referred to. However, it is not necessarily true that goodwill trust is incompatible with additional incentives to be granted to the trustee. The relationship can be complementary.

8. One senior manager admitted that he once warned a competitor organization about a former consultant to his company, but considered that exceptional. Information was not normally shared outside the parent company and no established warning system existed.

REFERENCES

Bleeke, Joel and David Ernst (1992), *Collaborating to Compete*, New York: Wiley.

Brewis, Jo, Doug Foster and Andreas Hoecht (1998), 'Trust, risk, anthropomorphism and agency', paper presented at the 14th EGOS Colloquium, Mastricht, Netherlands, July 9–11, 1998.

Burt, Ronald S. (1999), 'Entrepreneurs, distrust, and third parties: a strategic look at the dark side of networks', in L.L. Thompson, J. Levine and D. Messick (eds), *Shared Cognition in Organizations. The Management of Knowledge*, London: Lawrence Elbaum, pp. 213–43.

Cartwright, S. and C.L. Cooper (1996), *Managing Mergers, Acquisitions and Strategic Alliances. Integrating peoples and cultures*, Oxford: Butterworth-Heinemann, 2nd edn.

Coleman, James (1990), *Foundations of Social Theory*, Cambridge, MA: Harvard University Press.

Creed, W.E. Douglas and Raymond E. Miles (1996), 'Trust in organizations: a conceptual framework linking organizational forms, managerial philosophies and the opportunity costs of control', in R. Kramer and T. Tyler (eds), *Trust in Organizations: Frontiers of Theory and Research*, London: Sage, pp. 16–38.

Das, T.K.and Bing-Sheng Teng (2001), 'Trust, control, and risk in strategic alliances: an integrated framework', *Organization Studies*, **22** (2), 251–83.

Deakin, Simon, Christel Lane and Frank Wilkinson (1994), 'Trust or law? Towards an integrated theory of contractual relations between firms', *Journal of Law and Society*, 21, 329–49.

Doz, Y. and Gary Hamel (1997), 'The use of alliances in implementing technology strategies', in M.L. Tushmann and P. Anderson (eds), *Managing Strategic Innovation and Change: A collection of readings*, New York: Oxford University Press, pp. 556–80.

Eisenberg, Rebecca S. (1987), 'Propriety rights and the norms of science in biotechnology research', *Yale Law Journal*, 97, 177–231.

Garsten, Christina and Christopher Grey (1998), 'Trust and post-bureaucracy', paper presented at the 14th EGOS Colloquium, Maastricht, Netherlands, July 9–11, 1998.

Giddens, Anthony (1990), *The Consequences of Modernity*, Cambridge: Polity Press.

Hagstrom, Warren O. (1965), *The Scientific Community*, New York: Basic Books.

Hoecht, Andreas and Paul Trott (1999), 'Trust, risk and control in the management of collaborative technology development', *International Journal of Innovation Management*, 3, 257–70.

Humphrey, Jeffrey and Hubert Schmitz (1998), 'Trust in inter-firm relations in developing and transition economies', *Journal of Development Studies*, 34, 32–61.

Lane, Christel and Reinhard Bachmann (1996), 'The social construction of trust: supplier relations in Britain and Germany', *Organization Studies*, 17, 365–95.

Latour, Bruno and Steven Woolgar (1979), *Laboratory Life: The Construction of Scientific Facts*, Princeton: Princeton University Press.

Lewicki, Roy J. and Barbara B. Bunker (1996), 'Developing and maintaining trust in work relationships', in R. Kramer and T. Tyler (eds), *Trust in Organizations: Frontiers of Theory and Research*, Thousand Oaks, CA: Sage Publications, pp. 114–39.

Liebeskind, Julia P. and Amalya L. Oliver (1998), 'From handshake to contract: intellectual property, trust and the social structure of academic research', in C. Lane and R.Bachmann (eds), *Trust Within and Between Organizations: Conceptual issues and empirical applications*, Oxford: Oxford University Press, pp. 118–45.

Luhman, Niklas (1979), *Trust and Power*, Chichester: Wiley.

Lupton, Deborah (1999), *Risk*, London: Routledge.

Mansfield, Edwin (1986), 'Patents and innovation: an empirical study', *Management Science*, 32, 173–81.

McMillan, G. Steve, R.A. Klavans and Robert D. Hamilton (1995), 'Firm management of scientific information: some predictors and implications of openness versus secrecy', *R&D Management*, 25, 411–19.

van der Meer-Kooistra, Jeltje and Ed. G. Vosselman (2000), 'Management control of interfirm transactional relationships: the case of industrial renovation and maintenance', *Accounting, Organizations and Society*, 25, 51–77.

Newell, Susan and Peter Clark (1990), 'The importance of extra-organizational networks in the diffusion and appropriation of new technologies', *Knowledge: Creation, Diffusion and Utilisation*, 12, 199–212

Nooteboom, Bart (1999), *Inter-firm Alliances. Analysis and Design*, London: Routledge.

Porter, Michael E. (1987), 'From competitive advantage to corporate strategy', *Harvard Business Review*, May–June, 43–59.

Powell, Walter W. (1990), 'Neither market nor hierarchy: network forms of organizations', *Research in Organizational Behaviour*, 12, 295–336.

Powell, Walter W., Kenneth W. Koput, and Laurel Smith-Doerr, (1996), 'Inter-organizational cooperation and the locus of innovation: networks of learning in biotechnology', *Administrative Science Quarterly*, 41, 116–146.

Sako, Mari (1992), *Prices, Quality and Trust: inter-firm relations in Britain and Japan*, Cambridge: Cambridge University Press

Sitkin, Sim B. and N. Roth (1993), 'Explaining the limited effectiveness of legalistic 'remedies' for trust/distrust', *Organization Science*, 4, 367–92

Williamson, O.E. (1993), 'Calculativeness, trust and economic organization', *Journal of Law and Economics*, 36, 456–83.

Zucker, Lynne G. (1986), ' Production of trust: institutional sources of economic structure, 1840–1920', *Research in Organizational Behaviour*, 8, 53–111.

Zucker, Lynne G., Michael Darby, Marilynn Brewer and Peng Yusheng (1996), 'Collaboration structure and information dilemmas in biotechnology: organizational boundaries of trust production', in R.Kramer and R.Tyler (eds), *Trust in Organizations: Frontiers of Theory and Research*, Thousand Oaks, CA: Sage Publications, pp. 90–112.

7. Trust in a dynamic environment: fast trust as a threshold condition for asymmetric technology partnership formation in the ICT sector

Kirsimarja Blomqvist

1. INTRODUCTION

Trust – or lack of it – has been seen as a 'make-or-break' factor in partnerships, technology cooperation and strategic alliances (Gambetta 1988; Larson 1992, Dodgson 1993; Young-Ybarra and Wiersema 1999 and Ariño et al. 2001). It has been identified as leading to cooperative behavior and constructive problem solving, which are necessary in long-term cooperation (Axelrod 1984; Young and Wilkinson 1989; Ring and van de Ven 1992; Morgan and Hunt 1984; Jones and George 1998). Trust reduces complex social realities economically and increases predictability, thus being an efficient mechanism to manage relational risks (Arrow 1974; Luhmann 1979; Ring and van de Ven 1992). Trust can be seen as 'implicit contracting' increasing the efficiency and effectiveness in relationships (Bradach and Eccles 1989).

Even though the research on trust has become popular recently, there is still confusion about the concept itself, and many researchers' approach to trust has been partial. Also Ring (2000), Koenig (1995) and Kelly et al. (2002) note that in the past the research of the informal processes leading to inter-organizational cooperation has been somewhat ignored. According to Ring (2000) research on the early dynamics of the partnership formation process is also scarce, and there are more studies on alliances that have come to being (the negotiations have not failed). Ring concludes that 'we have to open up the "black box" of alliance creation processes and shed more light on task, team and time issues...'. Also Luo (2001) proposes that there is no adequate understanding of the ways in which personal attachment is established, and how it affects the performance of international cooperative ventures.

Usually trust is seen as an outcome of a process, that is, trust relationships develop gradually. Trusting relationships develop with time as the actors get to know each other's capabilities and values. Trust is seen as evolving from past experience and current interaction (Deutsch 1973). Previous reputation and experienced similarity both in character and values enhance the experience of trust (Zucker 1986; Gulati 1995; Jones and George 1998). The social exchange theory (for example Blau 1964) explains trust by repeated interactions of increasing satisfaction. In general trust is believed to evolve slowly, through incremental investments and experiences.

2.   TRUST IN ASYMMETRIC TECHNOLOGY PARTNERSHIP FORMATION

The role of trust may be assumed to be especially important in asymmetric technology partnerships,[1] where complementary actors with different characteristics share and create new knowledge. However, asymmetry, that is, firm-specific heterogeneity and diverse knowledge bases, impede the natural evolvement of shared understanding and prediction needed for the evolution of trust. The ICT sector is also a highly dynamic environment, where predictability is low due to complexity and convergence, as well as high technological and market uncertainty. Convergence and subsequent consolidation are strong and the whole ICT sector is going through a rapid restructuring where the roles of the players are changing. Prediction based on potential partner organizations is also difficult: companies are in constant flux with respect to their focus and position in the ICT value network.

In a dynamic environment trust would seem like a rational and natural prerequisite for asymmetric technology partnership formation, but there is little basis for natural development of trust. The uncertainty and high pace of technological and market change contains a paradox for the evolution of trust-based relationships.

3.   RESEARCH DESIGN

The conceptualization and the illustrations in this chapter are based on research on asymmetric technology partnerships, in which eight small software firms' partnerships with globally operating ICT firms were analysed (Blomqvist 2002). The pattern of fast trust, and the critical role of fast and individual-based trust, emerged unexpectedly in the study. The purpose of the PhD study (Blomqvist 2002) was to increase the understanding of the role and nature of trust in asymmetric technology partnership formation. The main research question was: what is the role of trust in asymmetric technology partnership formation?

Qualitative methodology was applied in in-depth interviews. In the empirical interviews the small firms were software suppliers and the large corporations were telecom operators, software integrators and hardware manufacturers for computers and cellular phones. The large globally operating firms' product and service offerings varied. Some of the companies were active in telecom services, some in terminal manufacturing and electronics, and one of the companies was mainly an IT integrator. The small software companies were active in value-adding services like mobile games or offered mobile platforms and even intelligent middleware. The large firms were either looking for complementary value-adding products and services or leveraging the small firms' complementary knowledge. The small firms offered mainly specialized value-adding components and services related to electronic or mobile business.

The interviewees had direct knowledge and experience of asymmetric technology partnerships. The interviewees from the small software suppliers were mainly managing directors (decision-makers) or technology experts with customer/partner responsibility. The interviewees from the large ICT firms were managers responsible for the relationships with the small suppliers. In the large firms there were two to three interviews at both strategic and operative levels. The interviewees were chosen on the basis of the researcher's knowledge and all the interviews were conducted personally. Access and contacting was relatively easy despite the sensitive issues. The interviews were conducted in very open and trusting terms.[2]

The interviews were semi-structured. Special care was taken not to impact the interviewed persons' perceptions and ideas into giving socially acceptable answers (see also Blois 1999, on the sensitive handling of trust due to the fragility and complexity of the issue). Trust was first discussed indirectly in order not to impact the management's perception of the role of trust. The interviewer guided the discussion and returned later with some interesting questions or asked additional ones as the research project advanced. Only when the managers brought the issue to discussion was trust discussed openly, usually in the latter part of the second interview.

The components for the conceptualization of trust were found through *open questions*, for example: how do you evaluate your partner? What characteristics do you find important? What do you tell and highlight about you and your company when presenting yourself to a potential partner? How would you advise a small/large firm looking for a partner to present their company? How should the small/large firm be evaluated in your opinion? The developed conceptualization of trust was validated in follow-up interviews with the interviewed managers (Blomqvist 2002).

4. ASYMMETRIC TECHNOLOGY PARTNERSHIP FORMATION

In the following the asymmetric technology partnership formation process is studied as presented by Pettigrew (1987). According to Pettigrew the *process* itself, the process *content* and the *context* should be studied when researching process phenomena. The context answers the '*why*' question, what are the inner and outer factors leading to asymmetric technology partnership formation. The content explains '*what*' the parties plan to do and the process '*how*' the partnership forms and the role of trust in this process.

This section is divided into three parts. First the context for fast and individual-based trust, that is, the dynamic ICT sector, is described. Then the content of the cooperation, that is the nature of the R&D cooperation, is illustrated. Thereafter a model on the evolution of fast trust as a relationship development process from awareness to an emerging relationship is created.

4.1 Context: Dynamic, Uncertain and Complex ICT Environment

Due to convergence, de-regulation and blurring industrial boundaries the telecom, content and information technology industries are going through a major transformation and developing into an ICT industry. The simultaneous convergence of industries, technologies and equipment as well the related demand for interoperability create complexity (Day and Schoemaker 2000), as do the simultaneous management of different technology generations (for example cellular technologies) and emerging new standards. The complexity and systemic nature of the services set a natural demand for partnerships with complementary suppliers.

The global focus on innovation and simultaneous market transparency has shortened the time-to-market and subsequent product life cycles (Kenney 2000). Information about new innovations and technology is immediately available around the globe. The shortening product and service life cycles lead to concern on 'time-to-market' and 'fast-track' product development. It is expected that in such 'high-velocity markets' the competitive advantage may be only temporary, and time is an essential aspect of strategy (Best 1990; Eisenhardt and Martin 2000). Being a forerunner and being able to implement innovative new technology and business concepts fast is crucial.

The ability to leverage diverse knowledge from non-redundant networks may be a key source for weak signals enabling early information on competitor action or new technological development. Because of the developed communication technologies individuals are easy to reach immediately and directly (Evans and Wurster 2000). Non-hierarchical and lean organizations along with flexible job descriptions for knowledge-complex work create time pressure. Managers have to cope simultaneously with very many decisions and actions.

Technological discontinuities like the internet bring new innovative players, who try to break the rules of competition and seek the niches not noticed by the incumbent players. For incumbents the discontinuities pose a threat that may be turned to an opportunity through cooperating with innovative players and learning from them. Alliances, partnerships and looser industry cooperation are important and common tools in creating market-based industry standards. Small technology firms may utilize their large partners to push their technology towards dominant design and standardization. Large partners give credibility to the emerging new technology and small technology firms (see also Kotabe and Swan 1995).

In a business environment emphasizing speed and global competition there is also little room for the gradual development of relationships. In the high pace markets the window of opportunity disappears unless the actors are able to proceed fast. Subsequently, there is little time to learn or study the volatile markets or constantly emerging new technologies. The perception of available managerial time has compressed[3] and the subsequent compressed time orientation partly explains the need for fast trust.

4.2 Content: Integrating Diverse Knowledge and Capabilities of Asymmetric Actors

In the converging ICT sector the asymmetric technology partnerships quite often attempt to combine the actors' diverse knowledge bases. Communication is critical for coordination, and a common understanding for the description of tasks, assignments, roles and location of expertise is needed. Informal processes require a supportive environment for free and content-rich interaction. Emergent processes of informal interaction and joint problem solving are needed (Faraj and Sproull 2000, 1554–7). Software development teams are typically formed de novo for each new project, depending on the project requirements and availability of experts. Software development teams typically resemble 'temporary groups' (Goodman and Goodman 1976).

In the fast-changing and turbulent industry the present competencies do not guarantee a suitable state-of-the-art of future technological competencies and ability to respond to external challenges. Probing the other party with questions on, for example, their values, *willingness and true ability to cooperate*[4] is more challenging than issues on technological or business-wise competence. Thus, the specific personality of the individual actor and his or her capabilities of, for example, leveraging resources for the joint venture, are critical for the success.

The flows of information are simultaneously rich and far-reaching (see Evans and Wurster 2000). Individual actors and organizations receive more information and impulses than they are able to manage. Coping with the abundant information and increased individual decision-making becomes extremely challenging due to bounded rationality[5] and the limits of the managerial planning tools. Organizational planning needs to be changed from annual cycles to real-time information processing and feedback systems. Knowledge-workers enjoying the luxury of having 'the world in front of them' suffer from the limitations of human capacity to cope with the abundant information and possibilities. It may be that because of the ubiquitous and even contradictory information flows the decision makers make their decisions faster and increasingly based on intuition (see Goodman and Goodman 1976; Eisenhardt 1990).

In future-oriented R&D it is the state-of-the-art capabilities that are more important than the existing resources. Because of the high pace of change, the needed capabilities are also partly open and unpredictable. Because of the human bounded rationality, individual-based trust may become an important decision-making criterion in order to cope with the complexity. In this kind of situation the role of individual-based trust is accentuated.

4.3   Process: Evolution of Fast and Individual-Based Trust

In this sub-section *a conceptual process model* on the development of fast and individual-based trust is introduced. The model is based on earlier theory, case studies, reflection and analysis. Also observation and explanation (Lave and March 1975) have been used.[6] Theory review and empirical data collection were an iterative and continuous process throughout the research project. Thus the evolving model was continuously 'tested' against different cases to see how well the model described reality (Eisenhardt 1989). The additional information from new cases was added to the knowledge base to confirm or alter the conceptual model. The actors' interplay is described according to the iteration of the interviews, the literature on trust, participant observation and introspection.

Social exchange theory is used when describing the development of an intimate and mutual relationship from surface level awareness to a mutual relationship (Huston and Burgess 1979). In addition to the emerging theory on trust the model draws also on the interaction approach (Håkansson 1982). In the model (see Figure 7.1) the relationship development is divided into four phases: framebreaking, synchronization, improvisation and experimentation (the phases are marked in block letters). The process leading to fast trust emerges through interest, understanding, learning, adaptation and commitment. Subsequently the actors are willing to make decisions based on intuition and commit themselves to joint experimentation (improvised action). Thus the improvised action (phase 3) denotes the evolution of fast trust in the model.

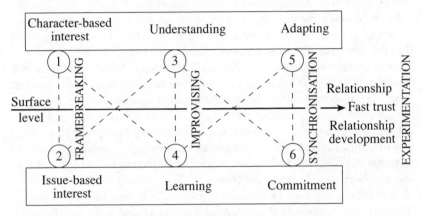

Figure 7.1   Evolution of fast and individual-based trust from awareness to an emerging relationship

However, because of the elusive and abstract nature of trust we may only try to understand it more in depth. Trust is always perceived, and is seen as both a situation and a person-specific inner attitude.[7] Therefore the presented model on the evolution of fast trust may be only an approximation of real-life attitudes and behavior. Also, the model should not be viewed as linear and sequential, but rather as iterative and cyclical.

In the following the different phases and their contents are described in detail:

Framebreaking
In asymmetric technology partnership formation the actors come from different backgrounds and have different organizational and individual characteristics. Therefore they need to be able to break the existing mental models, that is, be capable for *framebreaking* in order to appreciate other organizational cultures and contexts. Thus they have different histories, diverse knowledge and diverse potential socio-economic benefits of the

relationship. According to Scharmer (2001) the individual's ability for 'pre-sensing' (Scharmer 2000), that is, being intensively present in the interaction is critical for the evolution of trust. This is understandable, as interest in the other is visible already in the very first behavioral and attitudinal signs and signals. The individual actor's strong self-reference (Luhmann 1979) enables open and equal connection. In a similar vein Fukuyama (1995) discusses spontaneous sociability and social virtues (honesty, reliability, cooperativeness, and a sense of duty to other) in the context of trusting relationships. Also Eisenhardt (1990) notes the need for cohesive interaction and perception of equity in fast decision making.

In the framebreaking phase there is an interplay of two dimensions of trust: affect-based trust and cognitive trust. Affect-based trust means that the actor perceives the other actor as cooperative, equal, ethical and likeable (Huston and Burgess 1979). Affect-based trust also includes care (von Krogh 1998) and interest for the other actor's knowledge and character. In an asymmetric situation the interest in the other and potential affection demand breaking of existing stereotypes. Cognitive trust means that the actor has knowledge, on the basis of which s/he forms the prediction that it is worthwhile to trust the other; there are some social or economic benefits to be gained. This kind of cognitive trust is motivated by self-interest and has also been called calculative trust.

In the framebreaking phase the actor needs to be able to see beyond the diversity and appreciate the potential benefits arising from the diversity. Either affect-based or cognitive/calculative trust may arise first, but usually both exist simultaneously and are needed for the actor to become interested. As one of the interviewed persons indicated, the investment in understanding and learning is so high that the other person's likeability becomes a prerequisite for further negotiations. Therefore it is proposed that the evolution of fast trust also demands affect-based involvement and shared excitement between the committed actors. Some of the interviewed persons described the early phase as 'instantaneous', 'liking' or simply 'interest'. The metaphor of 'breaking the ice' describes this phase.

Synchronization
The synchronization phase could also be described as *indwelling* (von Krogh 1998). Based on intuitive knowledge, the parties try to *understand* and learn of each other and the mutual potential. According to a Finnish idiom the actor will 'try to stand in the boots of the other person'. This phase could be described as shifting towards each other: who are they? What do they want?

Also in the synchronization phase trust is both affect-based and cognitive, that is based on the actor's analytic thinking and evaluative knowledge.

Affect-based trust in the synchronization phase combines empathetic appreciation with an analytic attempt to understand what kind of a business model and strategy the other individual's organization has.

> I would not say that this is mechanic but it is an acknowledged thing. First you have the interest to find out what the other person knows, where s/he is good. That is clear and often done. But then you choose your questions in accordance with the person you have in front of you. You have an intuition that the other one is not a right kind of person. You perceive automatically that nothing comes out of this. You stay waiting, you may let the other person explain what the relationship will be like... (A development manager for large ICT Company A)

At the individual level the other actor's potential, limitations, organizational role and personality are evaluated. Also the basic assumptions (Schein 1992) or individual and organizational values may be assessed at a more cognitive level. For the parties to be able to understand the potential value-added of each other's knowledge, some reference points and shared language are needed. Understanding the other party's business model and his/her role creates a 'platform' on which to create understanding of what is possible and what is not from the point of view of the other. The actor's absorptive capacity and common reference points and language determine the speed and level of *learning* of the different knowledge base of the other. Questions like 'what are they capable of?' and 'what can we learn of them?' are raised. The actors' absorptive capacity determines common reference points and subsequent speed for understanding the common potential.

Improvising
Fast trust leads to an improvisation phase, where the parties consider mutual *adaptation* and improvise in order to test the relationship with some specific task or venture. Adaptation demands internal willingness to *commit oneself*. In the improvisation phase trust is behavioral, some indications of experienced and given trust must be shown at a fast pace. Also Eisenhardt and Martin (2000, 1112) call for iteration, experimentation and early testing as managerial capabilities to learn quickly and to compensate for limited knowledge bases. Active coping and proactive behavior may also enhance feelings of competence and control (Eisenhardt 1990, 52). The capability to improvise indicates the actor's ability to find innovative solutions and create new combinations, which are critical skills in the emerging cooperation based on the partners' diverse knowledge.

Experimentation
When the fast and individual-based trust has evolved, the parties are ready for some cooperative experimentation. Some specific tasks or ventures are

agreed on. The cooperation described in the interviews was tentative and based on short-term projects.

In general the intensity and openness of communication characterizes the evolution of fast trust in emerging business relationships. A synchronized interaction rhythm enhances the evolution. At its best the interaction is like an exciting and rather fast-step dance or a game of tennis between skilled and alert actors.

Shared vision, that is, whether the potential partners are able to share the same vision for the business to be created together, is critical for fast trust to evolve. It may be the most important and focal issue in the evolution of fast trust. In a dynamic environment the actors have to accept that there is no perfect information, and therefore decisions must be made partly based on tacit knowledge and intuition. In the empirical interviews the potential partners' *shared values and vision* were indicated as a key issue in the emergence of fast and individual-based trust due to the complexity and uncertainty in the ICT sector.[8]

> I evaluate a potential partner with feelings anyway. It is the first couple of minutes. Then, if it goes all wrong ... The first impression is important for how things will go ... and then how short a term they will present, whether they are really interested and have a vision. I also see whether they are able to communicate their vision and have self-respect. It is the feeling ... Yes, I don't know if I should have, but I don't have any systematic way of evaluating them. You listen to their story and evaluate whether this was credible or not. (Partner director for Large ICT company B)

> I test them with certain questions, as you must do as well, of what that person knows. Some questions on some perceptions s/he has. And then I see how s/he starts to approach those things. Is it a person who says I want, I want ... Or is a dialogue possible. Truly honest dialogue, which we both advance ... you have that, I have this and we are creating a partnership and have trust between us. You just cannot do that with every person. Some are more like they wanted everything themselves and want to be on the top all the time. That is part of their type (personality). According to research they are very clever and fast to take advantage, but never innovate themselves. (A development manager for large ICT Company A)

Therefore, it is expected that in order to cope with the dense contacts, complex issues, and subsequent flow of decisions the managers try to speed up their actions.

5.   FAST AND INVIDUAL-BASED TRUST – WHAT IS IT?

In this section the identified fast and individual-based trust is first compared to incremental and organization-based trust. After that the difference between swift (Meyerson et al. 1996) and fast trust is discussed. Finally the conceptualization of trust and fast trust is discussed.

Intuition and rationality are combined in evaluating trustworthiness. A person may *probe* the other one's trustworthiness with certain questions (for example on competence and ethics). Tyler and Kramer (1996, 9) refer to 'intuitive auditing', which seems similar to continuous assessment of trust. Individuals maintain mental accounts regarding the perceived history of trust-related behaviors involving themselves and others. Face-to-face meetings are needed to facilitate the strategy development of how to deal with the specific individual. Images are formed on the basis of clues from communication. People categorize others in order to understand them, for example according to gender, age, strong or weak, competent or incompetent and so on. On the basis of these images a model on a person's motives is created and an interaction strategy is developed. Strong feelings of, for example, trust or distrust are often formed in the first face-to-face interaction (Nohria 1992).

According to Cohen and Fields, trust found in the Silicon Valley is specific and somewhat similar to the fast trust found in this study. It is not based on common history but rather on reputation, and it is generated by performance. This performance-based trust is more open to outsiders, and can be extended to other cultures and even people with different ideas (Cohen and Fields 2000, 216–17, see also Kenney 2000).

5.1 Comparison to Incremental and Organization-Based Trust

Trusting behavior is believed to increase trust. Initial fast trust may be a strong force in asymmetric partnership formation. It may trigger mutual trust if the other party is able to take the risk of trusting at the outset of the relationship.

Fast trust is rather thin and fragile, as it is tested continuously. In the early phase of the relationship the ability to create fast trust may be critical for asymmetric technology partnership formation. Fast trust creates interest and enables initial investments for relationship building. According to the interviewed managers the negotiations either advance fast or stop, if the probing does not produce satisfactory answers. Then the turn to take the lead in the relationship building is given to other one, as the initiator hesitates (due to lack of fast developing trust). This may slow the development of the relationship remarkably or even create a situation where the relationship never develops further; the chance in the dynamic environment is lost.

> It [fast trust] is meaningful in two things. First, that you get a second meeting. You need to earn trust in that first meeting. You have to have the preconditions right: homework done, right people in the meeting, they need to behave right.

> The customer needs to see what this customer benefit is. Then a wider discussion starts. After that it goes through people. My role is to create trust in the top management. That is my personal task in a big partnership process. It means that if I do not succeed there, probably nothing happens. (Director for Large ICT company D)

> Trust is created much at first sight, determined by what the other person is capable of. If the person is good, the organization-related uncertainties are left behind … If the person driving the relationship is *not* credible and able to create trust and mutual understanding fast, the potential partnership formation enters the slow track.(Partner director for Large ICT Company B)

This fast trust is thin and fragile, however. The parties may have high expectations but also high reservations, and any cue for either trust or distrust is read fast (see also Meyerson et al. 1996, 184).

Incremental trust has also elements based on a deeper cognitive knowledge and behavioral experience of the other. It is based on both institutional and personal-based individual trust. It is assumed that incremental trust includes, for example, in-depth evaluation of the other party's goodwill, which the fast trust rather eliminates, as goodwill elements of trust are difficult to evaluate fast. Incremental trust is thicker and probably also more resilient than fast trust.

Ring and van de Ven (1993) have an interesting view on the institutionalization of a relationship. It is in line with the presented differentiating view on fast and incremental trust, where fast and individual-based trust initiates a relationship and incremental trust 'cements' the relationship to a partnership. Institutionalization could also be understood as a wide interface between the parties, that is, the relationship changes from individual-based to an organizational relationship.

Strong trust increases the persons' willingness to stretch their roles in the organization and to accept broad role definitions. It promotes orientation towards a common future, which is more than a calculated attempt towards short-term balance of favors. If the parties are able to reach strong trust, they may relax the control function and concentrate fully on the task to be accomplished. This creates a positive effect, which widens the way the parties see their role and tasks. Strong trust also increases mutual cooperation and lessens the cognitive trust based on self-interest, that is, calculation of gives and takes.

5.2   Fast Trust in Relation to Swift Trust

Meyerson et al. (1996) have introduced a close concept called *swift trust*, which can be found in some *temporary groups*[9] (R&D projects, theatre groups, Red Cross task force) as a unique form of collective perception and relating (Meyerson et al. 1996).

Meyerson et al. (1996) emphasize the role-based trust in the emergence of swift trust. In comparison to swift trust, fast trust also emphasizes affection and personalized interaction instead of solely role-based fast categorization. If the task is challenging (complex and demanding diverse knowledge), staying in a pre-set narrow role may not allow such a close connection as would be necessary for fruitful information exchange and knowledge creation. Extending the narrow occupational role could allow more full and empathetic information exchange. Narrow roles do not allow as full an understanding of the context and information of the background as more open information and interaction (see also Meyerson et al. 1996, 172). Goodman and Goodman (1976, 494) argue that role clarity would inhibit professional growth and innovation, whereas *blurring each member's role* enhances innovation. In a similar vein it is argued that in situations where creativity and open-mindedness are important, the more flexible roles bring benefits also in asymmetric technology partnership formation, where actors search for synergistic benefits from shared knowledge creation from different knowledge bases.

The fast trust found in asymmetric technology partnership formation and described in this chapter is different in the sense that it is not based on narrow roles and stereotype-based fast typologies only (for example doctor, computer specialist and so on). Fast trust seems to evaluate the characters and also emphasizes affect-based trust. If there is a chance for this *personal and individual-based trust* to emerge, the resulting fast trust is probably more productive, if the individuals can meet openly at the personal level and get into the complex problem solving as fast as possible.

5.3 Conceptualization of Trust and Fast Trust

In the asymmetric technology partnership context trust has been defined as: 'Actors' expectation on the self-referential actor's capability and, goodwill visible in mutually beneficial behavior enabling cooperation under risk' (Blomqvist 2002). Subsequently, the concept of trust can be divided into related components of trust (see Figure 7.2). In the asymmetric technology partnership formation context *capability* consists of technological capability, business capability, and a capability to cooperate. *Goodwill* implies a more abstract, yet a very important component of trust in asymmetric technology partnerships. It has been earlier defined as the 'partner's moral responsibility and positive intentions toward the other' (Blomqvist 1997).

Along time, when the relationship is developing, the actual *behavior*, for example that the trustee fulfills the positive intentions, builds trust (Lazarec

Trust under pressure

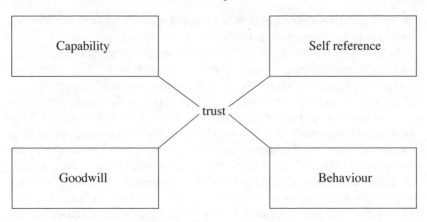

Figure 7.2   Components of trust

and Lorenz 1998a, 1998b; Bidault 2000; Miles et al. 2000). Through the partnering process (along time) the actual behavior, for example kept promises, becomes more visible and easier to evaluate. Thus the capability and goodwill become visible in the behavioral signals of trustworthiness. *Self-reference* is a rather complex but useful concept to understand trust in asymmetric technology partnerships. Luhmann (1979) has introduced the concept in the context of autopoetic (self-renewing) systems. Self-referential systems (for example human beings or organizations) are basically autonomous and independent of the environment. The system sets apart the environment and itself by conscious distinction of what the system is and what it is not (Luhmann 1995). Thus the system becomes aware of its identity and capabilities in relation to others. Self-reference is demonstrated in the system's ability to define 'one's own existence, the basic idea for being and doing, values, principles and goals ... knowing what is important and meaningful ... prioritizing', using others as reference and by self-reflection (Ståhle 1998, 94). Thus the word 'reference' in the concept self-reference means the system's ability to use others as a reference to self.

Fast trust includes the same components of trust as more general conceptualizations of trust described above. However, only inferences of the trustworthiness are intuitively drawn and signals and signs of trustworthiness are evaluated in the behavior. 'Fast' in fast trust means that trust evolves in the relationship during the actors' first meeting. Fast trust results in improvised action leading to further action, that is, experimentation. In asymmetric technology partnerships the actors' experimentation leads the relationship to tentative and project-based cooperation. If fast trust does not evolve, the relationship will not develop from the awareness level to a level of a potential partnership, and the chance for cooperation has been bypassed.

6. CONCLUSIONS

In a dynamic environment the role of individual-based fast trust gets highlighted. Fast trust seems to be evaluated through inferences and intuition rather than profound evidence. It is believed that the parties in an emerging relationship constantly, consciously or unconsciously, evaluate trustworthiness from signals in the other's speech and behavior. As an ultimate goal they want to see whether the other party would risk their well-being (for example act opportunistically or in a way which is not in mutual interest) or whether they can trust the other party's integrity in promoting the mutual good.

Shared values and vision were identified as critical for fast and individual-based trust to emerge in the asymmetric technology partnership formation context. It seems natural to trust individuals who are perceived to share one's vision of technological, economic and social development. Also the expected capability to mobilize or create (internal renewal or external leverage) the complementary capabilities needed for the joint experimentation was important. The important role of the person, that is, the character-specificity and affect-based trust differentiate the identified fast trust from the concept of swift trust, which is based more on categorization on the basis of the other actor's clear and narrow role (for example doctors, see Meyerson et al. 1996).

Identified fast and individual-based trust is also different than the more traditional, incremental trust. Fast and individual-based action enables and initiates relationships, whilst the incremental and more organization-based trust makes the relationship more durable.

It is also argued that in the complex and uncertain ICT markets a critical managerial boundary rule could be the ability to trust another key individual fast and to be trusted. Without fast and individual-based trust there seems to be little chance for asymmetric technology partnership formation in the dynamic environment. Fast and individual-based trust seems like a critical threshold condition for emerging relationships in the dynamic environment.

NOTES

1. Complementary actors with different characteristics are denoted as asymmetric, that is, having 'difference in skills, capabilities and power as well as management and organizational culture of actors' (Blomqvist 2002).
2. The trust may have partly developed through earlier contacts in almost all of the cases. Because of the working experience in the field I had many suitable contacts available.
3. A trend of time compression has been identified in the network society (Himanen 2000).

4. As Metcalfe and James (2001, 42) argue, a 'great deal of the competitive value of knowledge depends on matters of organization and activity'.
5. Bounded rationality limits the 'powers of individuals to receive, store, retrieve, and process information without error (and limits individual abilities to articulate their knowledge or feelings by the use of words, numbers, or graphics) in ways which permit them to be understood by others' (Williamson 1975, 21–22). Originally by Simon (1957, 198) 'The capacity of the human mind for formulating and solving complex problems is very small compared with the size of the problems whose solution is required for objectively rational behavior in the real world – or even for a reasonable approximation to such objective rationality'.
6. A model is a simplified picture of a part of the real world. It is a systematic set of conjectures about real world observations (Lave and March 1975, 2–4).
7. In line with Bagozzi and Burnkrant (1979) trust is seen as a multi-dimensional attitude and construct consisting of cognitive, affective and behavioral dimensions. However, as noted earlier, trust is an inner attitude and the importance of the dimensions varies between individuals.
8. Aldrich (1999, 231) notes that pioneering founders (start-ups) cannot rely on information and prior behavior or objective external evidence, but must base their initial trust-creation strategies on 'framing the unknown in such a way that it becomes believable'.
9. A temporary group is 'a set of diversely skilled people working together on a complex task over a limited period of time'. Temporary groups have no shared history or shadow-of-the-future for future relationships. They usually consist of diverse people with complementary skills and therefore lack the commonly found trust based on similar characteristic, for example professional background, enhances relationship creation (Goodman and Goodman 1976, 494).

BIBLIOGRAPHY

Aldrich, Howard E. (1999), *Organizations evolving*, London: Sage Publications.
Anderson, James C. and James A. Narus (1990), 'A model of distributor firm and manufacturer firm working partnerships', *Journal of Marketing*, 54, 42–58.
Ariño Africa, José de la Torre and Peter Smith Ring (2001), 'Relational quality: managing trust in corporate alliances', *California Managment Review*, **44** (1), Fall, 109–31.
Arrow, K. (1974), *Limits of Economic Organization*, New York: Norton.
Axelrod, R. (1984), *The Evolution of Cooperation*, New York: Basic Books.
Bagozzi, R.P. and R.E. Burnkrant (1979), 'Attitude organization and the attitude–behavior relationship', *Journal of Personality and Social Psychology*, **37** (6), 913–29.
Barney, J.B and M.H. Hansen (1994), 'Trustworthiness as a source of competitive advantage', *Strategic Management Journal*, 15, 175–90.
Best, Michael H. (1990), *The New Competition, Institutions of Industrial Restructuring*, Cambridge: Polity Press.
Bidault, Francis (2000), 'The New Economy', a keynote speech at FINTRA Annual Seminar, 8 February, Helsinki.
Bidault, F. and C.J. Jarillo (1997), 'Trust in economic transactions', in Francis Bidault, Pierre-Yves Gomez and Gilles Marion (eds), *Trust: Firm and society*, London: Macmillan Press.
Blau, P.M (1964), *Exchange and Power in Social Life*, New York: Wiley.
Blois, K.J (1999), 'Trust in business-to-business relationships: an evaluation of its status', *Journal of Management Studies*, **36** (2), 197–217.

Blomqvist, K. (1997), 'The many faces of trust', *Scandinavian Journal of Management*, **13** (3), 271–86.

Blomqvist, Kirsimarja (2002), 'Partnership in the dynamic environment: the role of trust in asymmetric technology partnership formation', *Acta Universitatis 122*, Lappeenranta University of Technology, Finland.

Bradach, J.L. and R.G. Eccles (1989), 'Price, authority and trust: from ideal types to plural forms', *Annual Review of Sociology*, 15, 97–118.

Bromiley, P. and L.L. Cummings (1992), 'Transactions costs in organizations with trust', Discussion Chapter 128, Strategic Management Research Center, University of Minnesota.

Burns, T. and G.M. Stalker (1994), *The Management of Innovation*, Oxford: Oxford University Press.

Burt, Ronald S. (1992), 'The contingent value of social capital', *Administrative Science Quarterly*, 42, 339–65.

Casson, Mark (1995), *Entrepreneurship and Business Culture: Studies in the economics of trust, Volume One*, Aldershot, UK and Brookfield, US: Edward Elgar.

Chiles, Todd H. and John F. McMackin (1996), 'Integrating variable risk preferences, trust, and transaction cost economics', *Academy of Management Review*, **21** (1), 73–99.

Cohen, Stephen S. and Stuart E. Fields (2000), 'Social capital and capital gains: an examination of social capital in Silicon Valley', in Martin Kenney (ed.), *Understanding Silicon Valley: The anatomy of an entrepreneurial region*, Stanford: Stanford University Press.

Day, George, and Paul J.H. Schoemaker (2000), 'Avoiding the pitfalls of emerging technologies', in George S. Day, Paul H. Schoemaker and Robert E. Gunther (eds), *Wharton on Managing Emerging Technologies*, New York: John Wiley and Sons.

Deutsch, Morton (1973), *The Resolution of Conflict: Constructive and Destructive Processes*, London: Yale University Press.

Dibben, Mark R. (2000), *Exploring Interpersonal Trust in Entrepreneurial Venture*, Basingstoke: MacMillan Press

Dodgson, M. (1993), 'Learning, trust, and technological collaboration', *Human Relations*, **46** (1), 77–94.

Doz, Yves L. (1988), 'Technology partnerships between larger and smaller firms: some critical issues', in Farok J. Contractor and Peter Lorange (eds), *Cooperative Strategies in International Business*, Massachusetts: Lexington Books, pp. 317–38.

Eisenhardt, Kathleen M. (1989), 'Building theories from case study research', *Academy of Management Review*, **14** (4), 532–50.

Eisenhardt, Kathleen M. (1990), 'Speed and strategic choice: how managers accelerate decision making', *California Management Review*, **32** (3), 39–54.

Eisenhardt, Kathleen M. and J.A. Martin (2000), 'Dynamic capabilities: What are they?', *Strategic Management Journal*, **21** (10–11), 1105–21.

Erikson, Erik (1950), *Childhood and Society*, New York: Norton

Evans, Philip and T.S. Wurster (2000), *Blown to Bits: How the new economics of information transforms strategy*, Harvard: Harvard Business School Press.

Faraj, Samer and L. Sproull (2000), 'Coordinating expertise in software development teams', *Management Science*, **46** (12), 1554–68.

144   *Trust under pressure*

Ford, David (1998), 'Two decades of interaction, relationships and networks', in Peter Naudé and Peter W. Turnbull (eds), *Network Dynamics in International Marketing*, London: Pergamon, pp. 3–15.

Ford, David, L.-E. Gadde, H. Håkansson and I. Snehota (1998), *Managing Business Relationships*, Chichester: John Wiley & Sons.

Fukuyama, F. (1995), *Trust, the Social Virtues and the Creation of Prosperity*, London: Penguin.

Gambetta, Diego (1998), *Trust: Making and Breaking Cooperative Relations*, Oxford: Blackwell.

Goodman, R.A and L.P. Goodman (1976), 'Some management issues in temporary systems: a study of professional development and manpower – the theater case', *Administrative Science Quarterly*, 21, 494–501.

Gulati, Ranjay (1995), 'Does familiarity breed trust? The implications of repeated ties for contractural choice in alliances, *Academy of Management Journal*, **38** (1), 85–112.

Håkansson, Håkan (1982), *International Marketing and Purchasing of Industrial Goods: An interaction approach*, Chichester: Wiley.

Himanen, Pekka (2001), *The Hacker Ethic and the Spirit of the Information Age*, New York: Random House.

Huston, Ted L. and Robert L. Burgess (1979), 'Social exchange in developing relationships: an overview', in Robert L. Burgess and Ted L. Huston (eds), *Social Exchange in Developing Relationships*, New York: Academic Press.

Johnston, Wesley J., M.P. Leach and A.H. Liu (1999), 'Theory testing using case studies in business-to-business research', *Industrial Marketing Management*, 28, 201–13.

Jones, G. and J. George (1998), 'The experience and evolution of trust: implications for cooperation and teamwork', *Academy of Management Review*, **23** (3), 531–46.

Kelley, Michael J., Jean-Louis Schaan and Héléne Joncas (2002), 'Manging alliance relationships: key challenges in the early stages of collaboration', *R&D Management*, **32** (1), 11–22.

Kenney, Martin (2000), 'Introduction', in Martin Kenney (ed.), *Understanding Silicon Valley: The anatomy of entrepreneurial region*, Stanford: Stanford University Press.

Koenig, Christian (1995), 'Emerging cooperation: the dilemma of trust vs. calculativeness', a chapter presented at the EGOS Colloqium at Istanbul, July 6–8.

Kotabe, Masaaki and Scott K. Swan (1995), 'The role of strategic alliances in high-technology new product development, *Strategic Management Journal*, **16** (8), 621–36.

Krogh, Georg von (1998), 'Care in knowledge creation', *California Management Review*, **40** (3), 133–53.

Larson, Andrea (1992), 'Network dyads in entrepreneurial settings: A study of the governance of exchange processes', *Administrative Science Quarterly*, 37, 76–104.

Lave, C.A. and J.G. March (1975), *An Introduction to Models in the Social Sciences*, New York: Harper & Row, pp. 1–84.

Lazaric, Nathalie and Edward Lorenz (1998a), 'Introduction: the learning dynamics of trust, reputation and confidence', in Nathalie Lazaric and Edward Lorenz (eds), *Trust and Economic Learning*, Cheltenham, UK and Northampton, MA, USA: Edward Elgar.

Lazaric, Nathalie and Edward Lorenz (1998b), 'Trust and organizational learning during inter-firm cooperation', in Nathalie Lazaric and Edward Lorenz (eds), *Trust and Economic Learning*, Cheltenham, UK and Northampton, MA, USA: Edward Elgar.

Lewicki, Roy J. and B.B. Bunker (1995), 'Trust in relationship, a model of development and decline', in B.B. Bunker and J.Z. Rubin and Associates (eds), *Conflict, Cooperation and Justice: Essays inspired by the work of Morton Deutch*, San Fransisco: Jossey-Bass Publishers.

Lewis, David J. and Andrew Weigert (1985), 'Trust as social reality', *Social Forces*, **63** (4), 967–85.

Lorenz, E.H. (1988), 'Neither friends nor strangers: informal networks of subcontracting in French industry', in D. Gambetta (ed.), *Trust – Making and Breaking Relationships*, Oxford: Basil Blackwell, pp. 194–210.

Luhmann, N. (1979), *Trust and Power*, Chichester: Wiley.

Luhmann, N. (1995), *Social Systems*, Stanford: Stanford University Press.

Luo, Yadong (2001), 'Antecedents and consequences of personal attachment in cross-cultural cooperative ventures, *Administrative Science Quarterly*, **46** (2), 177–201.

Metcalfe, J.S. and A. James (2001), 'Knowledge and capabilities: a new view of the firm', in Foss, N.J. and P.L. Robertson (eds), *Resources, Technology and Strategy: Explorations in the resource-based perspective*, London: Routledge, pp. 31–52.

Meyerson, Debra, K.E. Weick and M.R. Kramer (1996), 'Swift trust and temporary groups', in Roderick M. Kramer and Tom R. Tyler (eds), *Trust in Organizations, Frontiers of Theory and Research*, London: Sage Publications, pp. 166–95.

Miles, R.E., C.C. Snow and G. Miles (2000), 'TheFuture.org', *Long Range Planning*, **33** (3), 297–474.

Morgan, Robert M. and Shelby D. Hunt (1984), 'The commitment–trust theory of relationship marketing, *Journal of Marketing*, **58** (3), 20–38.

Nohria, Nitin (1992), 'Introduction: Is a network perspective a useful way of studying organizations', in N. Nohria and G.R. Eccles (eds), *Networks and Organizations: Structure, form and action*, Cambridge, MA: Harvard Business School.

Nonaka, I. and N. Konno (1998), 'The concept of "Ba": building a foundation for knowledge creation', *California Management Review*, **40** (3), 40–54.

Nonaka, I. and H. Takeuchi (1995), *The Knowledge-Creating Company: How Japanese companies create the dynamics of innovation*, Oxford: Oxford University Press.

Pettigrew, Andrew M. (1987), 'Introduction: researching strategic change', in Andrew M. Pettigrew (ed.), *The Management of Strategic Change*, Oxford: Blackwell, pp. 1–13.

Pisano, Gary P. (1990), 'The R&D boundaries of the firm: an empirical analysis', *Administrative Science Quarterly*, 35, 153–76.

Puumalainen, Kaisu, J. Varis, S. Saarenketo, J. Niiranen, K. Blomqvist, O. Kuivalainen, K. Kyläheiko, J. Porras, P. Savolainen, V.-M. Virolainen and T. Äijö (2001), 'Tietoliikennetekniikan PK-lisäarvopalvelutuottajat Suomessa – tutkimusraportti', *Research Reports 3*, Telecom Business Research Center, Lappeenranta University of Technology.

Ring, Peter Smith (1992), 'The role of trust in the design and management of business organizations', a chapter presented at the Annual Meeting of the International Association of Business and Society, Leuven, Belgium, June 14–16, 284–92.

Ring, Peter Smith (1993), 'The role of trust ex ante contract', Proceedings of International Association for Business and Society, San Diego, California, March 19–21, 326–31.

Ring, Peter Smith (2000), 'The three T's of alliance creation: task, team and time', *European Management Journal*, **18** (2), 152–63.

Ring, Peter Smith and A.H. van de Ven (1992), 'Structuring cooperative relationships between organizations', *Strategic Management Journal*, 13, 483–98.

Ring, Peter Smith and A.H. van de Ven (1993), 'Developmental processes of cooperative interorganizational relationships', Strategic Management Research Center, University of Minnesota.

Rothwell, Roy (1994), 'Industrial innovation: success, strategy, trends', in Mark Dodgson and Roy Rothwell (eds), *The Handbook of Industrial Innovation*, Aldershot, UK and Brookfield, US: Edward Elgar Publishing, pp. 33–53.

Rotter, J.B. (1967), 'A new scale for the measurement of interpersonal trust', *Journal of Personality*, 35, 651–65.

Rousillon, Sylvie (1997), 'Confidence building: origins, processes and consequences', in Francis Bidault, Pierre-Yves Gomez and Gilles Marion (eds), *Trust: Firm and society, essays in honour of Dr Roger Delay Termoz*, Basingstoke: MacMillan Press.

Scharmer, Claus Otto (2000), 'Presencing: learning from the future as it emerges', paper presented at the Conference on Knowledge and Innovations, 25–6 May, Helsinki School of Economics, Helsinki, Finland.

Scharmer, O. (2001), A Presentation on the Workshop Meeting for a Conference on New Forms of Global Firms and Innovations, August 13–15.

Schein, Edgar H. (1992), *Organizational Culture and Leadership*, San Fransisco: Jossey-Bass Publishers.

Schein, Edgar H. (1996), 'Three cultures of management: the key to organizational learning', *Sloan Management Review*, Fall, 9–20, **37**, 50–56 (borrowed by Spekman and Wilson 1990).

Simon, Herbert (1957), *Models of Man, Social and Rational*, New York: John Wiley & Sons.

Ståhle, Pirjo (1998), *Supporting a System's Capacity for Self-Renewal*, a Doctoral dissertation, Research reports 190, Helsinki: University of Helsinki.

Ståhle, Pirjo and M. Grönroos (1999), *Knowledge Management – Tietopääoma yrityksen kilpailutekijänä*, Porvoo: WSOY.

Sydow, Jörg (1998), 'Understanding the constitution of interorganizational trust', in Christel Lane and R. Bachman (eds), *Trust Within and Between Organizations: Conceptual issues and empirical applications*, Oxford: Oxford University Press.

Teece, David J. (1998), 'Research directions for knowledge management', *California Management Review*, **40** (3), 289–92.

Tyler, Tom R. and Roderick M. Kramer (1996), 'Wither Trust?', in Roderick M. Kramer and Tom R. Tyler (eds), *Trust in Organizaions, Frontiers of Theory and Research*, Thousand Oaks California: Sage Publications.

Virolainen, Veli-Matti (1998), *Motives, Circumstances, and Success Factors in Partnership Sourcing*, PhD thesis, Research Chapters 71, Lappeenranta: Lappeenranta University of Technology.

Williamson, Oliver (1975), *Markets and Hierarchies: Analysis and antitrust implication*, New York: The Free Press.

Young, Louise C. (1996), 'Can we trust in our measures of trust', a chapter presented in the work-in-progress section of the 1996 International Marketing and Purchasing Conference, University of Karlsruhe, Germany.

Young, Louise C. and I.F. Wilkinson (1989), 'The role of trust and co-operation in marketing channels: a preliminary study', *European Journal of Marketing*, **23** (2), 109–22.

Young-Ybarra, C. and M. Wiersema (1999), 'Strategic flexibility in information technology alliances: the influence of transaction cost economics and social exchange theory', *Organization Science*, **10** (4), 439–59.

Zaheer, A., B. McEvily and V. Perrone (1998), 'Does trust matter? Exploring the effects of interorganizational and interpersonal trust on performance', *Organization Science*, **9** (2), 141–59.

Zucker, L.G. (1986), 'Production of trust: institutional sources of economic structure, 1840–1920', *Research in Organizational Behavior*, 8, 53–111.

8. Trust as a market-based resource: economic value, antecedents and consequences[1]

Bruno Busacca and Sandro Castaldo

1. INTRODUCTION

Trust has become a relevant subject in management literature since the increasing complexity of technology, consumer behaviour and competition has shown the need for new theoretical approaches, that can take account of the critical importance of intangible resources in the generation of competitive advantages and economic value. The *resource-based view* (for example Penrose, 1959; Rumelt, 1984; Wernerfelt, 1984; Barney, 1986 and 1991; Itami, 1987; Dierickx and Cool, 1989; Grant, 1991 and 1996; Vicari, 1991 and 1992; Amit and Schoemaker, 1993; Peteraf, 1993; Hunt and Morgan, 1995) has shown that these intangibles can be of a different nature. Although there is much debate between scholars about the best way of classifying intangible resources, these are principally of two related types: *knowledge* and *trust*. Knowledge refers to the cognitive schemes that a firm possesses internally and that are sufficiently stable to allow the whole business system to function. Trust refers to the cognitive models that relate to subjects outside the firm (for example customers, distributors, suppliers, and financial institutions). Knowledge resources which are contained in the memory of the firm are 'intellectual' assets, while trust which is contained in the memories of outside entities, is based on the certainty of behavioural expectations that the firm is able to generate in other subjects (Vicari, 1991; Srivastava et al., 1998).

Firms that are committed to the 'improvement' of knowledge and trust are best able to make strategic and management choices, and thus continuously generate economic value. A firm's capacity to organise production, transform products, interpret signals coming from the market, manage personnel, finance its own development, and win and hold customer loyalty, all depends on *knowledge* and *trust resources*.

From the point of view of intangible resources, the firm's process of value creation can be seen as the creation, accumulation, reproduction and increase of resources. During this process the use of trust relationships follows the formation of knowledge. It is through these trust-based relationships that knowledge, in the 'concrete' form of goods and services, is brought to market. A firm which is able to create customer value and shareholder value nourishes both a learning potential and a trust potential; the former produces new knowledge, the latter strengthens and broadens the relationship network.

In the light of these theoretical considerations it is fundamental for the firm to understand:

(1) the economic value of trust;
(2) to frame its antecedents and consequences, in order to define a model for trust building in market relationships.

In the following pages, after more fully explaining the role of trust in the process of value creation (section 2), the antecedents and consequences of trust will be identified, with particular focus on the marketing literature (sections 3 and 4). A general model will be suggested that is aimed at understanding the evolutionary dynamics of trust in the market relations. A part of this model was tested experimentally with reference to four different types of buyer–seller relationships, with the aim of identifying the main trust's antecedents (section 5).

2. TRUST, SHAREHOLDER AND CUSTOMER VALUE: A TRUST-BASED VIEW OF THE FIRM'S VALUE CREATION PROCESS

Originally, the concept of trust has almost exclusively been studied in social psychology, particularly in works concerned with group behaviour and interpersonal relationships. It has even been demonstrated experimentally that trust in these cases plays a significant role in the interpretation of the functioning of the individual's cognitive mechanisms and the behaviour that follows from it. Management theories later recognised the significance of the construct in the interpretation of certain specific contexts. Specifically, organizational theories deepened the concept of trust in order to understand the functioning of inter- and intra-organizational relationships (for example Zaheer and Venkatraman, 1995; Zaheer et al., 1998; Gatti, 1999). Studies in marketing focused in particular on the specificity of the concept in interpreting buyer–seller relationships in different contexts. It has been recognised that trust plays a crucial role in these situations, 'as every commercial transaction contains an element of trust within itself, and this is certainly true for every transaction that is conducted over a certain period of time'.[2] Indeed trust influences the firm's capacity both to form new relationships and to maintain relationships, thus improving the size and quality of the customer base. This means that increasing the trust also increases the *stability* (measured by the rate of retention of customers) and *reproductivity* (measured by the rate of attraction of new customers) of the relational network. In order to clarify the impact of trust on the stability of the firm relational network, it is important to understand which functions this resource can perform within the consumer's cognitive system.

First of all, several empirical researches (for example Kiel and Layton, 1981; Punj and Staelin, 1983) over the years have shown that there is a negative relationship between the level of trust and the informational effort that a consumer has to make during the buying process. Hence trust can act as a substitute for information, thus reducing the consumers' exposure to the marketing communications of other companies and stabilizing the relationship with the trusted firm. Secondly, trust toward a firm, built by the repeated confirmation of consumers' expectations, translates into a sort of *cognitive inertia*, based both on strong beliefs about the firm's capability to satisfy consumption needs and the desire to avoid the onset of clashing information with these beliefs.

On the other hand, the impact of trust on the widening of the firm's relational network can be directly referred to the transferability of this resource. If the trust that a firm develops is confirmed by a high number of consumption experiences, this means that it can activate a process of abstraction and generalisation that transfers the link between the expectations of satisfaction and a specific phenomenon to a wider level. The specific phenomenon is the consumption experience of a particular product of the firm's. The wider level is the set of possible experiences of interaction with the firm itself. One obvious example of the process of generalisation is the inter-industry transfer of the trust related to a particular brand (a transfer that is naturally linked to the cognitive fit with regard to its capabilities). Category extension strategies, which consist of the use of an existing brand to sustain the introduction of a new product in a new industry, are based on this kind of generalisation process.

That being stated, if one focuses on the relationships with the two basic types of stakeholders (customers and shareholders), the role of trust in the process of value creation can be better understood by considering how this resource contributes to the virtuous circle shown in Figure 8.1.

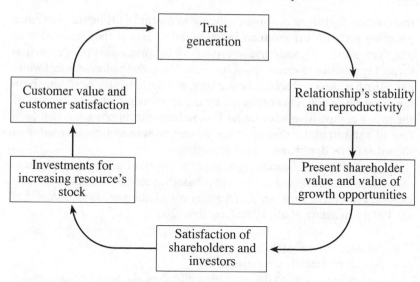

Figure 8.1   The trust virtuous circle

Improving the stability and reproductive capacity of the relational network stimulates the *net present shareholder value*. Its development is due to the impact of trust on the fundamental cost and income components of customer relationships.[3] Researchers have studied this subject for some time, and their work has resulted in greater knowledge of:

*   the correlation between certain indicators of the solidity of the firm's relational network (for example, the rate of customer retention and the level of customer satisfaction) and the profitability of the network itself (Reichheld and Sasser, 1990; Reichheld, 1991–1992 and 1996; Carrol, 1991–1992; Anderson et al., 1994);
*   the contribution of the firm's relational resources (*market-based assets* in the terminology of the authors) to the creation of shareholder value (Srivastava et al., 1998);
*   the value of the *customer base*, with particular reference to loyal customers (Wang and Splegel, 1994);
*   the estimate of customer *life time value* (for example Dwyer, 1989; Keane and Wang, 1995; Berger and Nasr, 1998) and *customer equity* (Blattberg and Deighton, 1996; Wayland and Cole, 1997).

Summarising the most significant results of these studies, we can say that the impact of trust on the *net present shareholder value* is due to the positive effect of this resource on the stability of relationships. Increasing trust means that there is also an increase in customer willingness to pay a premium price for the products bought, and to extend the relationship to other categories of goods and/or services in the firm's portfolio, as well as spreading positive referrals about the firm. The growth of customer loyalty has a further, direct effect on the duration of relationships, increasing both the duration of the rents produced by the relationship and the solidity of the firm's competitive advantage. This reduces entrepreneurial risk (and cost of capital) and increases either the net present shareholder value or the value of its opportunities for growth.

The present value of capital is, however, strongly influenced by the quality of the customer base, and this in turn is based on certain distinctive features of loyal customers, for example (Anderson and Sullivan, 1993; Johnson et al., 1995; Srivastava et al., 1998; Costabile, 2001):

- reduced price sensitivity;
- higher propensity to consumption;
- higher sensitivity to the marketing efforts of the firm, such as quicker response to new products;
- higher propensity to spread positive communications about the firm;
- higher willingness to *trading up*, that is the purchase of greater quality within the same product line, and to *cross buy*, that is the acquisition of other goods and/or services offered by the firm;
- reduced cost of sales and assistance;
- higher willingness to *knowledge sharing*, that is the activation of co-evolutionary processes between demand and offer, based on the exchange and integration of the knowledge that has been developed in specific contexts.

Relationship stability influences capital profitability, as well as the rate of profit. This can be expressed by the difference between *return on equity* (ROE) and the *capitalisation rate*. This rate is reduced thanks to the reduction of entrepreneurial risk that is the result of the greater solidity of the firm's competitive advantage because of customer loyalty. ROE, on the other hand, is increased thanks to the benefits that are due to the quality of the customer base (increased income, greater duration of relationships, reduction of customer acquisition and development costs). The positive impact of customer loyalty on the duration of normal expected profit should be added to this. It is directly due to the causal links between the loyalty rate of customers and the prospective longevity of the relationships.

3. ANTECEDENTS OF TRUST

Having clarified the main elements to define the economic value of trust, and its importance in interpreting market relations, it is worthwhile identifying the principal antecedents of trust in market relationships. This allows for the identification of the factors that have to be taken into account as part of possible strategies for increasing trust resources and, as a direct consequence, the firm's economic value. This was a very difficult task, above all because there was no clear and shared definition of trust itself. Trust was often defined by some authors by reference to elements that were considered by others to be simply the determinants of trust.

It was thought necessary, in the face of this difficulty, to clarify the boundaries of the construct, so as to arrive at a definition that could be taken as a starting point for identifying the determining elements. In our perspective trust is considered as a cognitive synthesis that indicates the capacity of the counterpart to perform the tasks he has taken on. It takes the form, however, of a perceptive construct that overlays the elements that define it. 'Trusting' is information that helps the subject to control uncertainty. The mental representation depends on the motivations and perceived knowledge of the individual, his reputation, and his behaviour in similar situations. These are often defined in terms of *chunks of information* that make it possible to infer trust. The profound meaning of the concept remains unchanged, although its determinants may change; the determinants should be considered, for this reason, as external to the construct although they have a decisive conditioning influence on it.

A fundamental role is played by past experience, which is one of the main determinants of trust. The knowledge that a subject accumulates about the behaviour of a counterpart is one of the main presuppositions for the creation of trust resources (for example Schurr and Ozanne, 1985; Swan and Nolan, 1985; Ganesan, 1994). Past experience, however, as will be made clear in what follows, is more than simply a genuine determining element – it is a necessary condition for the construction of trust.

The other antecedents of trust that are most often taken into account in the models aimed at showing the construct in the context of marketing relations, include the following – apart from past experience:

(a) The abilities and competencies of the counterpart;
(b) The motivations driving the behaviour of the subject, in particular the absence of opportunistic motivations;
(c) The behaviours and personal characteristics of the subject;
(d) The satisfaction obtained in past interactions with the counterpart;
(e) Partnership behaviour;
(f) Communication.

Each of the antecedents listed above will be treated briefly in the pages that follow.

(a) The abilities and functional competencies needed to create the *outputs* that can lead to the *trustor* satisfaction are the basic element for the development of a trust relationship (Andaleeb, 1992; Ganesan, 1994; Mayer et al., 1995; Doney and Cannon, 1997). A subject's credibility therefore depends on the beliefs of the buyer that the seller will have the knowledge that is required to perform his role efficiently and reliably. The firm's resources of competence, its *know-how* and its *knowledge*, are therefore an essential element in the trust concept (Vicari, 1991; Rullani, 1992). This confirms the circular causal relationship between knowledge and trust we underlined in the first section.

(b) The second trust antecedent concerns the system of motivations that governs behaviour. This is represented by the certainty that the counterpart will not behave opportunistically, and that his actions will on the contrary be aimed at producing mutual benefits (for example Martin, 1991; Andaleeb, 1992; Morgan and Hunt, 1994; Zaheer and Venkatraman, 1995; Rich, 1997). With the increase of similar attitudes, values, and above all motivations underlying the behaviour of the subjects involved, the relationship becomes more satisfying for the parties concerned. This is because the expectations that behaviour will lead to the achievement of shared goals increase. In situations, however, where a subject sees a significant amount of opportunism in the behaviour of the counterpart, this naturally leads to a failure to trust because of the egoistic motivations underlying the counterpart's behaviour.[4]

(c) Many authors have shown the importance of characteristics like honesty, sincerity, frankness, reliability and affinity between the parties as elements that can have an effect on trust (for example Swan and Nolan, 1985; Swan et al., 1985; Crosby et al., 1990; Martin, 1991; Moorman et al., 1993).[5] Many of the authors who showed these antecedents of trust relationships referred to contexts where the interaction was predominantly between individuals, as in the case of services and buyer–seller personal relationships. In practice these elements are not to be ignored for two reasons. Firstly, it should be considered that firms relationships are often governed by individuals who play the role of 'gatekeeper' for the firm (for example Zaheer et al., 1998). Secondly, another reason why personal characteristics cannot be neglected as the antecedents of trust is that these can be transferred to the firm as part of its image, although caution is necessary. It is possible, on the basis of this, to then determine the firm's level of reliability.

(d) The satisfaction experienced in past interactions with a firm is one of the factors that most authors think crucial to the creation of trust. It is the clearest indicator of the firm's capacity to keep its own promises (for example Anderson and Narus, 1990; Martin, 1991; Busacca, 1994; Ganesan, 1994; Garbarino and Johnson, 1999). A buyer's satisfaction derives from having obtained a level of output that is consistent with, or even exceeds, the expectations created by the firm (promises). It is therefore a further reason for firms to orient themselves towards *customer satisfaction* and to carry out a continuous monitoring of the level of their customers' satisfaction, thus acting in time to fill the possible gaps that might occur between the quality that customers desire and expect, and that which they perceive as having obtained (perceived quality) (Valdani and Busacca, 1992; Busacca, 1994). Doing this increases the level of satisfaction and thus increases trust. The relationship between trust and satisfaction is not a simple and direct causal one, but a circular one – anything that strengthens the trust relationship between the parties also has an indirect effect on the level of satisfaction (Crosby et al., 1990; Martin, 1991).

(e) There is the same uncertainty about the type of causality with regard to co-operation as there is with regard to satisfaction and trust (for example Anderson and Narus, 1990; Martin, 1991). At first sight it would seem beyond doubt that co-operative behaviour is a consequence of trust rather than, as some authors argue, one of its antecedents.[6] Empirical studies carried out in the context of games theory,[7] have proved that co-operation is an antecedent of trust (for example Rotter, 1967). Using this theory, Crosby et al. (1990) argue that the perceptions of customers about the seller's intention to co-operate have an effect on the trust that is placed in the seller by demand. In practice, although co-operation can be defined as an antecedent of trust, and 'although Axelrod argues that co-operation can develop without trust … it is inconceivable, in relation to human beings, without at least a predisposition towards trust' (Gambetta, 1989).[8] Where there is a lack of trust, or one-sided trust, it is impossible to pursue behaviours based on reciprocal co-operation. We argue that this case as well is really one of circular causality.[9]

(f) Finally, the connection between communication and trust has been one of the most deeply surveyed subjects by those interested in the trust dimension of market relationships. The authors have not reached unanimous conclusions about the type of relationship that brings the two variables together. Some authors consider that trust, or more precisely the *trust climate* that is a feature of the relationship, can facilitate communication between the parties, and at the same time make

the communication more credible (Zand, 1972; Lorey, 1980). Mohr and
Nevin (1990) have proposed a model that explicitly considers the forms
that communication takes at different levels of trust and co-operation
within a distributive channel. As well as making communication more
'fluid', trust also makes communication sources more credible, and
thus contributes to making the messages themselves more credible.[10]
In the cases that have been cited communication has been considered
the consequence of trust, and not one of its antecedents (for example
Dwyer et al., 1987; Mohr and Nevin, 1990).[11] Most of the marketing
scholars, on the other hand, have shown the role of communication as a
determinant of the process of creating a trust relationship, considering
communication as an antecedent of trust (for example Bialeszewski and
Gillaourakis, 1985; Anderson et al., 1987; Anderson and Narus, 1990;
Morgan and Hunt, 1994). When communication is transparent and
effective, it helps to resolve conflicts that can arise in the relationship.
Communication can align the expectations and perceptions of the
parties (Morgan and Hunt, 1994) and thus play an indirect role on
the level of trust.[12] Perceptions play a determining role in the creation
of trust. A difference of perception between the parties can easily
occur where the subjects 'interpret' the surrounding environment or
external phenomena in a different way. This can result in a lessening
of trust. It is only correct to consider transparency of communication
as an antecedent of trust where a static view of the situation is taken.
Empirical studies have shown that past communication (at time t_{-1})
between the parties effects the level of trust that is a feature of the
relationship at time t_0 (the present). Looking at the phenomenon in
dynamic terms, however, it becomes impossible to ignore the time flow
as one of the determining elements in the model that necessitates a
circular and recurrent relationship between communication and trust.
As shown earlier, if past communication (at time t_{-1}) increases the level
of trust in the present (at time t_0), this leads to the inevitable recognition
that consolidating the trust relationship improves communication itself.
There is thus interdependence between the two variables.

Analysis of the marketing literature shows additional elements to those
of the antecedents of trust. These other elements have to be regarded
as secondary, because they are less frequently cited in the literature, and
because they also have features in common with the elements that have
already been discussed. The categories of antecedent include: the level
of investment in the relationship (Ganesan, 1994), similarity between the
partners (Crosby et al., 1990) and above all the sharing of values (Morgan
and Hunt, 1994; Heide and John, 1992), reputation (Ganesan, 1994), the

partners' organizational structure and culture (Moorman et al., 1993), the features of the object of the transaction, and in particular its degree of complexity and the difficulty of expressing evaluations about its qualitative level (Moorman et al., 1993), brand value (Schurr and Ozanne, 1985), the degree of *customer orientation* of the *partners* (Swan et al., 1985) and so on (Mayer et al., 1995).

We try to summarize this discussion of the determinants of trust – defined as certainty about other people's behaviour – by arguing that it is above all conditioned by the information, past experience and consequent beliefs about:[13]

- The capacity of the counterpart to behave in a way that is consistent with what he has promised,
- His reasons for pursuing joint objectives without resorting to opportunistic behaviours and
- His capacity to act in such a way that his behaviour contributes to the achievement of joint objectives.

These seem to be the fundamental determinants of trust, as they emerge from an analysis of marketing literature. Where there is a high degree of personal interactions these determinants are conditioned by the behaviours and personal characteristics of the subjects involved in the relationship. It is not, however, the case that these variables are the only or even the most significant components of the cognitive scheme of trust. As already said, this cognitive scheme can take very different forms, depending on the individual and on the situation.

The satisfaction produced by interactions with the counterpart, the predisposition to collaborative behaviour, and communication, are undoubtedly antecedents of trust. They cannot, however, be considered exclusively as antecedents. They determine the level of trust and at the same time they are subject to conditioning by trust, so that, in a dynamic perspective (see Wilson, 1995; Jap, 1999; Costabile, 2001), they generate circular causal relationships. There is a process of self-generation of the resources connected to the relationship. The relationships take this form because they are 'recurring processes of the self-creation of trust, starting from the trust that is created in earlier interaction' (Vicari, 1991).

4.   CONSEQUENCES OF TRUST

Once the antecedents that contribute to the creation of trust have been clarified, the next step is to understand the consequences of trust. This means understanding the variables or constructs on which trust can display its effects. This will be useful for understanding the value of trust in relational activities. Analysis of the models dedicated to understanding the causal relations between trust and the elements connected to it shows the crucial role that this intangible resource plays. Trust is capable of:

(a) reducing the degree of decisional uncertainty;
(b) increasing the degree of *commitment* of the subjects involved;
(c) reducing the level of conflict;
(d) bringing about the greater use of non-coercive power sources;
(e) increasing the level of satisfaction and the quality of the relationship;
(f) making communication more efficient;
(g) collaborative behaviours.

A brief analysis of each of these effects follows.

(a) The reduction of decisional uncertainty was mentioned earlier, when it was emphasised that trust, like its opposite, makes the subjects' decisional process more certain by allowing the behaviour of a counterpart to be predicted (for example Baccarani, 1995; Mayer et al., 1995; Ugolini, 1999).
(b) We argue that the crucial importance of *commitment* requires further mention. Commitment indicates the effort made by individuals, and shows itself in a relationship which a party considers significant enough to make the maximum efforts to maintain.[14] This implies a desire to establish a stable relationship with the counterpart, and a willingness to make the short-term sacrifices needed to consolidate the relationship (*serial equity*), relying at the same time on the relationship's stability (Anderson and Weitz, 1992; Ganesan, 1994; Garbarino and Johnson, 1999). Three models suggested by Anderson and Weitz (1992), Morgan and Hunt (1994) and Garbarino and Johnson (1999) have aroused great interest in understanding the relationship between trust and *commitment*. These models provide an opportunity for considering the commitment of each of the counterparts, as a way of understanding the 'quality' of the market relation.
(c) The significance of testing the effects of trust on conflict[15] reduction springs from the fact that conflict is one of the main elements that can have a negative effect on the possibility for collaboration. It has been hypothesised that the more conflict there is between counterparts in a system, the less will be their level of satisfaction. The system

will also be less effective, and conflict is one of the main causes of relationship termination. Conflict does not always, however, produce negative results. While most authors trace a negative linear relationship between conflict and *performance*, this does not mean that conflict always acts in this way. Some scholars in fact suggest that there is a *cut-off point*. They theorise that there is a positive relationship between conflict and performance up to a certain point, beyond which the correlation becomes negative (Lusch, 1976; Rosenberg and Stern, 1971; Rosenbloom, 1973). To this should be added the effort to qualify conflict as functional or dysfunctional according to the results that it produces in system performance and to evaluate conflict positively if it occurs within contained levels (for example Robicheaux and El Ansary, 1976). Trust can transform conflict in cases where there is potential tension, turning the dysfunctional into the functional, and is thus an element that favours the co-ordination of individual actions within the *network*.[16]

(d) The contributions of Martin (1991) and Morgan and Hunt (1994) are particularly important in a consideration of the relationship between power and trust. These authors argue that trust is responsible for the counterparts' exercise of non-coercive power.[17] It has thus been shown that non-coercive sources of power (which are used most often in relationships that are based on trust) produce positive effects on the satisfaction and performance of the two parties, and thus avoid the emergence of conflict.[18]

(e) (f, g) Regarding the effects of trust on the level of satisfaction with the relationship, on the quality of communication, and the opportunity for co-operation, see the preceding section which emphasises the circular causality between the above variables.

Other results include the greater likelihood of allocating resources in favour of subjects who are trusted (Anderson et al., 1987), the greater ease of persuading or influencing the other part (Swan and Nolan, 1985; Swan et al., 1985) and the greater sales that follow from it.

Figures 8.2 and 8.3 summarise the arguments developed in this and previous sections. Figure 8.2 contains a synthesis of the antecedents of trust and its consequences, as these have been hypothesised in the principal models within the field of marketing and strategic management. The antecedents more cited in this literature are: past experience and length of the relationship; skill and competencies; individual variables; power and dependence; communication (transparency and frequency). Within the most cited consequences we have found: commitment; sales performances;

satisfaction and cooperation. On the basis of this literature review we framed a first model (Figure 8.3) including the principal components of the cognitive scheme underlying trust and their main relationships. It distinguishes between cognitive and behavioural constructs. More precisely, it is intended to show the role of past experience as a behavioural determinant, and reliability, competencies, and the subject's motivations (non-opportunistic) as cognitive determinants. These elements are the ones that make the largest contribution to trust creation. The model identifies the main cognitive effects of trust in reducing decisional uncertainty, increasing *commitment*, reducing dysfunctional conflict, and use of non-coercive power. It is easy to theorise that the behavioural consequence of trust in such a relationship is the greater probability of a relationship based on mutual collaboration. Finally, the model is intended to show the circular nature of the relationships that connect the level of satisfaction, the quality of communication, and the degree of collaboration with trust, so as to show the character of the 'self-generative resource' (Vicari, 1991 and 1992).

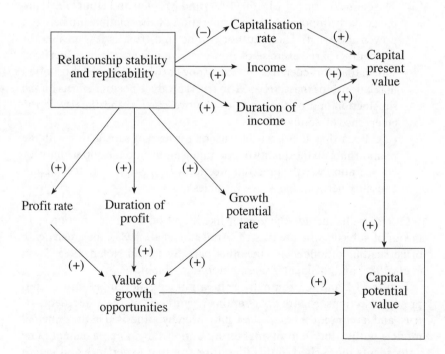

Figure 8.2   From the relationship stability to the capital potential value

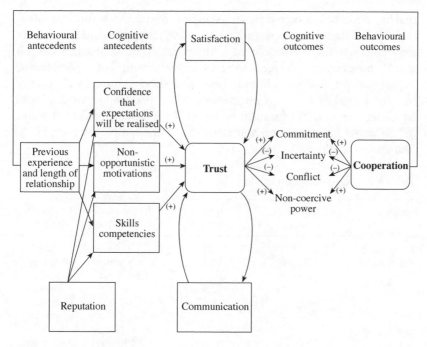

Source: Castaldo (2002, 240)

Figure 8.3   Trust in market relationships: a conceptual framework

5.   A FRAMEWORK FOR TRUST-BUILDING STRATEGIES: AN EXPLORATIVE RESEARCH

The model that has been described in the previous section was tested experimentally with reference to different types of buyer–seller relationships, with the aim of identifying the trust's main antecedents. The empirical research was carried out with reference to four types of relationship in consumer markets where there was a high level of 'trust intensity'. The four sets of relationships referred to two categories of goods and two of services. Buyer–supplier relationships were surveyed with respect to two types of service with a high intensity of trust, university training services and financial services, investigating the relationship between students and the university institution and that between the customer and financial consultant. The third choice was a category of grocery products, particularly beef (a sector that had never before been represented in trust resources – before, the survey had covered recent developments connected to the spread of BSE). Finally, the model was tested with regard to the purchase of a consumer durable good – an electronic device – to test the relationship between potential buyers and the producer's brand. Thus, four survey samples were carried out, for a total of 819 valid interviews (203 for financial services, 118 for education services, 274 for meat buyers, 224 for durable products). Some details about the dimension and structure of the sample for each of the four surveys are given in Table 8.1.

Table 8.1   Research sample

Sector	Financial services	Training services	Consumers non-durables	Consumer durables
Total number	203	118	274	224
Relationship	Clients of a company	Fourth-year university students	Purchasers of fresh meat	Potential purchasers with some knowledge of product
Average age	47	23	36% (41–50)	33% (20–30)
Sex	58% male	60% female	80% female	62% male
Profession	24% professionals	100% students	75% housewives	35% students
Year survey taken	1996	1995	1997	1994

The methodology used in the survey provided for the use of personal interviews on a pre-tested questionnaire, while the analysis of data and testing of the research hypothesis were performed by applying the Lisrel model (Joreskog and Sorbom, 1989). This allowed the 'theoretical empiricism', that is a characteristic of this analytic approach (Bagozzi, 1994), to be used during the research.[19] The main results of the survey are shown in Table 8.2, which summarizes the principal cognitive antecedents of trust with regard to the four types of relationship being empirically tested. It is clear from these results that, unlike relational contexts of reference, the drivers of trust have changed. Thus, while there is no change in the latent construct of trust itself, there is significant change in the *semantic network* of the underlying variables. This verifies the hypothesis put forward earlier regarding the definition of trust. This was verified by the cross-category survey with its identical set of starting hypotheses, although it used situation-specific variables as the object of measure. These results are only experimental, but they do reveal *the situation-specific* dimension of the cognitive antecedents of trust.

Table 8.2   Lisrel's results

	Financial services	Training services	Consumer non-durables	Consumer durables
Perceived competence	0.518*	0.644*	0.233*	
Shared values	0.399*			
Non-opportunistic motivation	0.240*	0.828*		
Emotive variables			0.597*	
Brand image		0.586**		0.551*
Assumption that expectations will be realized				0.220
AGFI (Adjusted Goodness of Fit Index	0.865	0.748	0.923	0.759
TCDE (Total Coefficient of Determination for Structural Equation)	0.964	0.844	0.835	0.978

Notes:
*   < 0.05
**   The relationship identifies trust as a brand image antecedent

In particular in the financial services case the perceived consultant's competencies and value sharing have been noticed as the main antecedents. For undergraduate training services the competencies are considered slightly less relevant as the driver for trust than non-opportunistic motivation for faculty behaviour. In the cases of grocery goods (meat) – a typical experience good – the relationship with the salesperson together with his perceived competencies have been found as the main antecedents. Finally, in the case of the consumer durable goods (electronic appliances) brand image is the main construct underlying trust. From this result some interesting managerial implication could be drawn for the trust-building strategies. For example, in the case of financial services it should be relevant for the companies to focus on the competence-building processes of salesmen and to consolidate their perceived integrity. In the case of undergraduate students the research has noticed the centrality of faculty motivation and competencies as the main trust antecedents. To invest in the perceived knowledge of professors and to implement incentive mechanisms for minimizing opportunistic behaviours towards the classroom should be the main priorities to develop students' trust in their university. In the cases of goods, it should be a managerial priority to invest in the sales personnel empowerment and feeling (for meat) and in company brand image (for durables). From these short considerations on managerial implication drawn by the exploratory research it is easy to imagine the potential of trust's studies and the managerial usefulness of semantic network analysis of trust for increasing firm performance, resources and economic value, as illustrated in the second section of this chapter. The synthetic model introduced at the end of the previous section could be considered a valid starting-point for the study of trust in its specific relational contexts.

NOTES

1. The authors wish to thank two anonymous referees for their useful suggestions, which allowed them to improve the structure and the content of this work.
2. See D. Gambetta (1989, 299). The original quote is from K.J. Arrow (1972), *Gift and Exchanges, Philosophy and Public Affairs*, **1** (4), 343–62.
3. The value of customer relationships (customer equity), in analytic terms can be expressed in the following way (Wayland and Cole, 1997, 103–6):

$$W_{RC} = \sum_{t=1}^{n} Q_t \pi_t / (1+i)^t + \sum_{t=1}^{n} (D_t + R_t) / (1+i)^t - A_1$$

where:

W_{RC} = the value of customer relationships (customer equity);
Q_t = the volume of purchases in each time period ($t_1, t_2, \dots t_n$)
π_t = the after-tax margin per unit purchased;
D_t = the costs of customer relationship development;
R_t = the costs of customer retention;
A_1 = the costs of acquiring customers;
i = the rate of discount;
n = the number of time periods taken into consideration, on the basis of the expected duration of the relationship.

4. Regarding opportunism as a (negative) antecedent of trust is particularly important from the theoretical point of view, because it challenges one of the fundamental hypotheses of the theory of transactional costs. This postulates that the presence of egoism in human behaviours means all aim at the astute achievement of an individual's own interests (see Williamson, 1985).
5. Authors with a social psychology background have made considerable efforts to identify the personal variables that are most directly correlated to the individual's predisposition to trust. This would allow for considerable reinforcement of the predictive capacity of the models proposed by theory and their application for practical purposes. Rotter identified some significant correlation between the individual's propensity to trust and the individual's role in the family, his socio-economic level, and the religion he followed. The same author showed that high trusting individuals are generally more reliable, happier, and more peaceful than low-trusters (see J.B. Rotter, 1967 and 1980).
6. A good proportion of the psychological and sociological studies favour this kind of relationship. For more on the debate see, among others, Loomis (1959) and Sacconi (1990).
7. Axelrod (1984) shows that, even in the absence of trust or in the presence of very weak trust relationships and situations in which the parties find it impossible to communicate, co-operative relationships between the parties can still develop.

8. Deutsch (1962, 302) is even more explicit about this point. He argues that 'the initiation of co-operation requires trust whenever the individual, by his choice to co-operate, places his fate partly in the hands of others'. Galeotti (1990, 122) maintains that 'even if trust ... were only a spontaneous result of co-operative relationships, it could function to maintain co-operation, replacing the more costly initial conditions'.

9. 'The cooperation–trust linkage exhibits spiral reinforcement, in that successive successful (unsuccessful) co-operative episodes in the relationship lead to higher (lower) levels of trust in the relationship' (Martin, 1991).

10. For the vast literature about the ways in which trust's response to sources impacts on message reliability, see Hovland and Weiss (1951); Schulman and Worrall (1970); Heesacker et al., (1983).

11. Many sociologists and psychologists have theorised various cause and effect relationships between communication and trust, and have also offered experimental testing. For a summary of these studies see Loomis (1959).

12. 'The ambiguity and manipulability of the symbolic pattern of communication and the interpretation can often make it difficult to construct and extend trust' (Roniger, 1988, 385).

13. As explained earlier, some authors have defined a greater number of trust determinants, these being antecedents or consequences of trust. For more on the determinants, see Frost et al. (1978); Butler and Cantrell (1985).

14. See Morgan and Hunt (1994, 23). Moorman et al. (1992, 316) suggested a similar definition. They state that 'commitment to a relationship is defined as an enduring desire to maintain a valued relationship'.

15. Conflict is a state that derives from a situation in which one component of the dyadic system perceives that the behaviour of the other component impedes the achievement of the first component's objectives, or makes it impossible for the first component to perform his role in the system efficiently. This gives rise to a state of frustration that can develop into open conflict. See Stern and Gorman (1969, 156).

16. 'However, we posit that it is trust that leads a partner to perceive that future conflictual episodes will be functional' (Morgan and Hunt, 1994, 26). 'Another posited consequence of trust is *functionality of conflict*, which can be defined as an evaluative appraisal of the results of recent efforts to resolve disagreements' (Anderson and Narus, 1990, 45). Martin (1991) shares this view.

17. Non-coercive power means the use of sources of power (for example those based on rewards) that make it possible to offer contributions to the counterpart, thus favouring the achievement of the counterpart's own objectives. Sources of coercive power, on the other hand, are potential punishments that make pursuing the same objectives more difficult. With regard to the relationship between power and trust see also Solomon (1960) and Hunt and Nevin (1974).

18. We argue that the relationship between power and trust is much more complex than is suggested by the authors whose work has been referred to. Its importance for interpreting market relations means that it should be further studied.

19. 'If one had to characterize the general philosophy of SEMs (Structural Equation Models) in an ideal way, the term 'theoretical empiricism' would be apt because of the need to emphasize the integration of theory with method and observations' (Bagozzi, 1994, 317).

REFERENCES

Amit, R. and P.J.H. Schoemaker (1993), 'Strategic assets and Organizational Rent', *Strategic Management Journal*, **14** (1), 33–46.

Andaleeb, S.S. (1992), 'The Trust Concept: Research Issues for Channel of Distribution', in J.N. Sheth (ed.), *Research in Marketing*, Vol.11, Jai Press Inc., pp. 1–34.

Anderson, E.W. and M.W. Sullivan (1993), 'The Antecedents and Consequences of Customer Satisfaction for Firms', *Marketing Science*, Spring, 125–43.

Anderson, E. and B. Weitz (1992), 'The Use of Pledges to Build and Sustain Commitment in Distribution Channel', *Journal of Marketing Research*, **XXIX**, February, 18–34.

Anderson, E.W., C. Fornell and D.R. Lehmann (1994), 'Customer Satisfaction, Market Share and Profitability: Findings from Sweden', *Journal of Marketing*, July, 53–66.

Anderson, E., L. Lodish and B. Weitz (1987), 'Resource Allocation in Conventional Channels', *Journal of Marketing Research*, **24**, February, 85–97.

Anderson, J.C. and J.A. Narus (1990), 'A Model of Distributor Firm and Manufacturer Firm Working Partnerships', *Journal of Marketing*, **54**, January, 42–58.

Axelrod, R. (1984), *The Evolution of Cooperation*, Basic Books, New York.

Baccarani, C. (1995), 'Riflessioni sulla fiducia', in M. Ugolini, *La natura dei rapporti tra imprese nel settore delle calze per donna*, Cedam, Padova, pp. XI–XXII.

Bagozzi, R.P. (1994), 'Structural Equation Models in Marketing Research: Basic Principles', in R.P. Bagozzi (ed.), *Principles of Marketing Research*, Blackwell, Cambridge, MA, pp. 317–85.

Barney, J.B. (1986), 'Strategic Factor Markets: Expectations, Luck and Business Strategy', *Management Science*, **32** (10), 1231–41.

Barney, J.B. (1991), 'Firm Resources and Sustained Competitive Advantage', *Journal of Management*, **17** (1), 99–120.

Berger, P.D. and N. Nasr (1998), 'Customer Lifetime Value: Marketing Models and Application', *Journal of Interactive Marketing*, 1, winter, 17–30.

Bialeszewski, D. and M. Gillaourakis (1985), 'Perceived Communication Skills and Resultant Trust Perceptions Within the Channel of Distribution', *Journal of the Academy of Marketing Science*, 13, Spring, 206–17.

Blattberg, R. and J. Deighton (1996), 'Manage Marketing by the Customer Equity Test', *Harvard Business Review*, **74** (4), 136–44.

Busacca, B. (1994), *Le risorse di fiducia dell'impresa. Soddisfazione del cliente, creazione di valore, strategie di accrescimento*, Utet, Torino.

Butler, J.K. Jr. and S.R. Cantrell (1985), 'A Behavioral Decision Theory Approach to Modeling Dyadic Trust in Superiors and Subordinates', *Psychological Reports*, **55**, 19–28.

Carrol, P. (1991–1992), 'The Fallacy of Customer Retention', *Journal of Retail Banking*, 4, Winter, 15–20.

Castaldo, S. (2002), *Fiducia e relazioni di mercato*, Il Mulino, Bologna.

Costabile, M. (2001), *Il capitale relazionale*, McGraw Hill, Milano.

Crosby, L.A., K.R. Evans and D. Cowles (1990), 'Relationship Quality in Services Selling: An Interpersonal Influence Perspective', *Journal of Marketing*, **54**, July, 68–81.

Deutsch, M. (1962), 'Cooperation and Trust: Some Theoretical Notes', in J.R. Marshall (ed.), *Nebraska Symposium on Motivation*, Vol. 10, University of Nebraska Press, Lincoln.

Dierickx, I. and K. Cool (1989), 'Asset Stock Accumulation and Sustainability of Competitive Advantage', *Management Science*, **35** (12), 1504–11.

Doney, P.M. and J.P. Cannon (1997), 'An Examination of the Nature of Trust in Buyer–Seller Relationships', *Journal of Marketing*, 61, 35–51.

Dwyer, F.R. (1989), 'Customer Lifetime Valuation to Support Marketing Decision Making', *Journal of Direct Marketing*, 3, Fall, 9–15.

Dwyer, R., P. Schurr and S. Oh (1987), 'Developing Buyer–Seller Relationships', *Journal of Marketing*, **51**, April, 11–27.

Frost, T., D.V. Stimpson and M.R. Maughan (1978), 'Some Correlates of Trust', *Psychological Reports*, **99**, 103–8.

Galeotti, A.E. (1990), 'Fidarsi è bene', *Stato e Mercato*, 28, April, 117–26.

Gambetta, D. (1989), 'Possiamo fidarci della fiducia?', in D. Gambetta (ed.), *Trust. Making and Breaking Cooperative Relations*, Basil Blackwell Ltd., Oxford., pp. 275–309 of Italian version.

Ganesan, S. (1994), 'Determinants of Long-Term Orientation in Buyer–Seller Relationships', *Journal of Marketing*, **58**, April, 1–19.

Garbarino, E. and M.S. Johnson (1999), 'The Different Roles of Satisfaction, Trust, and Commitment in Customer Relationships', *Journal of Marketing*, 63, 70–87.

Gatti, M. (1999), 'Fiducia e generazione di conoscenza nelle relazioni tra imprese: il caso "ST"', *Sinergie*, 50, 129–61.

Grant, R.M. (1991), 'The Resource-Based Theory of Competitive Advantage: Implications for Strategy', *California Management Review*, 22, 114–35.

Grant, R.M. (1996), 'Toward a Knowledge-Based Theory of The Firm', *Strategic Management Journal*, 17, 109–22.

Heesacker, M., R.E. Petty and J.T. Cacioppo (1983), 'Field Dependence and Attitude Change: Source Credibility Can Alter Persuasion By Affecting Message-Relevant Thinking', *Journal of Personality*, **51** (4), December, 653–66.

Heide, J.B. and G. John (1992), 'Do Norms Matter in Marketing Relationships?', *Journal of Marketing*, **56**, April, 32–44.

Hovland, C.J. and W. Weiss (1951), 'The Influence of Source Credibility on Communication Effectiveness', *Public Opinion Quarterly*, Winter, 635–50.

Hunt, S.H. and R.M. Morgan (1995), 'The Comparative Advantage Theory of Competition', *Journal of Marketing*, **59**, April, 1–15.

Hunt, S. and J.R. Nevin (1974), 'Power in a Channel of Distribution: Sources and Consequences', *Journal of Marketing Research*, **11**, May, 186–93.

Itami, H. (1987), *Mobilizing Invisible Assets*, Harvard University Press, Cambridge, MA.

Jap, S.D. (1999), 'Pie-Expansion Efforts: Collaboration Process in Buyer–Supplier Relationships', *Journal of Marketing Research*, **36**, November, 461–75.

Johnson, M.D., E.W. Anderson and C. Fornell (1995), 'Rationale and Adaptive Performance Expectations in a Customer Satisfaction Framework', *Journal of Consumer Research*, March, 695–707.

Joreskog, K.G. and D. Sorbom (1989), *LISREL 7: A Guide to Program and Applications*, second edition, SPSS Inc., Chicago, Ill.

Keane, T.J. and P. Wang (1995), 'Applications for the Lifetime Value Model in Modern Newspaper Publishing', *Journal of Direct Marketing*, 2, Spring, 59–66.

Kiel, G.C. and R.A. Layton (1981), 'Dimension of Consumer Seeking Behavior', *Journal of Marketing Research*, May, 233–39.

Loomis, J.L. (1959), 'Communication, the Development of Trust, and Cooperative Behavior', *Human Relations*, 12, 305–15.

Lorey, W. (1980), 'Mutual Trust is the Key to Open Communication', in S. Ferguson and S. Deveraux Ferguson (eds), *Intercom: Readings in Organizational Communication*, Hayden Book Company, Rochelle Park, New Jersey, pp. 115–20.

Lusch, R.F. (1976), 'Channel Conflict: Its Impact on Retailer Operating Performance', *Journal of Retailing*, 52 (2), Summer, 3–12, 89–90.

Martin, G.S. (1991), 'The Concept of Trust in Marketing Channel Relationship: A Review and Synthesis', in Gilly, M. et al. (eds), *Enhancing Knowledge Development in Marketing*, Chicago, IL, American Marketing Association, pp. 251–9.

Mayer, R.C., J.H. Davis and F.D. Schoorman (1995), 'An Integrative Model of Organizational Trust', *Academy of Management Review*, **20** (3), 709–34.

Mohr, J. and J.R. Nevin (1990), 'Communication Strategies in Marketing Channels: A Theoretical Perspective', *Journal of Marketing*, October, 36–51.

Moorman, C., R. Deshpandè and G. Zaltman (1993), 'Factors Affecting Trust in Market Research Relationships', *Journal of Marketing*, **57**, January, 81–101.

Moorman, C., G. Zaltman and R. Deshpandè (1992), 'Relationship Between Providers and Users of Market Research: The Dynamics of Trust Within and Between Organizations', *Journal of Marketing Research*, **29**, August, 314–29.

Morgan, R.M. and S.D. Hunt (1994), 'The Commitment–Trust Theory of Relationship Marketing', *Journal of Marketing*, **58**, July, 20–38.

Penrose, E. (1959), *The Theory of the Growth of the Firm*, Wiley, New York .

Peteraf, M.A. (1993), 'The Cornerstone of Competitive Advantage', in *Strategic Management Journal*, 14, 179–91.

Punj, G.N. and R. Staelin (1983), 'A Model of Consumer Information Search Behavior for New Automobilies', *Journal of Consumer Research*, March, 366–80.

Reichheld, F.F. (1991–1992), 'The Truth of Customer Retention', *Journal of Retail Banking*, Winter, 21–24.

Reichheld, F.F. (1996), *The Loyalty Effect*, Harvard Business School Press, Boston.

Reichheld, F.F. and W.E. Sasser, Jr., (1990), 'Zero Defections: Quality comes to Service', *Harvard Business Review*, Sept./Oct., 105–111.

Rich, G.A. (1997), 'The Sales Management as a Role Model: Effects on Trust, Job Satisfaction and Performance of Salespeople', *Academy of Marketing Science*, **25** (4), 319–28.

Robicheaux, R.A. and A.I. El Ansary (1976), 'A General Model for Understanding Channel Member Behavior', *Journal of Retailing*, Winter, 13–30.

Roniger, L. (1988), 'La fiducia. Un concetto fragile, una non meno fragile realtà', *Rassegna italiana di sociologia*, 3, July–September, 383–402.

Rosenberg, L.J. and L.W. Stern (1971), 'Conflict Measurement in the Distribution Channel', *Journal of Marketing Research*, **8**, November, 437–42.

Rosenbloom, B. (1973), 'Conflict and Channel Efficiency: Some Conceptual Models for the Decision Maker', *Journal of Marketing*, **37**, July, 26–30.

Rotter, J.B. (1967), 'A New Scale for the Measurement of Interpersonal Trust', *Journal of Personality*, **35**, 651–65.

Rotter, J.B. (1980), 'Interpersonal Trust, Trustworthiness, and Gullibility', *American Psychologist*, **35** (1), January, 1–7.

Rullani, E. (1992), 'Economia delle risorse immateriali: una introduzione', *Sinergie*, 29, September–December, 9–47.

Rumelt, R.P. (1984), 'Toward a Strategic Theory of the Firm', in R.B. Lamb (ed.), *Competitive Strategy Management*, Prentice Hall, Englewood Cliffs, pp. 566–9.

Sacconi, L. (1990), 'Razionalità di fidarsi o fidarsi razionalmente?', *Rassegna italiana di sociologia*, 4, October–December, 543–70.

Schulman, G.I. and C. Worrall (1970), 'Salience Patterns, Source Credibility, and the Sleeper Effect', *Public Opinion Quarterly*, **34** (3), Fall, 371–82.

Schurr, P.H. and J.L. Ozanne (1985), 'Influences on Exchange Processes: Buyers' Preconceptions of a Seller's Trustworthiness and Bargaining Toughness', *Journal of Consumer Research*, **11**, March, 939–53.

Solomon, L. (1960), 'The Influences of Some Types of Power Relationships and Game Strategies upon the Development of Interpersonal Trust', *Journal of Abnormal and Social Psychology*, **61** (2), 229.

Srivastava, R.K., T.A. Shervani and L. Fahey (1998), 'Market-Based Assets and Shareholder Value: A Framework for Analysis', *Journal of Marketing*, January, 2–18.

Stern, L.W. and R.H. Gorman (1969), 'Conflict in Distribution Channels: An Exploration', in L.W. Stern (ed.), *Distribution Channels: Behavioral Dimensions*, Houghton Mifflin Co., New York, pp. 288–305.

Swan, J.E. and J.J. Nolan (1985), 'Gaining Customer Trust: A Conceptual Guide for the Salesperson', *Journal of Personal Selling & Sales Management*, November, 39–48.

Swan, J.E., I.F. Trawick and D.W. Silva (1985), 'How Industrial Salespeople Gain Customer Trust', *Industrial Marketing Management*, 14, 203–11.

Ugolini, M. (1999), 'Tecnologie dell'informazione e fiducia: la nuova sfida per l'impresa', *Sinergie*, 50, 63–89.

Valdani, E. and B. Busacca (1992), 'Customer satisfaction: una nuova sfida', *Economia & Management*, 2, 8–27.

Vicari, S. (1991), *L'impresa vivente. Itinerario in una diversa concezione*, Etas Libri, Milano.

Vicari, S., (1992), 'Risorse aziendali e valore', *Sinergie*, 29, September–December, 81–93.

Wang, P. and T. Splegel (1994), 'Database Marketing and its Measurements of Success', *Journal of Direct Marketing*, 2, Spring, 73–81.

Wayland, R.E. and P.M. Cole (1997), *Customer Connections: New Strategies for Growth*, Harvard Business School Press, Boston.

Wernerfelt, B. (1984), 'A Resource-Based View of The Firm', *Strategic Management Journal*, 5, 171–80.

Williamson, O.E. (1985), *The Economic Institution of Capitalism*, New York, Free Press.

Wilson, D.T. (1995), 'An Integrated Model of Buyer–Seller Relationships', *Journal of the Academy of Marketing Science*, **23** (4), 335–45.

Zaheer, A. and N. Venkatraman (1995), 'Relational Governance as an Interorganizational Strategy: An Empirical Test of the Role of Trust in Economic Exchange', *Strategic Management Journal*, 16, 373–92.

Zaheer, A., B. McEvily and V. Perrone (1998), 'Does Trust Matter? Exploring the Effects of Interorganizational and Interpersonal Trust and Performance', *Organization Science*, **9** (2), 141–59.

Zand, D.E. (1972), 'Trust and Managerial Problem Solving', *Administrative Science Quarterly*, **17**, 229–39.

9. Store and advertiser reputation effects on consumer trust in an Internet store: results of an experimental study

Peter Kerkhof, Nadine Vahstal-Lapaix and Hans Caljé

INTRODUCTION

Web shopping has some clear advantages over shopping in regular shops: web shops are open 24 hours a day; the prices of products can be easily compared and are often lower than regular prices; the choice of products is often larger; and consumers don't have to leave their homes to buy something. Still, web shopping has developed at a much slower rate than expected and the amount of money spent online is only a very small percentage of the money spent in regular shops, even in countries where web shopping is popular (for example the USA). Apparently, besides the many advantages, there are also disadvantages to buying products over the web. For example, consumers can neither touch nor see the real products, the medium of the Internet is impersonal (there is no contact with a salesperson), and many people doubt the safety and privacy of online shopping (Palmer et al., 2000).

Underlying many of the disadvantages of online shopping seems to be a lack of trust associated with many aspects of the Internet. For example, lack of trust seems to underlie the refusal of many people to leave their email address to companies requesting it, one of the problems in using email as a marketing tool (Kerkhof et al., 2004). Lack of trust is also apparent when it comes to using information that is electronically available. For example, online medical information is notoriously unreliable (Culver et al., 1997). Using an experimental design, Eastin (2001) showed how users of online information utilize information about the credibility of the source of medical information to evaluate the validity of the information provided on an Internet site, and thus try to prevent drawing false conclusions.

Lack of trust is typically associated with a reduced willingness to behave in a risky way. In their reviews of conceptualizations of trust in different fields, Rousseau et al. (1998, p. 395) state that the intention to accept vulnerability is typical for the definition of trust in several domains. Indeed, Jarvenpaa et al. (2000) show that lack of trust is an important determinant of the perception of risk concerning online buying, and that the perception of risk in turn is a good predictor of the intention to buy from an Internet store. In Jarvenpaa et al.'s study, the main factor influencing trust in an Internet store was the perceived reputation of the store. Internet stores that were perceived to have a good reputation were trusted far more than stores that lack a good reputation.

In this chapter we intend to contribute to our understanding of the origins of trust in an Internet store. First, we want to give the existing literature on reputation effects on online trust a stronger basis for drawing causal conclusions. Specifically, using an experimental procedure, we want to establish whether trust is indeed caused by the reputation of the Internet store. Moreover, we want to take into account not only the reputation of the store itself, but also of advertisers on the site of an Internet store. Before introducing our study, we will go into our conceptualization of online trust. Then, we will show how store and advertiser reputation may affect online trust.

ONLINE CONSUMER TRUST

Trust has long been recognized as an important factor in the decision to buy or not to buy a certain product at a certain store. Trust is defined by Doney and Cannon (1997, p. 36) as 'the perceived credibility and benevolence of a target or trust'. Credibility refers to the expectancy that the promises of the trustee can be relied on. Benevolence refers to the amount to which the trustee is perceived as genuinely interested in the trustor's welfare.

In the marketing literature, research has shown that consumer trust is a key element of the relation between buyers and sellers. For example, Swan et al. (1999) conducted a meta-analysis to show that consumers that trust a salesperson have a more positive attitude towards the salesperson, and a higher intention to buy from this salesperson. More importantly, in the end they do indeed buy more from a trusted than a distrusted salesperson. In another recent meta-analysis on trust in marketing channel relationships, Geyskens et al. (1998) show that trust also matters in a professional context where professional buyers buy from professional sellers.

The correlations between trust and its hypothesized consequences are not always very high. For example, the average correlation between trust and the intention to buy is 0.28 in Swan et al.'s (1999) meta-analysis. Doney and Cannon (1997) find no direct effect of trust on buying behavior. However, in many studies trust plays a key mediating role between buyer–seller channel characteristics and their consequences (Morgan and Hunt, 1994; Geyskens et al., 1998).

There is reason to assume that trust plays a more important role in an online context than in the traditional buyer–seller context. The main reason is that consumer trust is more difficult to establish in an online environment, because there is no physical interaction with the store, the salesperson or the product (Jasper and Quellette, 1994). All the cues that consumers have to check the trustworthiness of a store no longer work when they evaluate an online store. Moreover, the risk that something goes wrong with the product is larger because there is a time lag between buying the product and receiving it. When the product arrives, it has often undergone a long journey where much may have gone wrong.

Another reason that online trust is difficult to obtain, is that the investments needed to start an Internet store are lower, or perceived as lower, than the investments needed to start a traditional store. Even when the investments in an Internet store are high, they are less visible to the consumer, who does not get to see the buildings, salespersons and so on that come with a regular store (Doney and Cannon, 1997). The relatively low costs of starting an Internet store imply low costs of abandoning the store, making it relatively easy for an Internet entrepreneur to quit. Therefore, given the time lag between ordering a product and receiving it, and given the risk of a premature ending of the store, online consumers have few guarantees that the products they order will actually be theirs (Jarvenpaa et al., 2000).

Tan and Thoen (2001) distinguish two kinds of trust that matter in online buying: party trust and control trust. Party trust is similar to trust in the definition by Doney and Cannon (1997) mentioned earlier: it refers to trust in the other party. Control trust, on the other hand, refers to trust in the mechanisms that assure that you get what you have agreed upon with the other party, even if the other party is not able or not willing to deliver. For example, money-back guarantees offered by organizations other than the store itself may tell a consumer that, whatever goes wrong, the money paid to purchase a product will not be lost. Although the effect of reputation on trust is not per se limited to party trust, the way reputation effects have been treated in the literature typically refers to party, instead of control, trust. In the following, when we refer to trust, we mean party trust.

REPUTATION AND CONSUMER TRUST

Many companies already have a track record before going online. In fact, most of the companies that perform well on the Internet are companies that have a brand name that is known to people. Jarvenpaa et al. (2000) explain this phenomenon by referring to the reputation of the company: companies that go online without any indication of past performance have no reputation to lose. This makes it more risky to consumers to trust the company. On the other hand, companies that do have an off-line past, have a lot to lose by starting an Internet store that does not live up to its promises. Jarvenpaa et al. (2000) tested the reputation effect on online trust by having their participants surf to a selection of existing Internet stores that differed in reputation. They showed that the perceived reputation is strongly related to trust in the Internet store. The correlations they found ranged from 0.60 to 0.71.

Another interesting study of the effects of reputation in an online situation is provided by Standifird (2001). Standifird conducted a study among users of eBay, the world's largest online auction. The behavior of users of eBay gets rated every time they perform a transaction. The mean rating of their behavior by other users was used by Standifird as a measure of their online reputation. Standifird showed that a positive reputation had only a mild positive effect on the final bid price, but that a negative reputation had a strong negative effect on the final bid price. Although trust was not the dependent variable in this study, the study does show that reputation matters highly in online situations.

Reputation is defined by Fombrun (1996, p. 37) as 'the overall estimation in which a company is held by its constituents'. Doney and Cannon (1997) refer to several trust-enhancing processes that can explain the effect of reputation on trust. First, they refer to a calculative process that could mediate the effect of reputation on trust: reputation usually does not come without significant investments and firms will be reluctant to lose these investments by acting in an untrustworthy way. Doney and Cannon (1997) also mention the process of transference. Trust, they state, can be transferred from one trustor to another without actually having any interaction with the trustee. Trust is inferred from a third party's experiences with the trustee.

Although reputation in an online situation has been strongly associated with trust in several studies, and although there are sound theoretical reasons to assume that reputation causes trust, instead of vice versa, the relation between trust and reputation has never been studied in such a way that one can draw strong causal conclusions about the effect of reputation on trust. For example, as Jarvenpaa et al. (2000) note themselves, the sites of the Internet stores that they used in their study differed in many other aspects than just reputation. Ease of use and site design were not held constant and may well have an effect on consumer trust (Kim and Moon, 1998). Other studies of reputation and trust that were not conducted in online situations also use correlational data (for example Anderson and Weitz, 1989; Ganesan, 1994).

One aim of our study is to provide the literature with a stronger basis for drawing causal conclusions about the relationship between trust and reputation. This is important because correlations between trust and reputation could be the result of initial trust and a subsequent false consensus effect (Ross et al., 1977). Research on the false consensus effect typically shows that people tend to believe that most other people think about an issue in the same way that they do themselves. Trusting a company may lead us to believe that most other people trust this company, and, thus, that this company has a positive reputation. This way, trust causes a store's reputation, instead of the other way around. Therefore, the first aim of our study is to test whether the reputation of an Internet store does indeed have a causal effect on trust in the Internet store. We will test this by experimentally varying reputation while holding other factors constant. Our first hypothesis is:

H1: Trust in an Internet store is enhanced by a good reputation of the Internet store.

On an Internet site, the Internet store itself is in many cases not the only firm with a reputation. Many sites of Internet stores contain banners of other firms that also come with a reputation. We expect that the reputation of the advertiser may also have an effect on the trustworthiness of the Internet store. When online consumers enter an Internet store for the first time, they will look for cues that tell them something about the trustworthiness of the Internet store. This may be derived from the reputation of the Internet store itself, as we have already argued. Assuming again Doney and Cannon's (1997) transference and calculative processes, trust may also be derived from the reputation of the advertiser. When a banner comes from an advertiser with a good reputation, this may tell a consumer that a trusted third party cooperates with the potential trustee.

Of course, the reputation of an advertiser is less informative about the trustworthiness of an Internet store than the reputation of the store itself. However, we think that online consumers are no different from people in many other situations: they use all information that is readily available, and easy to process, to make up their minds. The judgment they derive from this information is good enough, rather than optimal (Fiske and Taylor, 1991). Thus, we expect that online consumers will not check the trustworthiness of an Internet store by checking all possible information that they can get their hands on, regardless of whether this information is easy to get, or easy to process. On the contrary: consumers are more likely to conduct a quick scan of the trustworthiness of an Internet store, especially when the stakes are not that high because there is not yet a strong intention to purchase a product online. In such a quick scan, the advertisers' reputation can be informative about the trustworthiness of the Internet store.

Bruner and Kumar (2000) showed that the attitude towards the banner is indeed correlated with the attitude towards the site. Although their study is not about reputation and trust, their results show that banners may have an effect quite different from what they typically aim at. The sentiment towards a banner and the company behind the banner may spread to the sentiment towards a site and, eventually, to the company supporting that site.

Therefore, our second hypothesis is as follows.

H2: Trust in an Internet store is enhanced by a good reputation of an advertiser on the site of the Internet store.

In an experimental study about the communication of trustworthiness, Elsbach and Elofson (2000) follow the reasoning by Fiske and Taylor (1991). They state that people are limited in their capacity to process information, and rely heavily on cues that enable them to come to an adequate, rather than an accurate, evaluation of trustworthiness (Elsbach and Elofson, 2000; Fiske and Taylor, 1991, p. 13). The process of looking at cues, Elsbach and Elofson state, is hierarchical: the trustworthiness cues are not processed at the same time, but evaluated separately. As soon as one cue is found to be a sign of trustworthiness, information processing stops. This indicates that having two cues that indicate trustworthiness, in our case a good reputation of both the Internet store and the advertiser, does not add to perceived trustworthiness when compared to a site with only one trustworthiness cue. This leads us to our third hypothesis about the interactive effects of both the reputation of the Internet store and the reputation of the advertiser. We expect that both the reputation of the advertiser and the reputation of the Internet add to the perception of trustworthiness when compared to a site with none of these cues. However, a site containing two trustworthiness cues will not be perceived as more trustworthy than a site with only one trustworthiness cue. Thus, our third hypothesis is as follows.

H3: The site of an Internet store with a good reputation and containing a banner of an advertiser with a good reputation will not be perceived as more trustworthy than a site with only one trustworthiness cue.

METHOD

Overview of the Study

To test our hypotheses, we used an experimental design. We made a fictitious site of an Internet store, and manipulated the reputation of the Internet store itself and the reputation of an advertiser on the site. This design enables us to test the hypotheses regarding the effects of reputation on trust in the Internet store. Moreover, by combining the two experimental manipulations we could also test the interactive effects of the reputations of both the Internet store and the advertiser. The four versions of the fictitious Internet site were shown to students, who first answered some questions regarding their Internet experience, then watched the Internet page, and then answered questions regarding their trust in the Internet store.

Participants and Procedure

The participants were 88 students at the Vrije Universiteit in Amsterdam, The Netherlands and consisted of 47 males and 41 females. More than half of the respondents were younger than 25 years. All of them had experience surfing on the Internet: 21.6 per cent surfed on the Internet for more than 10 hours per week, 54.5 per cent surfed between 2 and 10 hours, and 23.9 per cent less than two hours. Most participants (78.4 per cent) had never purchased a product over the Internet.

The participants were randomly assigned to one of four experimental conditions in a 2 (reputation of the Internet store, non-reputable store vs. a reputable store) × 2 (reputation of the advertiser, non-reputable advertiser vs. a reputable advertiser) between subjects design. The participants were asked to first answer some general questions (for example demographics, Internet use). Next, we showed them a color print of a fake webpage, containing our manipulation, of an Internet store selling computers. This was followed by questions about our main dependent variables.

The Experimental Design

In the 2 by 2 experiment we manipulated the reputation of both the Internet store and the advertiser. A webpage of a company selling computers over the Internet was designed. The reputation of the Internet store was manipulated by assigning to half of the webpages the name of a well-known computer seller (Compaq Computers) and the other half the name of a computer seller that is unknown in the Netherlands (Tiny Computers). The reputation of the advertiser was manipulated the same way. We designed an advertisement for a company providing financial loans. In one condition the advertisement came from a well-known Dutch bank (ABN AMRO), in the other condition the advertisement came from an unknown financial company called Optimaal Advies. This resulted in four webpages (see Table 9.1).

Table 9.1 Experimental design

Reputation of Internet store:	Reputation of advertiser	
	Reputable advertiser	Non-reputable advertiser
Reputable Internet store	Compaq Computers & **ABN AMRO**	Compaq Computers & Optimaal Advies
Non-reputable Internet store	Tiny Computers & **ABN AMRO**	Tiny Computers & Optimaal Advies

Measures

Trust in the Internet store was assessed using four items similar to those used in the studies of Jarvenpaa et al. (2000) and Doney and Cannon (1997): 'This Internet store is trustworthy', 'In my opinion, this Internet store lives up to its promises', 'If anything goes wrong with the product, this Internet store will deal with my complaints in a serious way' and 'I trust this Internet store not to take advantage of me' (1= strongly disagree, 5 = strongly agree, Cronbach's Alpha = 0.84, m = 3.24, SD = 0.67).

To validate our measure of trust in the Internet store, we also assessed two other variables from Jarvenpaa et al.'s (2000) study. *Risk perception* was assessed with four items that were introduced with the text: 'Suppose you wanted to buy a product at this Internet store, what are in your opinion the chances that something will go wrong with (a) the payment, (b) the working of the product, and (c) the physical state of the product (1 = very low, 5 = very high). Then, participants were asked 'How risky do you think it is to buy a product on the Internet at this organization? (1 = not risky at all, 5 = very risky; Cronbach's Alpha = 0.72, m = 2.84, SD = 0.59). The *intention to buy* at the Internet store was assessed using a single item: Suppose you wanted to buy a computer over the Internet. What would be the chance that you would go to this organization? (1 = very small, 5 = very large; m = 2.33, SD = 1.08).

To check whether our manipulations worked as intended, we included two manipulation checks. As a check for the manipulation of *reputation of the Internet store*, we asked the respondents to indicate their agreement with the item: 'This Internet store has a good reputation' ($m = 3.32$, $SD = 0.75$). As a check on our manipulation of the reputation of the advertiser, we assessed respondents' *attitude towards the advertiser* with a single item: 'What do you think of the site in terms of the advertiser?' (1 = very negative, 5 = very positive; $m = 2.99$, $SD = 1.02$).

Analyses

To test our three hypotheses, we conducted four separate analyses of variances (ANOVAs). ANOVA is the most common way of analyzing experimental designs (Kiess and Bloomquist, 1985). First, we conducted two ANOVAs to check whether the manipulations worked as intended. Second, to test the first two hypotheses, we conducted a 2 by 2 ANOVA with the reputations of the Internet store and the advertiser as independent variables, and trust in the Internet store as the dependent variable. Third, we conducted an ANOVA with a priori contrasts to test our third hypothesis regarding the combined effect of the reputation of the Internet store and the advertiser. Fourth, to validate our measure of trust in the Internet store, we conducted two extra ANOVAs to see whether, as in the study of Jarvenpaa et al. (2000), trust in the Internet store mediates the effect of reputation on risk perception and the intention to buy at the Internet store.

Since the demographic variables (for example sex, age) and experience with surfing on the Internet, or buying online products, showed no relation with our dependent variables, we report the results of the analyses where these variables were not included as covariates.

RESULTS

Manipulation Checks

To see whether our manipulations of the reputations of the Internet store and the advertiser worked as intended, we conducted two ANOVAs. As intended, the 2 by 2 ANOVA on the reputation of the Internet store revealed a main effect of our reputation manipulation, $F(1, 87) = 26.84$, $p < 0.001$. The reputation of the reputable computer seller is better than that of the non-reputable computer seller (resp. $m = 3.43$, $SD = 0.64$, and $m = 2.72$, $SD = 0.68$). There were no effects of the reputation of the advertiser, and no interaction effects of the reputations of the Internet store and the advertiser.

We also checked whether the attitude towards the advertiser was more positive in the reputable (vs. the non-reputable) advertiser condition. As intended, the 2 by 2 ANOVA revealed a significant main effect of the reputation of the advertiser manipulation, $F(1, 87) = 12.57$, $p < 0.001$. The attitude towards the non-reputable advertiser is more negative than the attitude towards the reputable advertiser (resp. $m = 2.64$, $SD = 0.99$, and $m = 3.34$, $SD = 0.94$). Unexpectedly, and interestingly, we also found a significant main effect of the reputation of the Internet store. Regardless of its content, the banner is judged more positively when it is placed on the site of the non-reputable (vs. the reputable) computer seller (resp. $m = 3.27$, $SD = 0.87$, and $m = 2.70$, $SD = 1.09$; $F(3, 84) = 8.57$, $p < 0.001$). Again, there were no interaction effects of the reputations of the Internet store and the advertiser.

Hypothesis Testing

To test our first two hypotheses, we conducted a 2 by 2 ANOVA on trust in the Internet store. Figure 9.1 shows the results. Regarding the effect

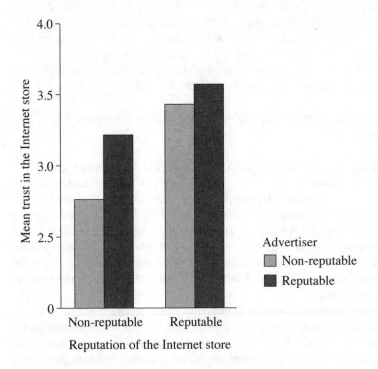

Figure 9.1 Reputation effects on trust in an Internet store

of the reputation of the Internet store on trust in the Internet store, the analysis revealed a main effect of the reputation of the Internet store, $F(1, 87) = 15.70$, $p < 0.001$. Trust in the Internet store is higher for the reputable computer seller ($m = 3.50$, $SD = 0.63$) than for the non-reputable computer seller ($m = 2.99$, $SD = 0.62$). This confirms our first hypothesis.

Regarding the effect of the reputation of the advertiser on trust in the Internet store, the analysis revealed a main effect of the reputation of the advertiser, $F(1, 87) = 5.24$, $p < 0.05$. Trust in the Internet store is higher when the banner comes from a reputable advertiser ($m = 3.39$, $SD = 0.63$) than when it comes from a non-reputable advertiser ($m = 3.10$, $SD = 0.69$). This confirms our second hypothesis.

In our third hypothesis we stated that the site of a reputable Internet store containing an advertisement of a reputable advertiser would not be perceived as more trustworthy than a site with only one of these trustworthiness cues. Finding a pattern of means in the four cells in which only the mean of the cell containing a non-reputable Internet store and a non-reputable advertiser deviates, would confirm this hypothesis. Figure 9.1 shows the pattern of means in the four cells.

Confirming our third hypothesis, an ANOVA with an a priori contrast (see Bobko, 1986) yielded the expected significant differences, $F(3, 84) = 7.49$, $p < 0.001$. Participants who viewed a site of a non-reputable Internet store, containing a banner from a non-reputable advertiser, reported less trust ($m = 2.76$), than respondents who viewed either a reputable Internet store, a reputable advertiser, or both (resp. $m = 3.43$; $m = 3.22$; $m = 3.57$).

Does Trust Mediate the Reputation Effects on Risk Perception and Intention to Buy?

To validate our measure of trust, we conducted an ancillary analysis to see whether our trust measure, as in Jarvenpaa et al. (2000), mediates the effect of reputation on risk perception and intention to buy at the Internet store. For this purpose, we conducted two 2 by 2 multivariate analyses of variance (MANOVAs), with risk perception and the intention to buy as dependent variables, and the reputation of the Internet store and the advertiser as independent variables. The first analysis was run without trust as a covariate, in the second MANOVA we included trust in the Internet store as a covariate.

The first analysis reveals a significant effect of the reputation of the Internet store on both risk perception and the intention to buy at the Internet store, $F(2, 83) = 9.14$, $p < 0.001$. The risk perception is lower among participants in the reputable Internet store condition ($m = 2.60$, $SD = 0.52$) than among participants in the non-reputable Internet store condition ($m = 3.08$, $SD = 0.56$; $F(1, 87) = 17.15$, $p<.001$). The intention to buy at the Internet store is higher among participants in the reputable Internet store condition ($m = 2.64$, $SD = 1.08$) than among participants in the non-reputable Internet store condition ($m = 2.22$, $SD = 1.00$; $F(2, 82) = 7.65$, $p < 0.01$). There are no effects of the reputation of the advertiser and no interaction effects on risk perception or the intention to buy.

In a second MANOVA we controlled for the level of trust in the Internet store by including trust as a covariate in the analysis. A strong reduction of the reputation effects on risk perception and the intention to buy would indicate mediation of these effects by trust, as in Jarvenpaa et al.'s (2000) paper. Indeed, the effects are reduced strongly by including trust as a covariate: the effect of reputation on the intention to buy is no longer significant, $F(1, 87) = 1.82$, ns, and the F-value of the effect of reputation on risk perception had reduced from 17.15 to 5.93 ($p < 0.05$). Thus, trust in the Internet store appears to mediate the effect of reputation on risk perception and the intention to buy.

DISCUSSION

Before discussing our major findings, there are some limitations that should be noted before drawing conclusions. First, we used a simple pencil and paper experiment. It might be that showing the sites in their natural environment alters the effects we found. Furthermore, we used students as participants, and one should be careful about generalizing the results to the whole population of Internet users. Thirdly, our study used the (fictitious) site of a computer seller with a financial advertiser. Jarvenpaa et al. (2000) showed that the sector in which reputation and trust are studied affect the outcomes. Using only one sector may have affected our outcomes.

Still, we do think that our study adds to the literature on trust and reputation, and its application to online trust, in several ways. First, we showed that reputation matters when it comes to establishing trust in an Internet store. The reputation of an Internet store was found to be a reliable predictor of trust in the Internet store. This is important, because we also showed that trust is an important mediator between reputation, risk perception and the intention to buy at an Internet store. Jarvenpaa et al. (2000) already showed that the reputation of an Internet store company correlates with trust in the Internet store. In Jarvenpaa et al.'s study, and several others, the association between trust and reputation was shown using correlational data (for example Anderson and Weitz, 1989; Ganesan, 1994). Our study provides the literature with a stronger basis for drawing causal conclusions about the relationship between reputation and trust. This is important because correlations between trust and reputation could, as we argued in our introduction, very well be the result of the false consensus effect. Although our data do not exclude such a process, it makes a strong case for the reversed causal effect.

Even though our aim was to establish a stronger causal link between reputation and trust, one should not rule out alternative explanations for our findings. We manipulated reputation by referring to reputable companies vs. non-reputable companies. However, in the case of the computer seller being a large, rather than a small, company may have caused the participants to trust the store more. Future research should try to eliminate these differences that often come with differences in reputation, since they might affect the results. Using fictitious companies and describing the reputation while holding all other factors constant may be a fruitful way of avoiding confounds.

A second finding was that the reputation of an advertiser also matters when consumers judge the trustworthiness of an Internet store: trust in an Internet store is higher when the banner comes from a company with a good reputation. This result fits in with other recent research work focussing not on the intended effects of advertisements (ads) on consumer attitudes towards the ad, and the products that are being promoted, but on the attitudes about the environment the ads are placed in. For example, Fennis and Bakker (2001) showed that irritating ads influence how consumers value the subsequent ads. Also, Bruner and Kumar (2000) show that the attitude towards the banner correlates with the attitude towards the site. In the study we reported here, the ad influenced the amount of trust in an Internet store. All these studies imply that Internet store managers, or, more generally, managers of all media that place ads (for example television channels, newspapers) should be selective about the adds they place. Given the current shortage of investors in Internet, it can be tempting for a site to place any ad that is offered. Our study shows that this may backfire and might very well cost money, instead of generating it.

An unexpected finding in our study was that the attitude towards the advertiser is more positive when the ad is placed on the site of a firm without a good reputation. One explanation could be that there is a contrast effect: compared to the non-reputable Internet store, both advertisers, reputable or not, are judged in a relatively positive way compared to the Internet store. Another explanation might be that the respondents in our study think that a reputable company should not have banners on its site. Why would a large and rich company make a little extra money by offering other companies a place on its website? Including a control group without a banner in a follow-up study could shed new light on this question.

Another finding of our study is that consumers seem to stop processing trustworthiness information as soon as they find one cue. Extra trustworthiness cues do not add to more trust in an Internet store. This is interesting because it tells us something about the way consumers establish whether a store can be trusted or not. Our data indicate that, using the terms of Chaiken's (1980) heuristic–systematic model, judging the trustworthiness of an Internet store is an heuristic, rather than a systematic process: consumers don't seem to make a lot of effort when they try to establish an online store's trustworthiness. The next store is one click away, and the decision not to trust an Internet store is easily made. Especially when the brand name of an Internet store does not come with a good reputation, one should be very careful about the design of the site, the banners on the site, and so on. At least one of these needs to serve as a cue for trustworthiness. On the other hand, these features seem to matter much less when one does have a store with a good reputation: one trustworthiness cue is enough and extra efforts to communicate trustworthiness may not matter much.

Our findings with regard to how consumers judge trustworthiness may be the result of the fact that the participants knew that they were not going to buy something at the store. The lack of thoughtfulness that our data indicate may have been caused by the fact that, for example, there was no risk of losing money. It may be the case that the moment that consumers are planning to really purchase a product at an online store, they may do an extra check on the store's trustworthiness that may be more thoughtful than the first quick scan of trustworthiness that we reported in this chapter. More research is needed to see whether people are indeed this strategic when judging online trustworthiness.

One last remark should be made about the findings in our study. We chose to compare companies that have a good reputation with companies that do not have such a good reputation. Reputation effects could become much larger when companies with a good reputation are compared to companies with a bad reputation. The findings of Standifird (2001) clearly show that having a bad reputation has a much stronger effect than having a good reputation. Thus, our findings may underestimate the effects that reputation has in an online situation. Future studies could include companies with a good, a bad, and an absent reputation to see whether the reputation of, for example, an advertiser may indeed be much stronger than our data indicate.

REFERENCES

Anderson, E. and E. Weitz (1989), 'Determinants of continuity in conventional industrial channel dyads', *Marketing Science*, 8, 310–23.

Bobko, P. (1986), 'A solution to some dilemmas when testing hypotheses about ordinal interactions', *Journal of Applied Psychology*, 71, 323–26.

Bruner, G.B. and A. Kumar (2000), 'Web commercials and advertising hierarchy-of-effects', *Journal of Advertising Research*, 40, 35–42.

Chaiken, S. (1980), 'Heuristic versus systematic information processing and the use of source versus message cues in persuasion', *Journal of Personality and Social Psychology*, 39, 752–66.

Culver, J.D., R. Gerr and H. Frumkin (1997), 'Medical information on the Internet: a study of an electronic bulletin board', *Journal of General Internal Medicine*, **12**(8), 466–70.

Doney, P.M. and J.P. Cannon (1997), 'An examination of the nature of trust in buyer–seller relationships', *Journal of Marketing*, 61, 35–51.

Eastin, M.S. (2001), 'Credibility assessments of online health information: the effects of source expertise and knowledge of content', *Journal of Computer Mediated Communication*, **6**(4).

Elsbach, K.D. and G. Elofson (2000), 'How the packaging of decision explanations affects perceptions of trustworthiness', *Academy of Management Journal*, **43**(1), 80–89.

Fennis, B.M. and A.B. Bakker (2001), 'Stay tuned: we will be back right after these messages: Need to evaluate moderates the transfer of irritation in advertising', *Journal of Advertising*, 33, 16–26.

Fiske, S.T. and S.E. Taylor (1991), *Social Cognition* (2nd edn), New York: McGraw-Hill.

Fombrun, C.J. (1996), *Reputation: Realizing value from the corporate image*, Boston: Harvard University School Press.

Ganesan, S. (1994), 'Determinants of long-term orientation in buyer–seller relationships', *Journal of Marketing*, **58**(2), 1–19.

Geyskens, I., J.E.M. Steenkamp and N. Kumar (1998), 'Generalizations about trust in marketing channel relationships using meta-analysis', *International Journal of Research in Marketing*, 15, 223–48.

Jarvenpaa, S.L., N. Tractinsky and M. Vitale (2000), 'Consumer trust in an Internet store', *Information Technology and Management*, 1, 45–71.

Jasper, C.R. and S.J. Quellette (1994), 'Consumer perception of risk and the purchase of apparel from catalogs', *Journal of Direct Marketing*, 8, 23–36.

Kerkhof, P., E.H.H.J. Das, B.M. Fennis, J. Endenburg and M. de Nie-Vermeulen (2004), *Customer Trust versus Commitment as Predictors of the Adoption of Electronic Services*, Manuscript submitted for publication.

Kiess, H.O. and D.W. Bloomquist (1985), *Psychological Research Methods: A conceptual approach*, Boston: Allyn and Bacon.

Kim, J. and J.Y. Moon (1998), 'Designing towards emotional usability in customer interfaces – trustworthiness of cyber-banking system interfaces', *Interacting with Computers*, 10, 1–29.

Morgan, R.M. and S.D. Hunt (1994), 'The commitment–trust theory of relationship marketing', *Journal of Marketing*, 58, 20–38.

Palmer, J.W., J.P. Bailey and S. Faraj (2000), 'The role of intermediaries in the development of trust on the WWW: the use and prominence of trusted third parties and privacy statements', *Journal of Computer Mediated Communication*, **5**(3).

Ross, L., D. Greene and P. House (1977), 'The "false consensus effect": an egocentric bias in social perception and attribution process', *Journal of Experimental Social Psychology*, 13, 279–301.

Rousseau, D.M., S.B. Sitkin, R.S. Burt and C. Camerer (1998), 'Not so different after all: a cross-discipline view of trust', *Academy of Management Review*, **23**(3), 393–404.

Standifird, S.S. (2001), 'Reputation and e-commerce: eBay auctions and the asymmetrical impact of positive and negative ratings', *Journal of Management*, **27**(3), 279–95.

Swan, J.E., M.R. Bowers and L.D. Richardson (1999), 'Consumer trust in the salesperson: an integrative review and meta-analysis of the empirical literature', *Journal of Business Research*, 44, 93–107.

Tan, Y.-H. and W. Thoen (2001), 'Toward a generic model of trust for electronic commerce', *International Journal of Electronic Commerce*, **5**(2), 61–74.

10. Trust, distance and common ground

Elena Rocco

1. INTRODUCTION

A large number of heterogeneous human relations, like transactions, delegation, teamwork, promises, are based on trust. As a consequence, different disciplines have contributed from different perspectives to the study of trust (Rousseau et al. 1998; Kramer and Tyler 1996). A shared view in this multidisciplinary debate is that is that there is no trust without risk (Deutsch 1958; Currall 1990; March and Shapiro 1987). Formal control and coordination mechanisms have been devised to reduce the amount of risk associated to trust, for example, escrow account, control procedures and hierarchical control (Thompson 1967; Mintzberg 1979). Nevertheless, these mechanisms reduce risks to the extent we can identify and predict the range of threats to trust. In the face of an unforeseeable event, either intentional or unintentional, if the trustee does not behave as the trustor would have expected to, the trust-based relation is likely to be undermined. Economic models, like the agency theory (Alchian and Demsetz 1972) and the transaction costs perspective (Williamson 1985), have focused on opportunism as the main threat to trust. Opportunistic behavior often leads to intentional actions unknown to the trustor and detrimental to his own interest (Williamson 1985; Gambetta 1988). Beyond opportunism, other elements may undermine trust. Trust may indeed be weakened by unintentional action by the trustee. For instance, the employee may act in the interest of her manager but not as he would have expected to. Similarly, tacit coordination in teams works as long as individuals can rely on each other's convergence of expectations and related behaviors (Schelling 1960, p. 54).

Technically, in linguistics the sum of mutual ideas, beliefs and presuppositions (or assumptions) upon which one makes coordination choice, is called *common ground* (Clark 1993, 1996). This chapter intends to explore the role of common ground in the formation of trust-based relationships. Other studies have contributed to the debate on trust shedding light on social and psychological causes of trust formation. For instance, characteristic similarity (for example gender, age, race) is a fundamental premise for trust formation (Zucker 1986). Information about the other is the ground for the emergence of knowledge-based trust (Lewicki and Bunker 1996). Similarly, environmental norms can enforce trust as in the norm-based trust (Powell 1990). The commonality among these 'trust feeding' factors is their role as uncertainty reducers. In fact, characteristic similarity, information and norms contribute to common ground formation in that they facilitate expectations convergence among individuals, thus diminishing the perceived risk associated to trust. The first goal of this chapter is to analyse thoroughly the concept of common ground, investigating mechanisms of common ground formation and the relationship between trust and common ground. Secondly, the chapter aims to investigate how distance may affect common ground, and thus trust. A field study conducted in a geographically distributed organization helps to bring some evidence on the role of common ground to develop trust in highly unpredictable and dynamic group activities, such as software development. Co-located colleagues share common ground, trust each other and coordinate effectively. Distant colleagues share a weak common ground, do not trust each other very much and often fail to coordinate effectively. The chapter discusses the evidence collected in the field in the light of the framework developed earlier, that effective coordination may reflect whether people trust others when common ground is in place. In fact, empirical evidence indicates that remote colleagues lack opportunities for common ground formation compared to co-located ones. Finally, the chapter offers some guidelines for trust enhancement by distilling a managerial lesson from the linguistic approach to common ground formation.

The next sections are organized as follows. First, we present the literature on common ground and related concepts, and introduce a conceptual framework on the effect of distance on common ground and trust. Second, we present the field study and the methodology. The third session presents the findings. Finally, we discuss the main results and provide some guidelines to protect trust in a geographically distributed organization.

2. CONCEPTUAL FRAMEWORK

2.1 Expectational Assets and Common Ground in the Literature

In economic theories, opportunism is the main barrier to trust, as in the metaphor of the prisoners' dilemma (Dawes 1980). For instance, agency theory assumes self-interest (Alchian and Demsetz 1972; Jensen and Meckling

1976; Eisenhardt 1989), meaning that individuals strive to maximize individual utility and that principal (manager) and agent (employee) seek to minimize risks associated with the relationship. Therefore, to minimize agency risks, the principal needs to monitor the agent's behavior or base the agent's compensation on task outcomes to align the agent's goals with his goals. Similarly, the transaction costs perspective (Williamson 1985) declares that transaction costs are afflicted by opportunistic behavior in which a part tries to cheat at the expense of the other. As Ouchi observes: 'People must either be able to trust each other or to closely monitor each other if they are to engage in cooperative enterprise' (1979, p. 846). According to this perspective, trust turns out to be a strategic organizational resource to counteract the recurrent risk of opportunism and inability to control the other party. For instance, this is evident in research activities or inter-organizational collaboration (Zaheer et al. 1998).

Lately, behavioral economics has started to explore another perspective on trust. When two or more individuals share common interests, opportunism might not be an issue. Nevertheless, trust might be weak or absent. It is in this respect that Camerer and Knez (1994) talk about trust related to *expectational assets* or convergent expectations (Malmgren 1961; Camerer and Knez 1996). Expectational assets exist in people's heads. They consist in beliefs and assumptions shared by a group (or an organization) upon which its members base their coordination choices. It is the convergence among beliefs and assumptions that makes trust emerge. In fact, members trust that the others will behave in a certain way, on the premise of well-established and shared assumptions or beliefs about the others' behavior. As we discuss in the next sections, cultural rules and routines can be important drivers of trust as well as expectational assets in organizations.

An economic model of expectational assets can be found in coordination games, like the *weakest link game*. The game is an abstract representation of many group situations characterized by a common interest (for example, authors collaborating for publishing a book together, team members striving to meet an organizational deadline). In the coordination game, team members must decide the individual effort level. They can neither communicate, nor control *ex ante* each other's choice. We call this a 'weakest link game' because, like a chain whose strength depends on its weakest link, the group component of each player's payoff is determined by the lowest action anyone takes. For instance, one member's delay implies the whole team's delay. Players would like to coordinate tacitly on some equilibria. (An equilibrium is a set of choices, one by each player, which are all best responses to one another.) But they would like that equilibrium to be as high as possible. The game pits payoff-dominant actions against risk dominance: the higher the payoff the riskier it is. So coordination is useful for measuring whether people trust others to take the risk and choose the high payoff actions. The group could also 'coordinate' on a low effort's choice. But in that case, neither risk nor trust is implied.

In behavioral economics, the concept of expectational assets includes a large range of mechanisms, such as trust, reputation, brand-name equity, organizational rules (Camerer and Knez 1994).

In linguistics, a construct closely related to expectational assets is that of *common knowledge* (Lewis 1969) or *common ground* (Clark 1993, 1996). Kartunnen and Peters (1975), who introduced this term, described common ground as the set of propositions that: 'Any rational participant [in an exchange of talk] is rationally justified in taking for granted, for example, by virtue of what has been said in the conversation up to that point, what all the participants are in the position to perceive as true, whatever else they mutually know, assume, etc'. In general, common ground between two or more individuals has been defined as the sum of their mutual knowledge, beliefs, and mutual suppositions (Clark 1993, 1996). In society, conventions or greetings forms are typical examples of common ground (Clark 1993). In organizations, practices deriving from management-by-objectives, TQM and quality circles (Camerer and Knez 1994, 1996) are common ground, to the extent that everybody expects everybody else to apply the same principles at work and coordinate accordingly. Similarly, members of an organization should coordinate their actions based upon shared presuppositions deriving from a corporate culture, adequate work practices, routines and so on. Focal points (Schelling 1960) are another instance of common ground. Focal points constitute the implicit knowledge shared by two or more individuals that allows them to reach successful coordination. For instance, a meeting point chosen by both without a previous agreement represents a focal point. In the weakest link game, the team gets a high payoff when a high level effort is perceived as the team's focal point.

To sum up, we discussed the congruence between the concepts of expectational assets (behavioral economics) and common ground (linguistics). Both mechanisms refer to a large class of intangible resources that can curb uncertainty and level the ground to trust. The argument is that effective coordination requires a high level of trust when team members cope with unpredictability. In the rest of the chapter we will use the term common ground, as we are interested in exploring the linguistic approach to common ground formation. Understanding the origins of common ground is particularly important to diagnose situations characterized by unpredictability and the consequent problems of coordination and trust decline. A typical organizational context in which trust decline has been frequently observed is that of geographically distributed organizations, or *virtual organizations* (Handy 1995; Jarvenpaa and Leidner 1999). The study of common ground could suggest possible directions for new managerial practices aimed to sustain geographically distributed work.

2.2 Distance and Common Ground: a Framework

The literature distinguishes three main ways (or heuristics) common ground forms: community membership, linguistic co-presence and physical co-presence (Clark 1993). Community membership refers to the basic idea that everyone in a community knows and assumes that everyone else in that community knows something too (Durkheim 1893). In the broad community of educated Italians, for example, people assume that everyone knows such things as: cars drive on the right; Sunday is a festivity; 'hello' is used among friends but not when speaking with the elderly, especially if they are strangers. The problem is that one belongs simultaneously to more communities and sub-communities, each of which has its own distinct areas of knowledge. The trick is to judge community membership. In ordinary conversation people take the trouble to establish the communities of which they are members just so that their definitive references will succeed. Failing to judge community membership can end up in mistaken assumptions about how the other will behave.

Linguistic co-presence is stronger than community membership in developing common ground, and refers to conversation. It develops common ground as people gain awareness of things referred to during conversations, regardless of their location. Imagine one person saying to another 'I fixed the red bicycle Mr Sonnest brought here yesterday'. By uttering 'the red bicycle', he posits for the other the existence of a particular bicycle and the event 'the bike is now fixed'. If the other hears and understands the speaker correctly, he will come to know about the bicycle's existence at the same time the speaker posits it. From that instant on, every utterance referring to that bike will make sense in the light of this sentence and with consideration of this event. The speaker assumes that the listener takes into account that that particular bicycle has been fixed and incorporates the knowledge in his own behavior. Physical co-presence is the strongest heuristic for common ground formation (Clark 1993): when individuals are co-present, physical and perceptual evidence becomes very strong. Physical co-presence allows individuals to engage in face-to-face interactions whenever it becomes necessary. Attending to each other smoothes potential sources of ambiguity as individuals exchange a broad set of objects (for example, tables, drawings) and visual cues (for example, body gestures).

Physical co-presence, linguistic co-presence and community membership have a direct effect on common ground formation. But there is also an enforcement effect among the three (Clark 1993) (see Figure 10.1). In fact, when people are physically co-present, they better satisfy the assumptions of linguistic co-presence, establishing face-to-face contact, sharing the same artifacts, attending to each other. Moreover, both physical and linguistic co-presences permit individuals to overcome the difficulties posed by community membership, enabling the identification of which community the others belong to.

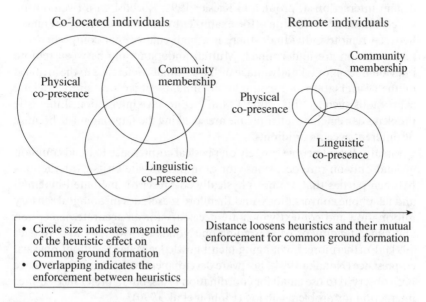

Figure 10.1   Framework on the heuristics for common ground formation and the impact of distance

Distance negatively affects all the three heuristics. First, at a distance community membership weakens. In fact, distant people are likely to belong to different sub-communities with their own behavioral norms, routines and work habits as outputs of history of the site, national and organizational culture (Narduzzo et al. 2000). The problem is that differences are subtle and they emerge unexpectedly while distant members interact. Misplaced community membership attributions leads to misinterpretations.

Second, distance weakens linguistic co-presence as a mechanism of common ground formation. In fact, linguistic co-presence is based on the assumptions of simultaneity, attention, and understandability. Distant people have difficulties in fulfilling these assumptions. First, they make large use of asynchronous mediated communication (for example, email, voice mail) that does not allow them to engage in simultaneous conversation. Time difference amplifies this problem when people are located in different countries. Consequently, information is communicated with delays (time lag between the sender and the receiver). Sometimes, it happens that information is not communicated at all, for various reasons (for example, work overload, oversight). This causes poor coordination as people work upon different assumptions until the communication gap is closed. Secondly, there is strong evidence that comprehension and attention decrease in distant interactions (Sproull and Kiesler 1991; Rocco 1998). Even during synchronous conversations (for example, by telephone, teleconference) between remote individuals, there is a high chance that comprehension and attention are undermined. Mutual understanding between remote individuals cannot take advantage of the automatic reference to the artifacts of the conversation (for example, documents, objects or simply deictic expressions such as 'this', 'that') as in face-to-face interaction. Linguistic problems can emerge even if people are speaking the same language because of different accents or idioms.

Finally, distant people can rely on physical co-presence to build common ground only on rare occasions (for example, off-site visits). Interactions between parties that are not physically co-present is mediated by email and telephone conversations, and therefore it excludes meaningful sensory information and context which are necessary for an accurate perception and understanding of what is going on (Nonaka, 1990; Lave and Wenger 1991). Furthermore, exchanging tacit knowledge is hard without physical co-presence (Nonaka 1994). Software development teams, for instance, have been observed to use email for coordination tasks, but to prefer face-to-face interaction for problem solving (Finholt et al. 1990).

To sum up, physical distance alters the main heuristics upon which common ground form: physical co-presence is limited to sporadic events (for example, work trips, plant visits, off-site training). Community membership blurs because of the presence of local sub-communities that often are ethnically and organizationally very heterogeneous. Thus, linguistic co-presence becomes the most important heuristic for common ground formation, through phone calls, teleconference meetings, email exchanges, and so on. Nevertheless, most linguistic co-presence suffers for asynchronous communication and reduced attention and understanding associated to mediated communication.

In the light of the conceptual framework just presented, we intend to investigate empirically the effect of distance on common ground, trust and coordination. As argued above when discussing the weakest link game, coordination is useful for measuring whether people trust others to take the risk and choose the high payoff actions. The research question is whether lack of common ground could explain lack of trust and, as a consequence, poor coordination. The study tries to collect some qualitative and quantitative evidence about the relationships between common ground, trust and coordination. When co-workers are distant (sometimes in different countries), interaction is mostly based on linguistic co-presence, while physical co-presence and community membership are fairly weak. In these circumstances, we expect coordination problems and moderate levels of trust to emerge. Conversely, when individuals are physically co-present, engage in face-to-face interactions and share the same community membership, common ground grows. Therefore, we can reasonably expect higher trust levels and smoother coordination. We now turn to an empirical study. We first describe the multi-site organization. Then, we focus on the software development process, providing some quantitative data on trust and some qualitative key examples on the role of trust for successful coordination.

3. THE EMPIRICAL STUDY

3.1 The Geographically-Distributed Organization

This field study took place from September 1997 to December 1999 within Lucent Technologies, a Fortune Global 100 telecommunication company headquartered in the United States. The research team focused on the Network Element Group (NEG, a disguised name) one of hundreds of departments within Lucent devoted to software engineering in support of telecommunication applications. The NEG department had 143 employees at the time of the study, located mainly in four sites: one in Germany (D), one in the United Kingdom (UK) and two in India (I).

The German site had been part of an independent company which, prior to its purchase by Lucent in 1996, was on the brink of bankruptcy. Most of the German workers were very experienced engineers having developed software development skills in the prior organization. They remained in the old facility. On average, they were 37 years old, and had 8.3 years of organizational tenure. In general, the broader experience in the field of software development and their focus on the last stages of the production process explained the German site's role of guidance within NEG.

In contrast to the German site, the British site was founded in early 1997 and occupied a completely new facility. Most employees were recent hires, and many were also recent university graduates. On average they were 33 years old and had two years of organizational tenure.

The NEG activities also relied heavily on two Indian sites located in Bangalore. The first Indian site was 'borrowed' on a long term from a local provider (Sycro, a disguised name). Employees were assigned full time to Lucent projects, observed confidentiality rules about the Lucent activities, worked in a separate building assigned to Lucent, and used to travel and meet European colleagues within NEG. The second site (BLDC) was created from scratch in a high-tech park and belonged to Lucent. As for the British site, employees were fresh graduates in computer science. For many of them, this was the first job. In general, Indian workers were 26.5 years old, with an organizational tenure of two years.

3.2   The Software Development Process

In theory, the software development process could be described as a sequence of well-defined tasks. Typically, the development process begins when a software production unit, like NEG, receives specifications for a particular release of the code for a particular program. From this point, the development process consists of six stages (Figure 10.2): (1) functional specification, (2) design, (3) coding, (4) unit test, (5) system integration, (6) testing and certification.

Functional specification (stage 1)	Design (stage 2)	Coding (stage 3)	Unit test (stage 4)	System integration (stage 5)	Testing and certification (stage 6)
UK, D	UK	UK, I, D	UK, I, D	D	D

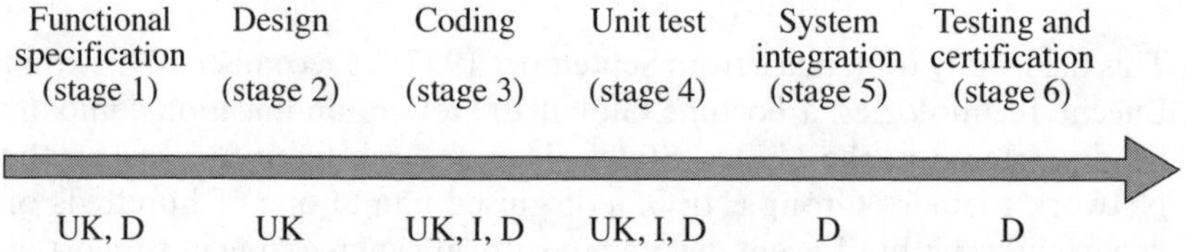

Note: D=Germany, UK=United Kingdom, I=India

Figure 10.2   Software development process and site contribution to the process

Strategic and cost-related reasons led NEG to locate the process worldwide. One or more teams, depending on the complexity of the stage, performed each stage. For instance, there were several teams dedicated to coding, given the plurality of modules to code. It is important to note that some teams overlapped, as the same individual could have belonged to two or more teams simultaneously. It meant that the same person could have had more than one leader at the same time. The dynamic nature of the product, indeed, forced the company to follow closely any market signals. As a consequence, new ad hoc teams were often constituted to explore new technical solutions.

In spite of the sequential nature of the software development process described above, in NEG, and likewise other software development firms, process complexity and unpredictable events demanded continuous adjustments and innovative solutions. In many cases, when modules had to be integrated, the integration plan turned out to be, in retrospect, very optimistic. Developers strove to adjust to the reality of the project that often resulted in a weekly redefinition of the plan. As a developer reported '[we] chopped and changed as things became ready'. In such a scenario, trust and common ground proved to be crucial for successful coordination.

3.3 Methodology

In the two-year investigation the research team spent several weeks in the field to acquire information on the software development process, division of work across sites, roles, technologies, procedures and coordination mechanisms (Rocco et al. 2001). The team conducted over 60 interviews in the four sites. Multiple visits allowed us to collect information by direct access to people, documents and meetings. We also collected detailed information on the organization by a Web-based survey. Questions covered topics like demographics (for example, age, national culture, education, organizational role), communication relationships (for example, who communicates with whom, communication frequency), coordination difficulties (for example, problems in sharing goals, plans and priorities), linguistic barriers (for example, fluency in English as corporate language), communication tools for distant interactions (for example, phone, email, fax). The respondents provided two answers per question: one with regard to local co-workers and the other with regard to distant co-workers. At the beginning of the questionnaire they were asked to select the most important distant site, that is, the site with which they interacted the most.

Trust
A part of the Web-based survey was devoted to trust. Overall, 92 individuals completed the questionnaire. We built a 6-item scale to measure trust. The theoretical construct was measured as mean of the items. Measures are based on 7-point Likert items, anchored by 1 = Strongly disagree, to 7 = Strongly agree. The items were derived from McAllister's (1995) and Pearce et al.'s (1994) questionnaires. Because of space constraints, we picked the items that reflected more closely the presence of trust in the software development organization. We also added two new items more fitting to the software development process (Table 10.1). While the multi-item scales referring to distant working relationship show satisfying reliability (Cronbach alpha >0.70), the same scales referring to relationships among co-located colleagues show slightly lower reliability. Reliability could have been improved by eliminating some items. Nevertheless, all the items were kept to conduct across-site comparisons.

Table 10.1   Trust measure, n = 92

Trust	local = 0.60	distant = 0.71
I feel comfortable sharing ideas and feelings about work with my co-workers (McAllister, 1995) I confide in my co-workers about difficulties that I am having at work (McAllister, 1995) I have close friendship with my co-workers (Pearce et al., 1994) I can rely on my co-workers to fulfill their commitments (e.g., meet deadlines, complete tasks) [reverse scored] (Pearce et al., 1994) My co-workers are always dependable at work My co-workers do their best to complete their task thoroughly [reverse scored]		

4.   FINDINGS

4.1   Effect of Distance on Trust

The trust measure used in the survey shows that remote co-workers trusted each other less than co-located ones (Table 10.2).

Table 10.2   Trust measured on a 7-point Likert scale, n = 92

	Co-located colleagues		Remote colleagues				
	Mean	SD	Mean	SD	Diff.	t	p
Trust	5.50	0.75	4.80	0.93	0.70	8.38	<0.005

Given the complexity and heterogeneous nature of the teams, we used interviews and direct observations to collect data about the relationships between trust and coordination. The following examples portray some evidence about the importance of convergent expectations (common ground) to solve successfully coordination problems characterizing different aspects of software development. In these examples, problems of coordination seem to explain low trust between remote people. As argued earlier, physical distance constituted a barrier to common ground formation negatively affecting heuristics of physical co-presence, linguistic co-presence and community membership.

4.2 The Role of Trust to Solve Coordination Problems in Software Development Processes

(a) Software development as a conjunctive task

A software product consisted of the assembly of modules that interact with each other. Each development team was responsible for one or more modules. If a team performed poorly (for example, delays, poor development, poor testing), the whole product failed. Like in the weakest link game, software development process can be described as a conjunctive task (Steiner 1972), in which the effort of the weaker jeopardizes the effort of the stronger. Naturally, external causes could slow down the activities, such as staff turnover, extreme schedule pressure, changing requirements. Nevertheless, at NEG people struggled to align their efforts with co-located and remote co-workers, in terms of timeliness and work practices. Both efforts were based upon *trust that community rules would have been respected.* On the one hand, engineers responsible for assembling pieces of code needed to trust that their co-workers engaged in the earlier stages would have respected the official deadlines and produced pieces on time. Similarly, a development team needed to trust that another development team would have communicated on time any change to allow the former to adjust to the new plan. On the other hand, everyone was expected to know and adopt the same procedures, regardless of responsibility and location. In reality, sources of differences included criteria for documentation, testing practices (see example above) and disagreement over the importance of particular bugs. Engineers often had to negotiate solutions – sometimes accompanied by very heated discussions over the urgency of fixing bugs in the current release, and the wisdom of postponing some bug fixes to a subsequent release. In these circumstances, the possibility to share a common set of presuppositions about each other's expertise, activity and priorities could facilitate coordination and rapid conflict solutions. In practice, people at one site lamented that team members at the other site made decisions independently and referring to different visions of how the final product should have looked. As a consequence, coordination failures were common, leading to low levels of trust.

(b) Interface management

As we already described, software development is based upon tightly coupled processes carried on by geographically distributed teams. Each individual module, developed by a team, had to interact with other modules developed elsewhere by other teams. In NEG, teams used to have regular meetings to discuss the most recent changes. But frequent inter-team discrepancies surfaced at the eve or during the integration stage (stage 4, in Figure 10.2). A main coordination failure was due to the poor interface management between modules. Teams used both interface specifications and simulators to predict how their sub-product would have interacted with the others. Interface specification reported event tracing, or 'fence diagrams' that showed sequences of messages among processes. Simulators represented components that another component had to interact with. Developers had to *trust that remote colleagues were building interfaces and simulators correctly*. For instance, team members had to trust that the other teams' interfaces reflected the necessary and updated information. Similarly, simulators reflected a team's assumptions about how the other components were functioning. Initially, teams trusted that assumptions were shared. In reality, both solutions proved to be insufficient, leading developers to realize that assumptions among teams were different and trust was misplaced. When components at the integration stage did not match as expected, discrepancies between teams' assumptions surfaced, proving that interface specifications and simulators lacked many essential details.

(c) Modification requests
The difficulty in reaching smooth coordination was evident in the course of testing the code, when engineers produced modification requests (called MRs) which were indications to engineers responsible for an offending module to clean up bugs that generated the MR. MRs surfaced differences among operations carried out at different sites. For instance, adversarial relationships emerged between functional groups, such as British software developers versus German testers. In this case, testers complained that the code should have been aggressively probed for errors, but that developers did not do it, leaving the test team with too many problems to solve. Developers, for their part, had different *expectations* about testing, and felt that the testers were over eager, posing unrealistically challenging tests for the finished code. Both groups claimed to have very little trust toward each other.

To sum up, trust formation and maintenance assume special significance in highly unpredictable, cognitively complex, tightly coupled tasks. On the one hand, complexity implies that formal coordination mechanisms (planning, predefined procedure and workflow systems) cope badly with the unpredictability of the process. Individuals must be able to trust that expectations about timing, working practices, problem-solving criteria and expertise are shared. On the other hand, when activities are tightly coupled, co-workers must be willing to collaborate openly, share, delegate and learn in a trustworthy environment. In these situations, developing trust is difficult and crucial: it requires fairly constant, small group activities that offer opportunities to observe others in action over time (Frey and Schlosser 1993). Other barriers to trust, like opportunism or lack of good faith, honesty, or benevolence (Cummings and Bromiley 1996) in carrying out work activities could have been present at NEG, but they were not lamented as the main threat to trust by the employees. Instead, poor coordination and the decline in trust toward remote colleagues seems to be explained by the reduced opportunities for interactions (in particular, informal interactions) and, thus, common ground building among distant colleagues.

5. DISCUSSION

This chapter extends the debate on trust in organizations exploring the role of convergent expectations or shared beliefs to build trust in unpredictable situations. We chose software development as a peculiar group activity characterized by unpredictability, due to the tightly coupled and cognitively complex nature of the work. In software development, individuals cope with a high rate of unpredictability, and, consequently, they need to produce *ad hoc* solutions while preserving coordination with other units or individuals. Trust is crucial in reaching effective coordination together, while traditional coordination mechanisms work only to a limited extent (Thompson 1967; Mintzberg 1979). But trust implies the acceptance of a risk. In this context, colleagues mainly faced the risk of carrying divergent expectations about how the activities should have been carried out and coordinated. Opportunism or lack of good faith, honesty, or benevolence was not lamented as the main threat to trust by the NEG employees.

We turned to coordination games (Schelling 1960), like the weakest link game, as representative of situations in which there is no risk of opportunism. Nevertheless, in coordination games, the highest payoff is reached if individuals trust others. Coordination reveals whether people trust others to take the risk and choose high payoff actions. Therefore, trust becomes the evidence of convergent expectations about how everybody in the game should act to reach the highest payoff. Software development is suitable to be studied as a coordination game. It could be described as a conjunctive coordination game: the group payoff depends on the proper coordination of individual actions, and the quality output is determined by the effort of the less well-performing member. If one individual delays in carrying out his responsibility, the time limit to market the new software product worsens. So, when expectations are not aligned, individuals select actions that other colleagues are not expecting them to take, leading to poor coordination or 'coordination decrements' (Steiner 1972). Common ground is a key resource for members of a virtual organization, as it guarantees them that expectations, knowledge and beliefs do converge. Nevertheless, common ground can only develop when precise conditions are in place.

In linguistics, the role of three conditions (or heuristics) responsible for common ground formation has been investigated: physical co-presence, linguistic co-presence and community membership. Physical distance deeply affects these heuristics. First of all, distance shrinks opportunities for physical co-presence. In fact, in the study, only co-located colleagues showed better coordination performance and, therefore, trusted each other more than remote colleagues, primarily thanks to the close physical proximity. Secondly, distant colleagues often belonged to different cultural or organizational communities. In the field study we observed, for instance, that the Indian community conceived even the same task (for example, the testing procedure) differently from the German or the British community. As a consequence, when Germans, Indians and Brits had to coordinate on the same task, different communities' conceptions led to different presuppositions about how tasks should have been done, causing in turn poor coordination, and inevitable frustration and reduced trust. With regard to the third heuristic, linguistic co-presence, remote colleagues largely rely on mediated communication by e-mail or telephone. However, as emerging from the personal experience of the people we interviewed, distance undermines the assumptions (simultaneity, attention and understanding) upon which linguistic co-presence is rooted. Using asynchronous tools of communication (for example, email) implied that information was shared in different times, or not read at all, or misunderstood. In any case, failure to communicate effectively and without ambiguity undermined the most frequently used heuristic for common ground formation among distant people. Fragility of linguistic co-presence at distance contributes to explain the low level of trust at a distance.

Managerial Implications

In this final session we try to distill some managerial lessons to support trust in geographically distributed, multi-cultural organizations. The core idea is that smoothing cultural, linguistic and behavioral differences will help trust by facilitating convergent expectations and, therefore, effective coordination.

Initial face-to-face interactions
Face-to-face interaction is important for trust building (Nohria and Eccles 1992; Handy 1995). Co-workers who are physically distant rarely interact on a face-to-face basis; in addition, this opportunity often occurs several

months after the working relationship started. At NEG, individuals reported that seeing their counterparts at distant sites helped to break down the syndrome of the invisible colleagues. Many wished that this face-to-face interaction had happened earlier. First, spending time at the other sites increased the acquaintance with strangers with different cultures and norms. Second, physical co-presence is the main heuristic for common ground formation, and it enhances the effect of the other heuristics (linguistic co-presence and community membership). In fact, when physically co-present, remote colleagues can develop a common frame of reference to share and enrich later on at distance. In particular, they can identify and converge shared expectations about work practices and timing procedure, satisfying better premises of simultaneity, attention and understanding. In addition, an earlier face-to-face meeting might provide an opportunity for later non-work-related interactions that we found to be positively associated to trust.

Liaison managers
Sometimes face-to-face interactions among remote colleagues are not feasible. Budget constraints or time issues prevent the opportunity of visiting the remote site. Furthermore, face-to-face presence could be necessary every time team members in different locations meet for reviews, discussions, problem solving, and so on. In this case, travelling for everybody would be costly and time consuming, causing additional delays. In these circumstances, organizations could adopt the practice of sending local representatives to remote sites. Within NEG, for instance, managers had an intuitive grasp of the importance of exchanges between sites through a practice that one manager described as 'hostage taking'. That is, in advance of critical cross-site conferences, managers would send a representative from each participating site to the opposite site (that is, the hostage). In this way, the representative could help translate and interpret both literally and culturally, within the call. The liaison would help to satisfy the premises of attention and understanding that are often lost in distant communication. In general, geographically distributed organizations could benefit from the presence of liaison managers from one site to another. On the one hand, liaisons would mediate the interaction between their local colleagues in the distant site, and the hosting site. This could be particularly useful for overcoming linguistic barriers. On the other hand, the liaisers could acquire valuable knowledge and expertise to diffuse once returned to their site. At NEG, for instance, those who had been to the opposite sites became unofficial guides to resources there. Finally, liaison managers assume the role of facilitators between sites. Time pressure creates local priorities that might differ among sites. In turn, colleagues in different sites develop divergent expectations

about when some task should be accomplished. The liaisons would help to maintain aligned expectations, avoiding the 'coordination decrements' mentioned above.

Expatriates as 'evangelists' of corporate culture

Sites of geographically distributed organizations are often characterized by different sets of norms and conventions. The culture clash problem is only one aspect of the problem: the characteristics of the site, its antecedents, and local routines contribute to creating local sets of conventions that are difficult to homogenize among sites. The same organizational norms (for example, documentation rules) could be interpreted differently in different sites, in the light of precedent experiences, local habits and local management decisions. As a convention's establishment depends on the frequency of interaction (Lewis 1969), different sites are likely to form different conventions, given less frequent interaction between remote colleagues than interaction among locals. Organizational members aware of the conventions and subtle differences emerging in different sites are in the best position to prevent sites' drifting. For instance, expatriates who spent years in the remote sites could be appointed the role of 'evangelists' once returned to the home site. In this way, they could facilitate the across-site convergence towards common standards of behavior. During our interviews in the Indian NEG site, for instance, the chief manager explained the importance of being an expatriate to diffuse the Western corporate culture into an Asian workplace. In fact, as an expatriate, he could understand the implicit assumptions embedded in different cultures.

Shared conventions for using collaborative technologies

During the study, we collected empirical evidence that the same technologies were adopted differently in the different sites. For instance, the British used to check their voice mail more times per day. Germans, on the other hand, used to do it once or twice a week. Many coordination breakdowns were attributed to the divergent expectations in terms of voice mail use. In general, explicit rules or conventions for using technologies appropriately would improve communication and coordination. For instance, email messages should contain vacation messages when somebody is out of the office reporting on whom to contact in case of urgency. In addition, every email should specify the date by when an answer is expected to reduce unintentional delays. The habit of sending an email with the description of the issue to discuss before calling the remote colleague might be useful in case of linguistic difficulties. In this way, people could talk during the phone conversations, making reference to a written document. This would improve understanding. In addition, the email message could indicate the time of the call, making it easier to find the remote colleagues available. In general, any geographically distributed organization should endorse shared rules to increase the benefit of collaborative technologies. Even more sophisticated technologies, such as calendar tools with culturally-specific information (for example, national holidays) or document-sharing applications (for example, NetMeeting) would lose effectiveness in distributed teams if members followed different rules.

6.   CONCLUSION

The chapter contributes to the literature on trust in two ways. First, it tries to explore threats to trust deriving from lack of convergent expectations or common ground among individuals, resulting in poor coordination. The linguistic literature on common ground helps to understand how shared beliefs and expectations form, and shows how when individuals cope with unpredictable events, lack of common ground might cause poor coordination, and consequently decline of trust. Second, the chapter develops a framework to explain how common ground weakens at a distance. Therefore trust at a distance is more cumbersome than trust among co-located individuals. The second part of the chapter tried to make sense of the decline of trust in a virtual organization exploring causes of coordination failures and explaining why distant colleagues missed common ground. The managerial practices we present are built upon the results of the study, and aimed to bridge organizational and human gaps in modern organizational forms.

ACKNOWLEDGEMENTS

The research presented in this chapter is part of a larger project sponsored by Lucent Technologies. I would like to thank all the people that made this chapter possible. In particular, I would like to thank Tom Finholt and Jim Herbsleb who offered me the opportunity to join the research and, above all, to get involved in a unique and instructive experience on the field. Their insightful comments inspired many ideas presented in the chapter.

BIBLIOGRAPHY

Alchian, A.A. and H. Demsetz (1972), 'Production, information costs, an economic organization', *American Economic Review*, 62, 777–95.
Axelrod, R.M. (1984), *The Evolution of Cooperation*, New York: Basic Books.

Camerer, C. and M. Knez (1994), 'Creating expectational assets in the laboratory: coordination in the "weakest link" game', *Strategic Management Journal*, 101–19.

Camerer, C. and M. Knez (1996), 'Coordination, organizational boundaries and fads in business practice', *Industrial and Corporate Change*, 5, 89–112.

Clark, H.H. (1993), *Arenas of Language Use*, University of Chicago Press.

Clark, H.H. (1996), *Using Language*, Cambridge University Press.

Cummings, L.L. and P. Bromiley (1996), 'The organizational trust inventory (OTI): development and validation', in Kramer, R.M. and T. R.Tyler (eds), *Trust in Organizations: Frontiers of Theory and Research*, Thousand Oaks, CA: Sage Publications, pp. 302–30.

Currall, S.C. (1990), *The role of interpersonal trust in work relationships*, Unpublished doctoral dissertation, Cornell University.

Dawes, R. (1980), 'Social dilemmas', *Annual Review of Psychology*, 31, 169–93.

Deutsch, M. (1958), 'Trust and suspicion', *Journal of Conflict Resolution*, 2, 265–79.

Durkheim, E. (1893), *The Division of Labor in Society*, New York: The Free Press.

Eisenhardt, K.M. (1989), 'Agency theory: an assessment and review', *Academy of Management Review*, 14, 57–74.

Finholt, T., L. Sproull and S. Kiesler (1990), 'Communication and performance in ad hoc task groups', in J. Galagher, R.E. Kraut and C. Egido (eds), *Intellectual Teamwork*, Hillsdale, NJ: Lawrence Erlbaum Associates, pp. 291–325.

Frey, S.C. and M. Schlosser (1993), 'ABB and Ford: Creating value trough cooperation', *Sloan Management Review*, 65–72.

Gambetta, D. (1988), *Trust: Making and breaking cooperative relations*, New York: Basil Blackwell.

Grabowski, M. and K.H. Roberts (1999), 'Risk mitigation in virtual organization', *Organization Science*, **10** (6), 704–21.

Handy, C. (1995), 'Trust and the virtual organization', *Harvard Business Review*, **73** (3), May/June, 40–50.

Herbsleb, J.D. and R.E. Grinter (1999), 'Architecture, coordination and distance: Conway's law and beyond', *IEEE Software*, **16** (5), Sept./Oct., 63–70.

Hofstede, G. (1997), *Software of the Mind: Intercultural Cooperation and its Importance for Survival*, New York: McGraw-Hill.

Jarvenpaa, S.L. and D.E. Leidner (1999), 'Communication and trust in virtual teams', *Organization Science*, **10** (6), 791–815.

Jensen, M.C. and W.C. Meckling (1976), 'Theory of the firm: managerial behavior, agency costs, and ownership structure', *Journal of Financial Economics*, 3, 305–60.

Kartunnen, L. and S. Peters (1975), 'Conventional implicature of Montague grammar', *Berkeley Linguistic Society*, 1, 266–78.

Kramer R.M. and T.R. Tyler (1996), *Trust in Organizations: Frontiers of theory and research*, Thousand Oaks, CA: Sage

Lave, J. and E. Wenger (1991), *Situated Learning: Legitimate peripheral participation*, Cambridge, UK: Cambridge University Press.

Lewicki, R.J. and B.B. Bunker (1996), 'Developing and maintaining trust in work relationships', in R.M. Kramer and T.R. Taylor (eds), *Trust in Organizations: Frontiers of Theory and Research*, Thousand Oaks: Sage, pp. 114–39.

Lewis, D.K. (1969), *Convention: A philosophical study*, Cambridge, MA: Harvard University Press.

Malmgren, H. (1961), 'Information, expectations and the theory of the firm', *Quarterly Journal of Economics*, 75, 399–421.

March, J.G. and Z. Shapira (1987), 'Managerial perspectives and risk taking', *Management Science*, 33, 1404–18.

McAllister, D.J. (1995), 'Affect- and cognition-based trust as foundations for interpersonal cooperation in organizations', *Academy of Management Journal*, 38, 24–59.

Mintzberg, H. (1979), *The Structuring of Organizations*, NJ: Prentice Hall.

Narduzzo, A., E. Rocco and M. Warglien (2000), 'Talking about routines in the field', in G. Dosi, R.R. Nelson and S.G. Winter (eds), *The Nature and Dynamics of Organizational Capabilities*, New York: Oxford University Press, pp. 27–50.

Nohria, N. and R. Eccles (1992), 'Face-to-face: making network organization work', in N. Nohria and R. Eccles (eds), *Networks and Organizations: Structure, form and action*, Boston, MA: Harvard Business School Press, pp. 288–308.

Nonaka, I. (1990), 'Redundant, overlapping organization: a Japanese approach to managing the innovation process', *California Management Review*, 32, 27–38.

Nonaka, I. (1994), 'A dynamic theory of organizational knowledge creation', *Organization Science*, **5** (1), 201–18.

Ouchi, W.G. (1979), 'A conceptual framework for the design of organizational control mechanisms', *Management Science*, 25, 833–48.

Pearce, J.L., I. Branyiczki and G. Bakacsi (1994), 'A person-based reward system: a theory of organizational reward practices in reform communist organizations', *Journal of Organizational Behavior*, 15, 261–82.

Powell, W. (1990), 'Neither markets nor hierarchy: network forms of social organization', in B.M. Staw and L.L. Cummings (eds), *Research in Organizational Behavior*, vol. 12, Greenwich, CT: JAI Press, pp. 295–336.

Rocco, E. (1998), 'Trust Breaks Down in Electronic Contexts but can be Repaired by some Initial Face-To-Face Contact', *Proceedings of the Conference on Human Factors in Computing Systems*, ACM Press, Los Angeles, CA, 496–502.

Rocco E., T.A. Finholt, E.C. Hofer and J.D. Herbsleb (2001), 'Out of sight, short of trust', Proceedings (cd-rom) European Academy of Management (EURAM), Barcelona 19–21 April.

Rousseau D.M., S.B. Sitkin, R.S. Burt and C. Camerer (1998), 'Not so different after all: a cross-discipline view of trust', *Academy of Management Review*, **23** (3), 393–404.

Schelling, T.C. (1960), *The Strategy of Conflict*, Cambridge, MA: Harvard University Press.

Sproull, L. and S. Kielser (1991), *Connections. New ways of working in the networked organization*, Cambridge, MA: MIT Press.

Steiner, I.D. (1972), *Group Process and Productivity*, New York: Academic Press.

Thompson, J.D. (1967), *Organizations in Action*, New York: McGraw Hill.

Williamson, O.E. (1985), *The Economic Institutions of Capitalism: Firms, markets, relational contraction*, New York: Free Press.

Zaheer, A., B. McEvily and V. Perrone (1998), 'Does trust matter? Exploring the effects of interorganizational and interpersonal trust on performance', *Organization Science*, **9** (2), 141–59.

Zucker, L.G. (1986), 'Production of trust: institutional sources of economic structure 1840–1920', in B.M. Straw and L.L. Cummings (eds), *Research in Organizational Behavior*, vol. 8, Greenwich, CT: JAI Press, pp. 53–111.

11. Does trust breed heed? Differential effects of trust on heed and performance in a network and a divisional form of organizing

Katinka Bijlsma-Frankema, Bastiaan W. Rosendaal and Gerhard van de Bunt

INTRODUCTION

In the past decades, several key authors within the field of trust research have argued that a trust-based network form of organizing is especially suitable for dealing with the external and internal challenges organizations face nowadays (Ouchi, 1979; Powell, 1990; Creed and Miles, 1996; Oliver, 1997). Oliver (p. 238), for instance, argues that internal and external networks are advantageous to organizations because 'they increase organizational flexibility and the ability to deal with contingencies, and allow organizational learning, features especially needed for complex organizations, operating in a highly complex environment'. In organizations that employ a high percentage of professionals with knowledge-intensive tasks, a network form of organizing can be particularly beneficial to both the organization and the professionals, because of the compatibility with the preferences of professionals for reduced administrative control and flexibility in evaluating outcomes next to the need to exchange specialized knowledge among them (Oliver, 1997, p. 227). Networks are seen as more efficient mechanisms of governance than hierarchies when tasks become increasingly complex and ambiguous, the value of the commodities exchanged is harder to assess and exchange relations are longer-term and recurrent (Powell, 1990). According to Powell, networks emerge in conditions of social similarity, complementary strengths, norms of reciprocity and high interdependence. In situations of recurrent exchanges, these conditions will enable learning and engender trust.

Creed and Miles (1996) argue that trust is critical to the functioning of network forms of organizing. As organizations move from functional forms to network forms of organizing, organizational performance becomes increasingly dependent on trustful relations between organizational members. A high level of trust within a network form is seen as a functional equivalent of building and maintaining control in functional forms (Powell, 1990; Miles and Snow, 1994; Creed and Miles, 1996; Sheppard and Tuschinsky, 1996; Oliver, 1997). The other side of the coin is that the costs of trust failure also rise if organizations move toward network forms of organizing. As Creed and Miles note, 'There is little question that within network forms trust requirements are high and the consequences of failing to meet them severe. Network members are expected to "forego the right to pursue self-interest at the expense of others" (Powell, 1990, p. 303) and recognize their co-dependence with upstream and downstream partners' (1996, p. 26). High levels of trust are needed to make organizational members abandon self-interested behaviors in favor of behaviors that take the interests of others into account as well. It is the task of management to embed a high level of trust within the organization, by showing genuine care for the wellbeing of organizational members, and by setting and maintaining standards for trustful behaviors. The idea that care can promote trust is confirmed by studies that have found care, or perceived organizational support, to be an antecedent of trust in co-members of the organization (von Krogh, 1998) and of trust in leadership (Dirks and Ferrin, 2002). If management fails to embed trust, there is no other in-built correctional mechanism against opportunistic behaviors (Creed and Miles, 1996). In other organizational forms, low levels of trust do not have such severe consequences, because in these forms hierarchy is more dominant as a mechanism of control: 'comparatively, in functional forms, trust failures reduce efficiency; in divisional forms, they reduce effectiveness and raise costs; in matrix forms they cause the form to fail; and in network forms they cause the firms to fail' (Creed and Miles, 1996, p. 26). In network forms, trust is thus seen as a stronger determinant of organizational performance than in other organizational forms.

However compelling this argument may be, empirical evidence to support it is still scarce. Besides, there is no research-based agreement on factors that may mediate the relation between trust and performance as yet, nor on organizational factors that may promote trust and performance. A related problem is that in discussions of trust in network forms, a distinction between trust in hierarchical relations and trust in relations between colleagues is not often made, while such a distinction would allow for differentiation between factors related to both forms of trust. Trust in managers may produce distinct effects compared to trust in colleagues.

The study presented here aims to enhance scholarly understanding of differential effects of trust on team performance by comparing two organizations, one with a divisional form and the other with a network form of organizing, that both employ mainly knowledge workers. By studying trust in vertical and horizontal relations simultaneously, differential effects of trust in managers and trust in colleagues can be explored. A second aim is to explore the role of two variables that may mediate the relation between trust and team performance, heedful interrelating (Weick and Roberts, 1993) and selfish behaviors. A last aim is to explore the consequences of perceived organizational support (POS), an organizational factor that is proposed to boost performance through promoting trust and heedful interrelating, and through curbing selfish behaviors. Combining the ideas of Powell, Creed and Miles, and Oliver about the network form, it can be argued that trust is more critical in a network form because it promotes behaviors that, in this organizational form, are critical to team performance, such as cooperation, learning behaviors and adequately dealing with contingencies. It is argued that the concept of heedful interrelating (Weick and Roberts, 1993) representing a specific mode of cooperation that implies constant learning and adequately dealing with contingencies, will mediate the trust–performance relation. Trust is also expected to promote performance indirectly by curbing self-directed behaviors in favor of behaviors that take the interests of others into account as well.

The research questions are:

(1) To what degree are trust in managers and trust in colleagues related to heedful behavior and team performance in both organizations? To what degree do a network form and a divisional form organization differ with respect to these relations?

(2) To what degree does heedful behavior mediate the relation between trust in managers and trust in colleagues, and performance? To what degree do a network form and a divisional form organization differ with respect to these relations?

(3) To what degree does the perception of selfish behavior of colleagues mediate the relation between trust in managers and trust in colleagues, and heedful behavior? To what degree do a network form and a divisional form organization differ with respect to these relations?

(4) To what degree does perceived organizational support (POS) indirectly influence team performance through a positive effect on trust in managers and trust in colleagues, and through a negative effect on selfish behaviors? To what degree do a network form and a divisional form organization differ with respect to these relations?

The network form organization offers web-related programs and services to other firms, the divisional form organization is a semi-public research institute. In both firms the employees can be typified as highly qualified professionals that have a great deal of autonomy in creating knowledge-based products.

The chapter will be structured into four parts. First, several conceptual and theoretical ideas that have guided the research will be briefly reviewed. In the second part the research design and techniques of data collection and analysis chosen will be discussed. In the third part the data and the results of analyses will be presented. In the final section conclusions will be drawn and some directions for future research will be formulated.

CONCEPTUAL FRAMEWORK

Concept of Trust

Most authors agree that the notion of risk is central to the concept of trust. According to Luhmann (1988), trust is a solution for specific problems of risk in relations between actors, because it is an attitude that allows for risk-taking: 'If actors choose one course of action in preference to alternatives, in spite of the possibility of being disappointed by the action of others, they define the situation as one of trust' (Luhmann, 1988, pp. 97–99). Dasgupta (1988, p. 51) similarly describes trust as 'connected to correct expectations about the actions of others that have a bearing on one's own choice of action when that action must be chosen before one can monitor the actions of those others'. The general definition of trust Gambetta (1988, pp. 217–18) introduced is close to the definitions of Dasgupta and Luhmann, but more explicit on the link between trust and cooperation: 'when we say we trust someone or that someone is trustworthy, we implicitly mean that the probability that he will perform an action that is beneficial or at least not detrimental to us is high enough for us to consider engaging in some form of cooperation with him'. Creed and Miles (1996) build on this definition, but their work is more focused on trust in organizations. Based on the work of Garfinkel (1967) 'considering engaging in cooperation with another' is widened to a positive inclination towards the demands of the social order within the organization: 'trust is both the specific expectation that another's actions will be beneficial rather than detrimental and the generalized ability to take for granted, to take under trust, a vast array of features of the social order'. Since this chapter focuses on trust in intra-organizational relations, this definition of Creed and Miles (1996, p. 17) was worked upon.

Trust is thus taken to represent a coordinating mechanism supporting cooperation. Trust begins where rational prediction ends (for example Luhmann, 1979; Gambetta, 1988), enabling actors to take a leap of faith beyond that which reason alone would warrant (Simmel, 1950; Bradach and Eccles, 1989; Lewis and Weigert, 1985). This leap of faith implies suspension of doubt about the possibility that another's action will be based on self-interest (that is, 'me' rationality) assuming that the other will reciprocate the 'us' rationality that is signaled by trust (Möllering, in this volume; Lewis and Weigert, 1985).

Bases of Trust

Trust can be embedded in the structure and culture of organizations to different degrees, as Creed and Miles (1996) argue. They conceive of trust as a function of three variables: (1) embedded predisposition to trust; (2) characteristic similarity; (3) experiences of reciprocity. In a similar vein, Zucker (1986) distinguishes three types of trust: (1) character-based trust, based on social similarities and shared moral codes; (2) process-based trust, based on experiences of reciprocity; (3) institution-based trust, flowing from institutional arrangements that evoke and sustain trustworthy behaviors. Broad societal norms, guarding institutional arrangements and organizational governance systems, can bring about varying degrees of embedded trust, of sharing norms and expectations, and of reciprocity. The latter two variables, sharing and reciprocal exchanges, point to two general principles of social integration that can be traced back to the work of Durkheim (1893), who coined the concepts of mechanical solidarity based on shared characteristics, and organic solidarity based on exchanging. By integrating both principles in a theory of trust, like Creed and Miles do, instead of treating them separately, a better understanding of trust can be formed. A similar point is made by Powell (1996, p. 63) in comparing rational (that is exchange) and social norm (that is sharing) models of trust, amending the latter with notions from the former: 'societal norm-based conceptions of trust miss the extent to which cooperation is buttressed by sustained contact, regular dialogue and constant monitoring'.

March and Olsen (1975) also relate sharing and exchanging to trust and social integration, adding a dynamic view to how trust and distrust develop. Positive exchange experiences are seen as antecedents of trust, facilitating sharing, seeing, and liking, which promote trust. Unlike most authors on trust, they include the notion of relevance in their theory of trust, a notion also found in the work of Weick (1995). They argue that people come to trust those who are perceived to bring about desirable events, or to prevent undesirable events, in areas that they experience as relevant. If people trust others, they seek interaction with them, tend to like what they like and see what they see, to share areas of relevance, thus furthering integration between them. Distrust creates discord, since, if others are distrusted, actors will tend to dislike what they like, tend not to share their areas of relevance and, to the degree that the structure permits them, tend to avoid interaction with them. In the process of developing trust or distrust, beneficial events will tend to be attributed to others that are trusted, detrimental events to those who are distrusted. Trust begets trust, while distrust begets distrust.

Trust and Performance

The relation between trust and performance is not uncontested. Although positive relations have been found (Costa et al., 2001; Connell et al., 2003), past research provides no more than 'mild, and/or inconsistent empirical results', as Dirks (1999, p.446) notes on the relation between trust in colleagues and team performance. A main aim of this study was to test the argument of Creed and Miles (1996) that in network forms performance is more dependent on trustful relations with 'upstream' and 'downstream' partners than in other forms. Maybe the mixed results found so far are due to an interaction effect with organizational form. Later on, hypotheses will be formulated to put the argument of Creed and Miles (1996) to an empirical test. Creed and Miles (1996) do, however, not differentiate between trust in superiors and trust in colleagues. Since positive relations have been found between team performance on the one hand and employee trust in managers (Connell et al., 2003) and employee trust in colleagues (Costa et al., 2001) on the other, it can be expected that in a network form performance will be more dependent on both forms of trust than in other organizational forms.

Trust, Heed and Performance

In the introduction the ideas of Powell, Creed and Miles, and Oliver about the network form, were discussed. Three factors were proposed to mediate the relation between trust and performance in network forms of organizing, cooperation, learning behaviors and adequately dealing with contingencies. It was argued that trust is more critical in a network form because in this organizational form, these trust-based behaviors are critical to team performance. Since the concept of heedful interrelating (Weick and Roberts, 1993) represents a specific mode of cooperation that implies constant learning and adequately dealing with contingencies, a new scale was developed in this study to measure heed. It will be hypothesized that heedful interrelating mediates the trust–performance relation. Since no empirical studies on heed are available to work upon, the hypothesis will be derived from studies on open communication, knowledge exchange and learning.

Learning behaviors are among the most important behaviors mentioned in the literature as critical to performance and to building competitive advantage. In line with the finding that trust furthers open communication between interaction partners (Currall and Judge, 1995; Smith and Barclay, 1997), it is argued and found that trust between equals, such as partners in a joint venture or co-workers, facilitates mutual learning because trust enables exchange of tacit knowledge on which most learning processes depend (Boisot, 1995; Nonaka and Takeuchi, 1995; Brown and Duguid, 1998; Nonaka and Konno, 1998; Janowicz and Noorderhaven, 2002; Bogenrieder and Nooteboom, 2004). In a similar vein, it is argued and found that trust in managers is positively related to learning behaviors (Dodgson, 1993; Bijlsma, 2001).

Learning and knowledge exchange, however, are not sufficient conditions to arrive at high performance. A certain level of collective thinking and acting is needed to make learning a critical success factor in organizations. Nonaka and Konno (1998) argue that in exchanging tacit knowledge to the benefit of the organization a shift to the group level of thinking must be made, in which emotional, experiential and mental thresholds between actors are removed. Furthermore, Weick and Roberts (1993), Kramer et al. (1996), and von Krogh (1998) argue that thinking and acting at the group level is a most important factor in enhancing team performance.

The problem of how to realize optimal team performance does thus touch upon the problem of collective action. Organizational members are 'expected to contribute their time and attention towards the achievement of collective goals, share useful information with other organizational members and exercise responsible constraint when using valuable, but limited organizational resources' (Kramer et al., 1996, p. 357). Creed and Miles argue that in network forms these expectations are most critical to performance: 'members must forego the right to pursue self-interest at the expense of others and recognize their co-dependence with upstream and downstream partners' (Creed and Miles, 1996, p. 26). High levels of trust are needed to make organizational members abandon self-interested behaviors in favor of behaviors that take the interests of others into account as well.

Weick and Roberts (1993) describe group performance as the result of interrelated activity, based on a collective mind, in which group members envision the interrelatedness of their actions. When people act like a group, they have a shared representation of the joint actions required. They interrelate their contribution with these actions, making their own activities subservient to the group process. Contribution and subordination presuppose a collective representation of the common endeavor, a collective mind in the words of Weick and Roberts (1993). They developed the concept of heed to clarify the relation between interrelatedness and team performance in situations that require nearly continuous operational reliability. They argue that heedful interrelating is also a relevant concept in organizations where task interdependence is high and task programmability is low, as is the case in the knowledge-intensive projects within the two organizations studied.

Heedful interrelating, to put it shortly, is described as attentiveness to the actions of other group members with regard to how these affect collective action and exchanging signals to improve the quality of the collective action. Heed thus implies a collective mind, speaking up in case of sub-optimal collective action and continuous learning, and consequently, mediates the relation between trust and team performance (Weick and Roberts): 'the more heed reflected in a pattern of interrelations, the more developed the collective mind and the greater the capacity to comprehend unexpected events ... . Heedful interrelating connects sufficient individual know-how to meet situational demands' (1993, p. 340). Heed mediates the relation between trust and team performance: 'Performance may require a well developed collective mind in the form of a complex attentive system tied together by trust' (ibid., p. 378). Based on these insights, the following hypotheses were formulated:

Hypothesis 1a: The higher the level of trust in colleagues, the higher the level of perceived team performance.

Hypothesis 1b: The higher the level of trust in colleagues, the higher the level of perceived team performance, mediated by the level of heed (that is an indirect effect).

Hypothesis 1c: The relations described in hypotheses 1a and 1b will be stronger in a network form than in a divisional form organization.

Hypothesis 2a: The higher the level of trust in managers, the higher the level of perceived team performance.

Hypothesis 2b: The higher the level of trust in managers, the higher the level of perceived team performance, mediated by the level of heed (that is an indirect effect).

Hypothesis 2c: The relations described in hypotheses 2a and 2b will be stronger in a network form than in a divisional form organization.

Trust, Selfish Behavior and Heed

So far, the argument of Creed and Miles that in network forms performance is more dependent on trust than in other forms of organizing has been explained by the idea that trust promotes performance-enhancing behaviors and cognitions that are intertwined in the concept of heedful interrelating. A related, yet slightly different, explanation is that trust can curb behaviors that diminish performance, like selfish behaviors.

Von Krogh (1998, p. 135) argues that the nature of interrelations between organizational members and the level of trust is a critical factor in processes that enables firms to boost organizational performance and to build competitive advantages: 'Untrustworthy behavior, constant competition, imbalances in giving and receiving information and "that's not my job" attitudes endanger effective sharing of tacit knowledge'. Selfish behaviors can be expected to diminish heedful interrelating, because these behaviors, based on self interest, undermine the collective mind on which heed is based.

Creed and Miles also state that in network forms, high levels of trust are needed to make organizational members abandon self-interested behaviors in favor of behaviors that take the interests of others into account as well.

The expectation that trust and selfish behaviors are inversely related is supported by reciprocity theory and theories of attribution. The theory of reciprocity (Gouldner, 1960) predicts that if an actor displays high trust in others this will be reciprocated with benevolent behaviors. While selfish behaviors can thus be a result of low trust displayed by an actor, trust will be reciprocated by unselfish behaviors, that is behaviors that take the interests of the trustor(s) into account, a necessary condition for building collective mind within a team. Alternatively, attribution theory predicts that once an actor trusts others, he or she will attribute positive motives (Kramer, 1996) and beneficial, or non-detrimental, events (March and Olsen, 1975) to those others. The following hypotheses are formulated:

Hypothesis 3a: The higher the level of trust in colleagues, the higher the level of heed.

Hypothesis 3b: The higher the level of trust in colleagues, the higher the level of heed, mediated by the perception of selfish behaviors of colleagues (that is an indirect effect).

Hypothesis 3c: The relations described in hypotheses 3a and 3b will be stronger in a network form than in a divisional form organization.

Hypothesis 4a: The higher the level of trust in managers, the higher the level of heed.

Hypothesis 4b: The higher the level of trust in managers, the higher the level of heed, mediated by the perception of selfish behaviors of colleagues (that is an indirect effect).

Hypothesis 4c: The relations described in hypotheses 4a and 4b will be stronger in a network form than in a divisional form organization.

Perceived Organizational Support, Trust and Selfish Behavior

A last matter included in the study is whether organizational factors can be found that promote trust and curb selfish behaviors, especially in network forms. Based on an exploration of the literature, perceived organizational support (POS) was included in the study to explore the effects of this most promising organizational factor, that von Krogh (1998) denominates as care. Von Krogh argues that care, broadly defined as 'serious attention, a feeling of concern and interest' is a key factor in shifting from 'self-commitment' to 'other-commitment'. Care builds trust, since it means helping others without the demand of immediate repayment. Besides mutual trust, behaviors furthered by care include active empathy, access to the help of others and lenience in judgment.

In accord with this notion, Creed and Miles (1996) argue that building a high level of trust in a network form is first and foremost dependent on management showing genuine attention to the wellbeing of organizational members. Bijlsma and van de Bunt (2002) found a strong relation between care and trust in managers. Furthermore, in a meta analysis of trust in leadership, Dirks and Ferrin (2002) found that POS is an important antecedent of trust in leadership. Therefore, POS was included in the study to measure care and genuine interest in organizational members. Since POS adds positively to what members receive, it can be expected that trust in managers is related to positive experiences of the leader–member exchange relation. It can be conjectured that POS will promote trust in colleagues as well, because if all team members that feel cared for and supported become other-directed, as von Krogh (1998) argues, the expectations of other's behavior will be positive and shared throughout the team, thus enhancing mutual trust. Three more hypotheses were thus formulated:

Hypothesis 5a: The higher the level of perceived organizational support, the higher the level of trust in colleagues.

Hypothesis 5b: The higher the level of perceived organizational support, the higher the level of trust in managers.

Hypothesis 5c: The higher the level of perceived organizational support, the weaker the perception of selfish behaviors of colleagues.

The combination of all hypotheses leads to the following structural equation model (see Figure 11.1: differences expected regarding the two forms of organization are not visualized).

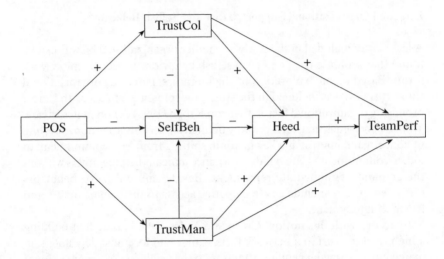

Note: + positive relation, – negative relation

Figure 11.1   Hypothesized structural equation model

RESEARCH DESIGN

The study was aimed at investigating the correlation structure of perceived organizational support, trust in managers, trust in colleagues, heedful and selfish behaviors, and performance of teams in two firms of two organizations, a professional bureaucracy (named Searchpro, a disguised name) and a professional network organization (named Netpro). The study, conducted in 2001, was part of a larger research project that focused on several modes of solidarity within firms. The firms are comparable regarding the type of employees, the nature of the tasks and the knowledge-intensive products delivered. In both firms the employees are highly qualified. They have a great deal of autonomy and, following Oliver's description, their work can be characterized as the work of professionals: 'transforming their commodity of expert knowledge and experience into the creation of knowledge-based products such as scientific papers and technological inventions' (1997, p. 228).

Interview and survey data were analysed to answer the research questions. First, the interview data (based on 27 interviews) and the literature were scanned for postulated relations between POS, trust in managers and colleagues, heedful interrelating and team performance. Second, a survey questionnaire was designed and administrated to a random stratified sample across five different departments at Searchpro. This resulted in a response of 48 per cent ($n = 97$). At Netpro all employees received a questionnaire. The response was 34 per cent ($n = 152$). Although the response, especially in the second organization, was moderate, the two samples showed an excellent representation of the different departments ($\chi^2 = 0.71$ and $\chi^2 = 0.78$, respectively; $p = 0.99$ in both cases). Reliability analyses were used to build the theoretical constructs on which the hypotheses were based. The variables were measured as multiple-item constructs, based on Likert scaling. The reliability of the scales fluctuates between 0.73 (for selfish behaviors) and 0.89 (for level of heed), ranging from satisfactory to good (see Appendix 11.1). Next, the relational hypotheses were combined to study paths of dependence and to compare the relative influence of trust in managers and trust in colleagues on team performance. Two structural equation models were designed to fit the data of each firm. The model fits were tested with a LISREL analysis (Jöreskog and Sörbom, 1989).

Case Description

Searchpro is a semi public research institute with a divisional form of organizing. It is a newer part of a larger organization, which was founded in 1930, with the aim of improving knowledge exchange between the academic world, government and companies. The firm, which can be typified as a professional bureaucracy, conducts applied research on health–labor relations in the commission of organizations in the public and private domain. Formerly, the firm depended almost entirely on assignments by the government for funding. In recent years it had to become more market-oriented in order to survive. The researchers are clustered into teams, called sectors, with a sector manager who is responsible for the quality and quantity of the sector output. They work on several projects simultaneously, most of the time in multi-disciplinary teams. Assessment of performance and feedback by management is individual-based, measured by the quality of output and the quantity of declarable hours delivered. In the interviews, it was reported that cooperation, exchanging knowledge and attentiveness to flaws in the team's processes are quite normal extra-role behaviors within the organization, which are promoted by managers as well. However, due to limited time resources, these relations are said to be restricted to a number of colleagues. Informal networks appeared to govern these relations and subsequent behaviors.

The second firm, Netpro, which offers web-related programs and ICT services to other firms, can be fully typified as a network organization. Netpro was founded in 1996 and has grown to 470 employees in 2001. Netpro is composed of 60 strongly autonomous mini-companies called business projects. The founders based the firm on the principles of self-management, autonomy and responsibility of employees. Employees are not assigned to pre-set functions. They are expected to form business teams with colleagues. These teams are expected to explore business opportunities in the market, make deals with clients and hire most new colleagues. The team decides on the allocation of roles, including the role of team manager, who acts as linking pin to the rest of the organization and monitors the internal processes.

Assessment of performance and feedback are partly team-based, partly individual-based. Each business project has its own account. If a team's business turns out not to be profitable in due time, the team is dissolved and team members must explore new business opportunities in another self-formed team. So, team members are strongly interdependent in realizing a profitable venture and in keeping the positive reputation that flows from membership of a successful team. The team also decides on how to spend or invest most of the profits made. Allocation of rewards, like salary raises and bonuses, is preferably based on the added value individuals contribute to the performance of the team. In the interviews, respondents, as in Searchpro, reported on cooperation, knowledge exchange and attentiveness to flaws in the team's processes. These behaviors were experienced as critical success factors regarding team performance. Unlike the Searchpro employees, however, Netpro employees, when talking about these extra-role behaviors, also mentioned the high degree of interdependence among team members to reach team goals. Members of successful teams reported high levels of these behaviors, members of unsuccessful teams reported sub-optimal levels.

RESULTS

Before analysing the correlation trust structure of Searchpro and Netpro, some similarities and dissimilarities of the two organizations are given. The demographic data mirror the clichés one can think of, describing a distinguished research organization and a young internet company. About 66 per cent of the employees in Searchpro are over 40 years old; 55 per cent of them have worked at least five years in this organization and 39 per cent even ten years or more. Netpro hosts a notably younger group of employees of which 78 per cent are below the age of 40, while 81 per cent of them have been employed by this company for less than three years. At Searchpro 41 per cent of the workers are female, while at Netpro this is no more than 15 per cent.

With respect to the five constructs (trust in managers and colleagues, perceived organizational support, and heedful and selfish behavior) and perceived team performance (see Table 11.1), quite sizeable differences between the two organizations were found. Only regarding selfish behavior no significant difference between the two organizations was found (η^2 = 0.002, F = 0.429; p = 0.513). Both companies employ rather autonomous knowledge workers who do not favor opportunistic behavior. For all other variables significant higher scores for Netpro were found. Employees at Netpro showed a more positive perception of the support that is provided by the organization (η^2 = 0.039, $F_{(1,247)}$ = 10.1; p = 0.002). Netpro employees also show more heedful behaviors (η^2 = 0.164, $F_{(1,247)}$ = 48.5; p < 0.001), put more trust in managers and in colleagues (η^2 = 0.059, $F_{(1,247)}$ = 15.6; p < 0.001, and η^2 = 0.0.122, $F_{(1,247)}$ = 34.6; p < 0.001, respectively), and report higher levels of team performance (η^2 = 0.0.039, $F_{(1,247)}$ = 10.1; p = 0.002).

Table 11.1 Differences between Searchpro and Netpro

	Mean Searchpro	Mean Netpro	F	p-value	partial η^2
Trust in managers	3.22 (0.90)	3.86 (0.77)	34.3	<0.001	0.122
Trust in colleagues	3.44 (0.69)	3.76 (0.57)	15.4	<0.001	0.059
Heed	3.41 (0.64)	3.95 (0.55)	48.5	<0.001	0.164
Perceived organizational support	3.08 (0.70)	3.63 (0.57)	46.5	<0.001	0.159
Selfish behavior	2.86 (0.72)	2.80 (0.64)	0.4	0.513	0.002
Perceived team performance	3.23 (0.67)	3.57 (0.93)	10.1	0.002	0.039

Notes: Mean scores of trust-related scales, standard deviations between brackets. All scales are positively formulated, except selfish behavior (scores between 1 and 5)

A Description of the Correlation Trust Structure of Searchpro and Netpro

For both organizations, the Pearson product moment correlations (ppmc) between the five trust-related variables and team performance are presented in Table 11.2. Most correlations are statistically significant. Remarkable, however, is that at Netpro and at Searchpro, team performance is differential related to trust. At Searchpro, team performance is only related to heed ($r = 0.20$; $p = 0.026$), whereas at Netpro, team performance is related to trust in managers ($r = 0.17$; $p = 0.017$), and heed ($r = 0.30$; $p < 0.001$).

However, simply examining the ppm correlations does not provide the knowledge and insights that are needed to make statements about differences between the two trust structures. A meta-analytical design, by comparing two correlations at the time, was used. In order to compensate for the number of tests (and therefore the number of false rejections), Holm's Sequential Bonferroni Method for multiple comparisons ($\alpha = 0.10$) was applied. For more details see Rosenthal (1984) and Cohen (1988). This analysis (see Table 11.2) showed that differences between Searchpro and Netpro are mainly due to differences in the relation between 'selfish behavior' and 'heed' (Searchpro, -0.57; Netpro, -0.23; $z = 3.07$, $p < 0.001$), 'trust in management' and 'heed' (Searchpro, 0.33; Netpro, 0.59; $z = 2.55$, $p = 0.003$), and 'trust in management' and 'trust in colleagues' (Searchpro, 0.48; Netpro, 0.18; $z = 2.57$, $p = 0.003$).

Table 11.2   The ppm correlations of the seven trust related concepts

	Heed	SelfBeh	TeamPerf	TrustCol	TrustMan	POS
Heed	1	**-0.57****	0.20*	0.45**	**0.33****	0.44**
SelfBeh	**-0.23****	1	0.02	-0.61**	-0.34**	-0.50**
TeamPerf	0.30**	-0.09	1	0.04	0.12	0.02
TrustCol	0.40**	-0.51**	0.09	1	**0.48****	0.73**
TrustMan	**0.59****	-0.08	0.17*	**0.18***	1	0.52**
POS	0.47**	-0.44**	0.07	0.55**	0.38**	1

Notes: ** $p < 0.01$, * $p < 0.05$
Searchpro: above diagonal; Netpro: below diagonal. Statistically significant differences are printed boldly

The Correlation Trust Structure of Searchpro and Netpro: a LISREL Analysis

Although Table 11.2 can be used in order to test most hypotheses on the surface, this is not the most favorable procedure. Therefore the correlation trust structures of Searchpro and Netpro have been analysed by means of LISREL. Figures 11.2 and Figure 11.3 show fitted models for Searchpro and Netpro, respectively. The fitted models only show 'paths' that, given the correlation trust structure, are statistically significant, that is, parameters that are at least twice as large as the corresponding standard errors (Jöreskog and Sörbom, 1989).

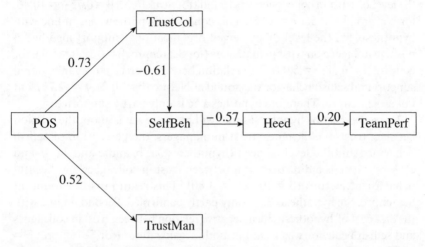

Notes: $\chi^2 = 12.12$, df $= 10$, $p = 0.28$ (model parameters are beta-coefficients)

Figure 11.2   Final LISREL model Searchpro

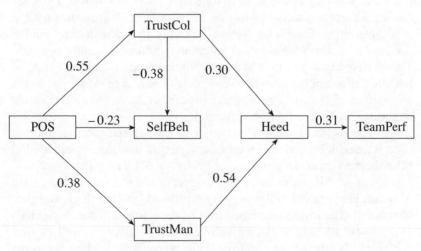

Notes: $\chi^2 = 7,32$, df $= 8$, $p = 0.50$ (model parameters are beta-coefficients)

Figure 11.3   Final LISREL model Netpro

   The examination of the two structural equation models will be based upon the postulated hypotheses. Since hypotheses 5a, b, and c do not assume a mediating effect, they will be discussed first. In both organizations a strong positive relation between the level of perceived organizational support and the level of trust in colleagues was found (for Searchpro: $\beta = 0.73$, $t = 10.46$; for Netpro: $\beta = 0.55$, $t = 8.16$). This conforms hypothesis 5a. In line with hypothesis 5b, the level of perceived organizational support also had a positive influence on trust in managers (for Searchpro: $\beta = 0.52$, $t = 5.93$; for Netpro: $\beta = 0.38$, $t = 5.09$). The relation between perceived organizational support and selfish behavior was found at Netpro ($\beta = -0.23$, $t = -2.79$), but not at Searchpro. Therefore hypothesis 5c is only partly supported.

   The second set of hypotheses that will be discussed is about the relation between trust in colleagues, trust in managers, the perception of selfish behaviors, and the level of heed (hypotheses 3a, b, and c and 4a, b, and c). First, there is a direct relation between trust in colleagues and heedful behavior at Netpro ($\beta = 0.30$, $t = 4.80$). This relation is not found at Searchpro. So, hypothesis 3a is only partly confirmed. Second, in line with the first part of hypothesis 3b, a negative relation between trust in colleagues and selfish behavior was found in both organizations (for Searchpro: $\beta = -0.61$, $t = -7.54$; for Netpro: $\beta = -0.38$, $t = -4.66$). Third, although it was hypothesized in the second part of hypothesis 3b, that the perception of selfish behaviors of colleagues has a negative bearing on heedful behavior, this effect was only found at Searchpro ($\beta = -0.57$, $t = -6.65$). Thus, for the larger part the analysis confirmed hypothesis 3b. Put together, trust in colleagues either directly (at Netpro) or indirectly (at Searchpro: via the perception of selfish behaviors of colleagues) influences heedful behavior. The observed indirect effect at Searchpro, in comparison to the sizes of the other effects in the Searchpro model, is of almost the same size as the direct effect at Netpro. This opposes hypothesis 3c, that the effect would be stronger at Netpro than at Searchpro.

   Hypothesis 4 is a somewhat different story. The only statistically significant effect is found at Netpro: the relation between trust in managers and heedful behavior is, as expected, positive ($\beta = 0.54$, $t = 8.62$). This partly confirmed hypothesis 4a. All other effects, either direct or indirect via the perception of selfish behaviors of colleagues, are not found (so hypothesis 4b is not confirmed). The results combined lead to the conclusion that hypothesis 4, except for the direct relation between trust in managers and heedful behavior at Netpro, is not confirmed. The perception of selfish behaviors of colleagues is not a mediating variable between trust in managers on the one hand, and heedful behavior on the other hand. Because of the only statistically significant effect at Netpro, hypothesis 4c is confirmed.

The final set of hypotheses (1a, b, and c, and 2a, b, and c), also assumes that there are direct and indirect effects from trust in colleagues and trust in managers on perceived team performance, and a difference in

Table 11.3 Summary of results in terms of the hypotheses

Hypotheses	Searchpro	Netpro
H1a: The higher the level of trust in colleagues, the higher the level of perceived team performance	–	–
H1b: The higher the level of trust in colleagues, the higher the level of perceived team performance, mediated by the level of heed (that is, an indirect effect).	–	+
H1c: The relations described in hypotheses 1a and 1b, will be stronger for a network form than a divisional form organization.	+	+
H2a: The higher the level of trust in managers, the higher the level of perceived team performance.	–	–
H2b: The higher the level of trust in managers, the higher the level of perceived team performance, mediated by the level of heed (that is, an indirect effect).	–	+
H2c: The relations described in hypotheses 2a and 2b will be stronger for a network form than a divisional form organization.	+	+
H3a: The higher the level of trust in colleagues, the higher the level of heed.	–	+
H3b: The higher the level of trust in colleagues, the higher the level of heed, mediated by the perception of selfish behaviors of colleagues (that is, an indirect effect).	+	–
H3c: The relations described in hypotheses 3a and 3b will be stronger for a network form than a divisional form organization.	–	–
H4a: The higher the level of trust in managers, the higher the level of heed.	–	+
H4b: The higher the level of trust in managers, the higher the level of heed, mediated by the perception of selfish behaviors of colleagues (that is, an indirect effect).	–	–
H4c: The relations described in hypotheses 4a and 4b will be stronger for a network form than a divisional form organization.	+	+
H5a: The higher the level of perceived organizational support, the higher the level of trust in colleagues	+	+
H5b: The higher the level of perceived organizational support, the higher the level of trust in managers	+	+
H5c: The higher the level of perceived organizational support, the less strong the perception of selfish behaviors of colleagues	–	+

Note: A '+' means that the corresponding hypothesis has been confirmed, whereas a '–' means that the corresponding hypothesis has not been confirmed strengths of the effects between the two organizations. In neither of the two organizations was a direct effect from trust in colleagues and trust in managers on perceived team performance found (so hypotheses 1a, and 2a are not confirmed). At Netpro, however, a positive relation between trust in colleagues and team performance, mediated by heed, has indeed been found ($\beta = 0.30 \times 0.31 = 0.09$, $t = 4.80$, and $t = 3.93$, respectively). At Searchpro, on the other hand, this relation is not observed. This partly confirms hypothesis 1b. Consequently, hypothesis 1c, which stated that the combined effect is stronger for Netpro than for Searchpro, is also confirmed. With respect to hypothesis 2b and c, similar conclusions can be drawn. At Netpro, trust in managers is positively related to team performance, mediated by heed ($\beta = 0.54 \times 0.31 = 0.17$, $t = 8.62$, and $t = 1.96$, respectively). So hypothesis 2b is partly confirmed, which automatically leads to confirmation of hypothesis 2c. Table 11.3 summarizes the results in terms of the hypotheses.

The combination of the above-described results suggests the following. In general terms the level of POS (the far left side of the structural equation model) is indirectly related to the level of heed and team performance (the far right side of the model). The two organizations differ, however, rather drastically. In both organizations, a higher level of organizational support results in higher levels of trust in both managers and colleagues. However, from this point on at Netpro two ways lead to a higher perceived team performance. Both trust in managers and trust in colleagues lead to more heedful behavior among colleagues, resulting in a higher perceived level of team performance. At Searchpro, on the other hand, trust in managers is a dead-end street. The level of trust in managers has no impact on either heedful behavior or perceived team performance. Also trust in colleagues is not directly related to heedful behavior. Only through the perception of selfish behaviors of colleagues, can heedful behavior and perceived team performance be reached. Thus, a higher level of trust in colleagues leads to a decrease of the perception of selfish behaviors of colleagues, which leads to more heedful behavior among colleagues, finally resulting in a higher perceived team performance. In other words, the management of Netpro has both more tools and a smaller distance to bridge in order to improve team performance, than the management of Searchpro has.

SUMMARY AND DISCUSSION

Summary

The aim of this study was to put some theoretical arguments about the distinct character of network organizations to an empirical test, including the argument of Creed and Miles (1996) that the trust requirements of network forms are higher than the trust requirements of other organizational forms. To this aim, two organizations, both employing professionals that perform knowledge-intensive tasks, were compared: Searchpro, an institute for applied research on health–labor relations, which can be typified as a professional bureaucracy, and Netpro, an e-business network organization. Apart from testing the validity of these arguments, the study aimed to contribute to the scholarly understanding of differential correlates of trust in colleagues and trust in managers by studying both types of trust simultaneously.

Based on open interviews with a sample of the organizational populations, and theoretical insights from the literature, a survey was developed, which contained several items regarding 'trust in managers', 'trust in colleagues', 'heed', 'perceived organizational support', 'selfish behavior', and a single item variable 'perceived team performance'. Reliability analyses confirmed all five multiple item variables.

The first research question was: *To what degree are trust in managers and trust in colleagues related to heedful behavior and team performance in both organizations? To what degree do a network form and a divisional form organization differ with respect to these relations?* The structural equation models (see Figures 11.2 and 11.3) showed that neither at Netpro nor at Searchpro were trust in managers and trust in colleagues directly related to perceived team performance. They also showed that at Netpro trust in managers and trust in colleagues are indeed related to the level of heedful interrelating. At Searchpro, however, no direct relation between trust and heedful interrelating was found.

The second research question was: *To what degree does heedful behavior mediate the relation between trust in managers and trust in colleagues, and performance? To what degree do a network form and a divisional form organization differ with respect to these relations?* The results differ extremely between the two organizations. At Searchpro no indirect effect between trust in managers and trust in colleagues on the one hand, and perceived team performance was found. At Netpro, however, both trust in managers and trust in colleagues are, via heed, positively related to perceived team performance. The higher the amount of trust put in colleagues (or managers), the higher the level of heed reported, the better the perceived team performance.

Almost similar but opposite results have been found with respect to the third research question: *To what degree does the perception of selfish behaviors of colleagues mediate the relation between trust in managers and trust in colleagues, and heedful behavior? To what degree do a network form and a divisional form organization differ with respect to these relations?* At Netpro no direct effect was found between the perception of selfish behaviors of colleagues and heedful behavior. This means that there is neither an indirect effect between trust in colleagues and trust in managers on the one hand, and heedful behavior on the other hand. At Searchpro the same conclusion can be drawn with respect to the indirect relation between trust in managers and heedful behavior. What was found, however, is that team performance is indeed achieved indirectly through perceived selfish behaviors of colleagues and heedful behavior. In other words, the more trust is put in colleagues, the less colleagues are perceived to show selfish behavior, the more heed.

The final research question was: *To what degree does perceived organizational support (POS) indirectly influence team performance through a positive effect on trust in managers and trust in colleagues, and through a negative effect on selfish behaviors? To what degree do a network form and a divisional form organization differ with respect to these relations?* In general, the analyses showed that in both organizations POS is positively related to trust in managers, and trust in colleagues. In both organizations the effect of POS on trust in colleagues is about one and a half times as strong as the effect of POS on trust in managers. At Netpro POS is also, though negatively, related to the perception of selfish behaviors of colleagues. Compared to the other two effects, this effect is the weakest. At Searchpro the latter relation was not found. At Searchpro the indirect relation between POS and perceived team performance was found to be a chain: an increase of POS leads to an increase of trust in colleagues; this leads to a decrease of perceived selfish behavior of colleagues, which results in an increase of heedful interrelating, and finally ends in an increase of the perceived team performance. At Netpro two chains, both shorter, lead from POS to perceived team performance: first, via trust in colleagues, heedful behavior to team performance, and second, via trust in managers, heedful behavior to team performance. Thus, perceived selfish behavior of colleagues is not part of either chain.

Discussion

By distinguishing between trust in horizontal and vertical relations, this study contributes to our understanding of the different effects of trust in managers and colleagues. Thanks to this distinction, differences between the firms' overall correlation structures appeared, that could not have been found by treating trust in an undifferentiated way, as most studies do. A striking difference between the two structural equation models is that at Netpro, trust in managers and trust in colleagues are directly related to the heedful behavior of colleagues. Since heed is strongly related to team performance, trust in managers and trust in colleagues appear to be important boosters of both these variables. In other words, at Netpro the perceived level of organizational support has, though not directly, a positive bearing on the level of heed, via the level of trust in managers and via trust in colleagues. At Searchpro, on the other hand, the level of trust in managers was not related to the level of heed, not even indirectly. These missing links between trust in managers and performance indicate that at Searchpro, trust in managers does not contribute much to the alignment of professional and organizational goals that in the view of Oliver (1997) is beneficial for both parties. In comparing both organizations, it can be concluded that the findings support Oliver's statement that 'trust-based networks have the potential to serve as important alternative governance mechanisms for regulating interactions and collaborations among professionals within organizational settings' (1997, p. 227).

Another difference found is that the effect of heed on team performance was slightly more prominent at Netpro than at Searchpro. At Searchpro the effect was relatively low, the lowest statistically significant parameter in the model ($t = 1.96$), whereas at Netpro the effect was somewhat more important ($t = 3.93$). These findings support the argument of Creed and Miles (1996) that trust is more of a critical success factor in network forms of organizing than in other forms.

A last difference is that at Searchpro selfish behavior of colleagues is a strongly negative function of the level of trust in colleagues, and a strong predictor of heedful behavior. At Netpro, selfish behavior is also a negative function of perceived organizational support, but has no relation with heedful behavior.

The differential parts that the two types of trust and selfish behaviors play in both organizations can be understood by the insights of von Krogh (1998) about modes of handling knowledge in high-care and low-care organizations. Although he discusses ideal types that will not be found in such pure forms, the Searchpro data disclose a significant lower level of care and significant lower levels of trust, heed and performance than the Netpro data. Although at Netpro, the higher care organization, the level of selfish behaviors of colleagues reported does not differ significantly from Searchpro, the model shows that these behaviors are without significant influence on heedful behavior and, consequently, team performance. Heedful behavior, which is displayed far more often at Netpro than at Searchpro, appears less a matter of individual choice in informal networks, as seems the case at Searchpro. These extra-role behaviors result from the POS, and trust in managers mainly, although POS through boosting trust in colleagues also furthers these behaviors. This explanation of the Netpro findings is, however, far from complete without considering the important part that the high level of interdependence and the reward system play in promoting trust, and heed. Only if their business project survives will the team survive, and only if the project thrives, will the team have the means to allocate individual rewards. Since extra-role behaviors are means to enhance the chance of success, and given the turbulent ICT market these projects must face, it is not surprising that team members willingly engage in mutual trust and heedful interrelating.

Limitations, Noted for Further Research

The findings of this study must be handled with caution because of the limitations of the study. First, only two organizations were compared, which is a very slim base for generalizing the conclusions to other organizations and other contexts. Second, the findings may be specific for professional–organization relations or for employees with knowledge-intensive tasks. The areas of relevance of professionals may differ from other kinds of employees. Referring to the study of de Gilder in this volume (Chapter 12), one can, for instance, wonder if contingent workers will respond differently to the organizational factors that seem to boost heed and performance. More research in other organizations and other contexts is needed to be able to generalize confidently on the findings presented in this chapter.

Several theoretical matters discussed in this study ask for further studies, besides related questions that can be raised. First, the influence of the phase of development of the organization on heed: Weick and Roberts (1993) suggest that heed is more often found in young firms or teams than in mature firms. Since Searchpro is an older firm and Netpro a young one, the age factor may have influenced our findings. Second, the role of the team manager in promoting heed needs exploring. In this exploration the mode of connectedness within teams may be included. Does the team manager function as a 'spider in the web' or do all members connect directly to all others? At Netpro this may explain differences between successful teams and less successful ones.

A third matter that deserves further attention is how heedful interrelating can be promoted, given the mediating role of heed in the trust–performance relation. Besides perceived organizational support and the reward structure, other organizational factors may surface as promoting heed, directly or indirectly. A factor that may play a part is that formation of business projects is left entirely to the initiative of employees. This may give rise to the fear of getting excluded from one project or another. Individuals that do not succeed in forming a team with others, for instance after membership of a unsuccessful team, do face the problem of exclusion relentlessly. Alternatively, those who are included in a project may show high levels of heed to keep project failure and the subsequent problem of exclusion at arm's length. Further research, however, may end up with the paradoxical finding that the risk of exclusion is a prime factor in promoting the inclusion of all in thinking and acting within a team.

REFERENCES

Bijlsma-Frankema, K.M. (2001), 'Enabling organizational learning and trust in top management', Paper presented at the EIASM workshop 'Trust within and between organizations', Amsterdam, November 29–30.

Bijlsma-Frankema, K.M. and G.G. van de Bunt (2002), 'In search of parsimony, A multiple triangulation approach to antecedents of trust in managers', *Research Methods Forum* 7, http://aom.pace.edu/rmd/2002forum.html

Bogenrieder, I. and B. Nooteboom (2004), 'Learning groups: what types are there? A theoretical analysis and an empirical study in a consultancy firm', *Organization Studies*, **25** (2), 287–313.

Boisot, M.H. (1995), *Information Space: A framework for learning in organizations, institutions and culture*, London: Routledge.

Bradach, J.L. and R.G. Eccles (1989), 'Price, authority, and trust: from ideal types to plural forms', *Annual Review of Sociology*, 15, 97–118.

Brown, J.S. and P. Duguid (1998), 'Organizing knowledge', *California Management Review*, **40** (3), 90–112

Cohen, J. (1988), *Statistical Power Analysis for the Behavioral Sciences* (2nd edn), Hillsdale, NJ: Erlbaum.

Connell, J., N. Ferres and T. Travaglione (2003), 'Engendering trust in manager–subordinate relationships; predictors and outcomes', *Personnel Review*, **32** (5), 569–88.

Costa, A.C., R.A. Roe and T. Taillieu (2001), 'Trust within teams, the relation with performance effectiveness', *European Journal of Work and Organisational Psychology*, **10** (3), 225–44.

Creed, W.E.D. and R.E. Miles (1996), 'Trust in organizations, a conceptual framework', in R.M. Kramer and T.R. Tyler (eds), *Trust in Organizations: Frontiers of theory and research*, London: Sage, pp. 16–39.

Currall, S.C. and T.H. Judge (1995), 'Measuring trust between organizational boundary role persons', *Organizational Behavior and Human Decision Process*, **64** (2), 151–70.

Dasgupta, P. (1988), 'Trust as a commodity', in D. Gambetta (ed.), *Trust: Making and breaking cooperative relations*, Oxford, UK: Basil Blackwell, pp. 49–72.

Dirks, K.T. (1999), 'The effect of interpersonal trust on work group performance', *Journal of Applied Psychology*, **84** (3), 445–55.

Dirks, K.T. and D.L. Ferrin (2002), 'The role of trust in organizational settings', *Organization Science*, **12** (4), 450–67.

Dodgson, M. (1993), 'Learning, trust and technological collaboration', *Human Relations*, **46** (1), 77–96.

Durkheim, E. (1893), *De la division du travail social: étude sur l'organisation des sociétés supérieures*, Paris: Alcan. [Translation, 1933.]

Gambetta, D. (1988), 'Can we trust trust?' in D. Gambetta (ed.), *Trust: Making and breaking cooperative relations*, Oxford, UK: Basil Blackwell, pp. 213–37.

Garfinkel, H. (1967), *Studies in Ethnomethodology*, Englewood Cliffs, NJ: Prentice Hall.

Gouldner, A.W. (1960), 'The norm of reciprocity: a preliminary statement', *American Sociological Review*, **25** (2), 161–78.

Janowicz, M. and N. Noorderhaven (2002), 'The role of trust in interorganisational learning in joint ventures', Paper, presented at the European Academy of Management Conference (Euram), May 8–10, Stockholm, Sweden.

Jöreskog, G. and Sörbom, D. (1989), *Lisrel 7: A guide to the program and applications*, Chicago: SPSS Inc.

Kramer, R.M. (1996), 'Divergent realities and convergent disappointments in the hierarchical relation, trust and the intuitive auditor at work', in R.M. Kramer and T.R. Tyler (eds), *Trust in organizations: Frontiers of theory and research*, London: Sage, pp. 216–46.

Kramer, R.M., M.B. Brewer and B.A. Hanna (1996), 'Collective trust and collective action. The decision to trust as a social decision', in R.M. Kramer and T.R. Tyler (eds), *Trust in Organizations: frontiers of theory and research*, Thousand Oaks, CA: Sage Publications Inc.

Krogh, G. von (1998), 'Care in knowledge creation', *California Management Review*, **40** (3), 133–54.

Lewis, J.D. and A. Weigert (1985), 'Trust as social reality', *Social Forces*, 63, 67–85.

Luhmann, N. (1979), *Trust and Power*, Chichester: John Wiley.

Luhmann, N. (1988), 'Familiarity, confidence and trust, problems and alternatives', in D. Gambetta (ed.), *Trust: Making and breaking cooperative relations*, Oxford, UK: Basil Blackwell, 213–37.

March, J. and J. Olsen (1975), 'The uncertainty of the past, organizational learning under ambiguity', *European Journal of Political Research*, **3** (2), 149–71.

Miles, R.E. and C.C. Snow (1994), *Fit, Failure and the Hall of Fame*, New York: Free Press.

Nonaka, I. and N. Konno (1998), 'The concept of "ba": building a foundation for knowledge creation', *California Management Review*, **40** (3), 40–55.

Nonaka, I. and H. Takeuchi, H. (1995), *The Knowledge-Creating Company*, New York: Oxford University Press.

Oliver, A.L. (1997), 'On the nexus of organizations and professions: networking through trust', *Sociological Inquiry*, **67** (2), 227–45.

Ouchi, W.G. (1979), 'A conceptual framework for the design of organizational control mechanisms', *Management Science*, **25** (9), 833–48.

Powell, W.W. (1990), 'Neither market nor hierarchy: network forms of organization', in B.M. Staw and L.L. Cummings (eds), *Research in Organizational Behavior*, Vol. 12, Greenwich: JAI Press, pp. 295–326.

Powell, W.W. (1996), 'Trust-based forms of governance', in R.M. Kramer and T.R. Tyler (eds), *Trust in Organisations: Frontiers of theory and research*, London: Sage, pp. 51–68.

Rosenthal, R. (1984), *Meta-Analytical Procedures for Social Research*, Applied Social Research Methods Series, 6, Beverly Hills, California: Sage Publications Inc.

Sheppard, B. and M. Tuschinsky (1996), 'Micro-OB and the network organization', in R.M. Kramer and T.R. Tyler (eds), *Trust in Organizations: Frontiers of theory and research,* London: Sage, pp. 140–66.

Simmel, G. (1950), *The Sociology of Georg Simmel*, New York: Free Press [German Original 1908].

Smith, J.B. and W.B. Barclay (1997), 'The effects of organizational differences and trust on the effectiveness of selling partner relationships', *Journal of Marketing*, **61** (3), 3–21.

Weick, K.E. (1995), *Sensemaking in Organizations*, London: Sage.

Weick, K.E. and K.H. Roberts (1993), 'Collective mind in organizations: heedful interrelating on flight decks', *Administrative Science Quarterly*, **38** (3), 357–82.

Zucker, L. (1986), 'Production of trust: institutional sources of economic structure', *Research in Organizational Behavior*, **6**, 53–111.

APPENDIX 11.1

Table 11A.1   Reliability of the trust-related scales

Name of scale: description (number of items)	Cronbach's Alpha
TrustMan: trust in managers (4)	0.88
Ex. 'My manager promotes mutual cooperation and team building.'	
TrustCol: trust in colleagues (5)	0.76
Ex. 'You have to take care of what you can tell to certain people in your working environment.'	
Heed: level of heed (10)	0.89
Ex. 'I feel free to criticize my colleagues in a constructive way.'	
POS: perceived organizational support (7)	0.84
Ex. 'The organization is genuinely interested in my wellbeing.'	
SelfBeh: selfish behavior (6)	0.73
Ex. 'Too many people join in here at the expense of other people's efforts.'	
TeamPerf: perceived team performance (single item)	

Note: Between brackets is the number of items on which the resulting scale is based. An example is given of each scale

12. Trust and contingent work: a research agenda

Dick de Gilder

INTRODUCTION

The studying of – and theorizing on – trust in organizational settings has taken flight in the past decade (for an overview, see Kramer and Tyler, 1996; Dirks and Ferrin, 2002). Clearly, there is a shared idea by social scientists that trust plays an important role in organizational life, that trust can be managed by organizations, that it could (or should?) be part of the human resource policies of organizations.

This idea is supported by a considerable number of studies directed at establishing the importance of trust in organizations. Particularly in the field of leadership, the antecedents and consequences of trust have been well documented. A meta-analysis (Dirks and Ferrin, 2002) has shown that trust in leadership is strongly related to correlates or antecedents such as leadership styles, different justice perceptions and perceived organizational support. Furthermore, trust in leadership appears to be strongly related to hypothesized outcomes, such as organizational commitment, job satisfaction and intent to quit, and less strongly, but significantly, related to organizational citizenship behavior (see Organ, 1988) and job performance. The meta-analysis on 106 independent samples thus yields the strongest support so far for the relevance of the concept of trust, although a critical discussion demonstrates the need for further research and the refining of the trust concept (Dirks and Ferrin, 2002).

An important potential limitation of much of the research performed so far, is that the settings that are studied seem to be dominated by samples that are relatively homogeneous. The starting point seems to be that there is a more or less stable relationship between the employer and the employee, or at least that such a stable relationship may emerge over time. However, a sizable part of the workforce does not have the perspective of a long-lasting relationship with their employers, such as contract workers, contingent workers and other types of temporary employees (see McLean Parks et al., 1998).

Although there are substantial differences among countries with regard to the size of the contingent workforce, the general observation is that the number of people with some sort of temporary contract has increased over the years (see for example Hartley, 1995; McLean Parks et al., 1998). Given these changes on the labor market, it seems worthwhile to investigate whether theory and findings on trust can be generalized to the contingent workforce. Although the amount of research on the effects of different job contracts is modest, theories on differences among categories of workers typically suggest that these may be substantial (Feldman, 1990; McLean Parks et al., 1998; van Dyne and Ang, 1998). It could be argued that the emergence of trust, and the effects of trust, also are not necessarily equal for all groups of employees. For instance, will two individuals, one with a permanent contract and one with a six-month contract without a prospect of a permanent contract, who start on the same job, have the same perspective of whom and what they should trust? The permanent worker may focus on the training opportunities that have been promised in the job interview. The contract worker, for whom training opportunities are unlikely as organizations are generally unwilling to invest in people who will leave the organization, may focus on the exact pay that has been promised and his/her relative pay in comparison to his/her colleague with the permanent contract.

This simple example raises the question whether the meaning of trust is the same for different categories of employees, or whether it is essentially different. In this chapter, I will elaborate on the relevance of the type of job contract for the emergence and consequences of trust in organizational settings. I will then present data on the potentially differential importance of trust for workers who have different job contracts. As these data should be regarded as a step towards a more extensive study on this topic, I will conclude this chapter by suggesting a research agenda for the study of trust among different categories of workers.

CONTINGENT WORK AND THE PSYCHOLOGICAL CONTRACT

The relationship between contingent workers and their employers is generally considered as transactional in nature (McLean Parks and Kidder, 1994). People do a task for a limited time, get paid for it, and leave the organization. It is exchange-based, very much like Taylor's ideas about the 'economic man' (Taylor, 1911). However, in the second half of the 20th century people in most developed economies had become used to a stronger relationship between them and the organization they were working for. People were typically working full-time, holding permanent and often life-time jobs: they had become 'organization men' (Whyte, 1960). Influenced by the human relations movement, both employers and employees became more interdependent. Gradually, a psychological or relational contract emerged, based on usually implicit expectations and beliefs about the mutual obligations of the parties involved (Rousseau, 1995).

The differences between transactional contracts and psychological contracts often may be less sharp than described above. The length of the contract, for instance, may affect the degree to which an individual contract worker perceives his/her contract as purely transactional. In a one-year contract, the sense of mutual obligations may be more developed than in a contract for one month. Furthermore, not all permanently employed workers will experience a psychological contract with their employer, as they also may define their relationship with their employer mainly as transactional. Given these qualifications, it becomes clear that the type of contract cannot be regarded as a static, objective element of the situation, but that it has a meaning to the perceiver of the situation. The evaluation of the contract one has is essentially a belief or perception by the individual in an employer–employee relationship, that may change as a consequence of his/her experiences with the other party (see Rousseau and Tijoriwala, 1998).

Although the contract an individual has, the situation s/he is in, will be defined for an important part by his or her perceptions of that situation, it does not mean that there are no systematic differences in these perceptions among groups of people that are employed under different contracts. That is, despite individual differences among people that may yield positive evaluations of the psychological contract by some contract workers, and negative evaluations by some permanent workers, having identical jobs in the same organization, there may be differences between contract workers and permanent workers that can be attributed solely to the differences in the objective contracts.

Despite the significant increase in contingent work (see for example Hartley, 1995; McLean Parks et al., 1998), there has been relatively little theoretical and empirical work set to understand the consequences of the changes in the organizations' workforce on job attitudes and work behavior (van Dyne and Ang, 1998) in general, let alone on trust. Looking at the empirical evidence on the effects of job status on job attitudes and performance on the job, the only conclusion one may draw is that the results are inconclusive. In some studies contingent workers show less favorable attitudes and poorer job performance than core employees (for example van

Dyne and Ang, 1998), whereas no effects of job status were found in others (for example, Pearce, 1993). In the results of the study I present below, the role of trust for contingent and core workers will be explored.

EVALUATING THE CONTRACT: JUSTICE AND TRUST

Given that trust and justice are related concepts and are often rather highly correlated (see Dirks and Ferrin, 2002), it is necessary to try to disentangle the concepts with regard to the role they might play in the comparison between contingent and core workers.

With regard to the consequences of contingent work for workers, the literature is diverse. Some researchers are outrightly negative about contingent work, suggesting it has grave consequences for contingent workers at the lower end of the job market, who have low job security and few chances for advancement (McLean Parks and Kidder, 1994; Rogers, 1995; Kalleberg et al., 2000). They generally argue that workers, in exchange for their poor treatment by the employers, are likely to have unfavorable job attitudes and to perform poorly in comparison to workers with a permanent contract. Other researchers contend that contingent employees are valuable resources to the organization who may contribute to innovation and the higher effectiveness of the organization (for example, Lepak and Snell, 1999).

The seemingly contradictory results of studies on the effects of job status reveal some problems in the literature. First, the concept of job status is much more complex than might be expected on the face of it. Contingent workers may differ from core employees in many other ways than in job status alone. Often it is difficult to compare employees with different job status, because the tasks both groups perform have a different content. Frequently, certain types of jobs, predominantly jobs requiring few skills and with relatively unfavorable task characteristics, are only performed by contingent workers and not by core employees (McLean Parks et al., 1998). Sometimes both groups of employees carry the same job title (for example, nurses), but still contingent workers may be given fewer responsibilities. Given the wide body of research indicating that task characteristics have a strong influence on job attitudes and job behavior (Hackman and Oldham, 1980; Mathieu and Zajac, 1990), differences in job content between employees differing in job status may by itself explain differences in outcome variables. This shows the necessity of studying samples in which comparisons between groups with different job status do not suffer from these flaws, something that will be done in the study presented here.

Perhaps as a consequence of this problem, there is little agreement on the process that describes the way job status affects job behaviors. However, there are some attempts to identify crucial variables that might intervene between job status and job behaviors. At a general level, apparently all contributions on contingent work emphasize the difference in the relationship between the employer and the different categories of employees. It is generally argued that it is much more difficult for contingent workers to establish a relationship with the employer and (temporary) colleagues than it is for core employees (for example, Beard and Edwards, 1995). An interesting line of work has been initiated by some authors (McLean Parks and Kidder, 1994; Guest, 1998) who incorporate a social justice perspective in the explanation of differences in job attitudes and job behaviors. In doing so, McLean Parks and Kidder (1994) use the well-known distinction between distributive justice and procedural justice. Distributive justice is 'the perceived fairness of the outcomes or allocations that an individual receives' (Folger and Cropanzano, 1998, p. xxi). Procedural justice 'refers to fairness issues concerning the methods, mechanisms, and processes used to determine outcomes' (Folger and Cropanzano, 1998, p. 26). As stated above, there is general agreement that the outcomes of contingent workers are usually worse than those of core employees.

McLean Parks and Kidder (1998) argue that procedural justice is more likely to be relevant to people who have a long-term relationship than to people who know the relationship will be short-lived and have a predominantly transactional character. They assume that, for contingent workers, it is difficult to build a relationship with the employer, since the contract essentially is of limited duration. They argue that contingent workers tend to focus on distributive justice when they decide how they will behave at work. If they evaluate the distribution of outcomes as just, they will show constructive behavior towards the organization. If the outcome is negative, they might display various levels of destructive behavior, ranging from negligence and shirking to even inflicting overt damage to the organization. For core employees, distributive justice is not irrelevant, but they have procedural justice considerations as well. As they do have a relationship with the organization, they might have more elaborate ideas about the organization's policies and will consider them more when preparing their behavioral response. Although there are, as yet, no data supporting these ideas, it seems to be worthwhile to explore whether the process leading from job status to behavior may be different for contingent and core employees. This exploration will take place in the study presented here.

Although justice research might give an interesting angle to study the effects of job status, a relatively recent line of theory and research emphasizes the role of trust in organizations (for an overview, see Kramer and Tyler, 1996). As with regard to justice, the relationship between employees and management is also highly relevant for the development of trust in organizations. Although there are several definitions of trust, an adequate definition is 'a state involving confident expectations about another's motives with respect to oneself in situations entailing risk' (Boon and Holmes, 1991, p. 194). Given that trust is associated both with justice considerations and with job attitudes and job behavior (for example Guest, 1998; Dirks and Ferrin, 2002), it should also be considered as a possible consequence of job status. In this respect, the crucial words in the above definition are 'confident expectations'. As in other definitions, trust is seen as a state that can be built by experiences. In an interesting analysis, Lewicki and Benedict Bunker (1996) propose that there may be different stages in the development of trust between individuals who are unfamiliar to each other. They call the first stage calculus-based trust, a stage in which the parties scrutinize each other's behavior in order to find out what the other expects. Because at this stage there is little knowledge about the other's trustworthiness, that is, there are no 'confident expectations', few negative or uninterpretable events need happen to disrupt beginning trust. The second stage is more stable, where knowledge-based trust is involved and where the other's behavior can be anticipated. This knowledge base develops from prolonged interaction between the parties and trust cannot be easily disrupted by minor incidents. The third stage is called 'identification-based', where the interactants identify with each other's intentions and have developed complete mutual understanding.

It can be assumed that it will be more difficult for contingent workers to develop trust towards their employer, because they usually don't have such an extensive knowledge base as core employees have. Furthermore, there is always some threat they will be dismissed, as contingent workers are usually the first employees to be laid off or replaced. In the framework of Lewicki and Benedict Bunker (1996), one would expect that trust by contingent workers be calculus-based. Accordingly, it can be expected that contingent workers' trust towards the employer is low relative to that of core employees (de Gilder, 2003).

The role of trust is investigated in three steps. First, mean differences between contingent and core workers are determined for trust, justice and several attitudes and behaviors that will be presented below. Second, a correlational analysis shows the strength of the relations between trust and the other variables in this study. Third, a correlational analysis is presented for the contingent and core workers separately, to find out whether the importance of trust depends on job status.

OTHER DEPENDENT VARIABLES: COMMITMENT AND BEHAVIORS

In research on effects of job status and research on organizational justice, several attitudinal and behavioral variables are measured as dependent variables. In this study, such variables are included to establish the role of trust as a potential correlate of attitudes and as a determinant of job behaviors.

There is a wide body of research on determinants and outcomes of affective organizational commitment (Mathieu and Zajac, 1990), the extent to which people experience a sense of identification and involvement with an organization (compare Allen and Meyer, 1990). Affective commitment is related to several behaviors, most notably the intention to leave the organization and to search for job alternatives, but also to turnover and job performance (Mathieu and Zajac, 1990).

In the different definitions of affective commitment to the organization, it is always assumed that the worker has a more or less permanent relationship with the organization, where the decision to stay in – or leave – the organization is made by the employee (for example, Mowday et al., 1979). For contingent workers this is not the case. It may therefore be expected that the level of affective commitment will generally be lower for contingent workers than for core employees. Consequently, it can also be expected that contingent workers show relatively less constructive behavior (for example, job performance) and more destructive behavior (for example, turnover). In the study by van Dyne and Ang (1998), contingent workers actually displayed lower organizational commitment.

In this study, commitment to the team is also included, as a specific measure may be a better predictor of job behavior than a general one (Ellemers et al., 1998; Mathieu and Zajac, 1990). Finally, continuance commitment was measured in this study. Continuance commitment refers to the costs associated with leaving the organization. People who think high costs are involved (finding another job, moving to another city) are less likely to leave the organization. Given that contingent workers know their position is temporary, they are more likely to be aware of the need to search for job alternatives, which implies they are likely to have lower continuance commitment.

Several job behaviors were included in this study. A general type of behavior that is frequently associated with the effects of the relationship between employee and employer is organizational citizenship behavior (OCB). OCB can be defined as behavior that is constructive, but that is not part of the formal job description of the employee (Organ, 1988), for instance, helping a colleague, volunteering to do extra chores, showing enthusiasm.

Extensive research has demonstrated the worth of OCB for organizational effectiveness (for example Podsakoff and MacKenzie, 1997).

Other types of behavior have a more specific nature. Hirschmann (1970) proposed that important behaviors of employees in organizations are *exit*, which refers to turnover intentions, and *voice*, referring to the active and constructive efforts to improve the situation at work. *Loyalty* is a passive but positive behavioral style, such that loyal employees remain positive about the organization under all circumstances and wait passively until the effects of negative events are extinguished. Later, *neglect* was recognized as potentially important behavior (Rusbult et al., 1988), referring to people silently allowing that things get worse in the organization, for instance by showing up late and by spending little effort. Exit and voice are considered active behaviors, whereas loyalty and neglect are passive behaviors. Voice and loyalty are seen as constructive behaviors, while exit and neglect are destructive behaviors (Rusbult et al., 1988). It is expected that contingent workers show less constructive behaviors (voice, loyalty, OCB) and more destructive behaviors (exit, neglect, labor market activity) than do core employees.

For the correlational analyses, it may be expected that trust will be correlated to several other dependent measures in a similar way as in the meta-analytical findings by Dirks and Ferrin (2002). Trust is likely to be positively correlated to justice, affective commitment and positive behaviors, and negatively to negative behaviors. It is more difficult to make explicit predictions for the correlational analyses on the data for contingent and core workers separately, as there are no theoretical foundations available for such an exercise. These analyses will therefore be exploratory.

METHOD

Procedure

Data for this study were collected from workers at two hotels that were part of an international hotel chain. The jobs of the workers were all service-related in the hotels' bar, restaurant, reception and catering. Importantly, contingent workers had identical jobs to core employees.

Survey data were collected from workers and an evaluation of their OCB by their supervisors. Questionnaires were personally handed over to the workers, in order to make sure the number of questionnaires were evenly distributed among core employees and contingent workers. All surveys were completed during working hours. Respondents were guaranteed their data would remain confidential.

Data were collected from 64 employees, 33 from contingent workers, 31 from core employees. In order to avoid common method variance, data on OCB were not collected using employee surveys. Supervisors were asked to fill out a 6-item OCB questionnaire for each of their employees who had returned their questionnaire. All employees were asked to write down their name on the questionnaire, to be able to relate the questionnaire data to the OCB measurement.

Men and women were roughly equally represented among the respondents (55 per cent men, 45 per cent women), which is representative for the organization. The mean age was 26.9 years for the core employees and 22.4 years for the contingent employees. Many of the contingent workers (26) were engaged in some sort of education, besides working in the hotel. Hourly pay and gratuities were somewhat lower for the contingent workers and core employees had better fringe benefits. Age differences and differences in fringe benefits between core and contingent workers are rather typical (for example, Nollen and Axel, 1996).

Questionnaire

Almost all items were of the Likert scale type. Respondents were instructed to indicate their agreement with a series of statements, using 5-point scales (1 = strongly disagree, 5 = strongly agree). These statements were presented in random order. To measure the affective and continuance commitment, items (five and four items, respectively) were taken from the Dutch translation (de Gilder et al., 1997) of the Allen and Meyer (1990) scales. Sample items are 'I feel emotionally attached to this organization' (affective commitment) and 'I feel I have too few alternatives at the moment to quit my job'. Items measuring team commitment (7 items) were taken from the scale developed by Ellemers et al. (1998). A sample item is 'I try to invest effort into a good atmosphere in my team' (team commitment).

Items measuring distributive justice (5 items), procedural justice and trust (4 items in each scale) were pretested by the author and had previously shown satisfactory reliabilities. Sample items are 'Given the responsibilities I carry, the pay I receive is fair' (distributive justice); 'The way my job performance is evaluated, is fair' (procedural justice); 'I know I can trust my employer completely' (trust).

Items measuring exit, voice, loyalty and neglect were adapted from the work of Rusbult et al. (1988). Sample items are 'I would rather work elsewhere than in this hotel' (exit); 'I have ideas about changing the feedback system and I would like to help implementing the changes' (voice); 'I intend to say positive things about this organization, even if others are criticizing it' (loyalty); 'I might report sick if I don't feel like working' (neglect).

As exit is an intention and actual turnover could not be measured in this case study, a measure of labor market activity was included, which is closer to actual behavior. The labor market activity scale consists of four dichotomous items, measuring whether or not the respondents had, in the past six months, (a) read personnel ads, (b) had an internal career interview, (c) applied for a job outside of the organization, (d) informally received information on career opportunities elsewhere. All scales yielded satisfactory reliabilities, with Cronbach alphas ranging from 0.64 to 0.92.

RESULTS

In a first analysis, the effects of job status on the dependent variables were determined by conducting t-tests (see Table 12.1). For trust and justice, the results were not in line with our expectations. Trust and procedural justice are equal for the two groups of employees but, surprisingly, contingent workers judge their distributive outcomes as more just than the core employees do, despite seemingly objectively less favorable conditions.

The other variables show marked differences between contingent and core workers. Contingent workers' team commitment and organizational commitment are substantially lower in comparison to the core

Table 12.1   T-test results for the effect of job status on the dependent variables

	Core employees	Contingent workers	t-value	df	p (one-tailed)
Trust	3.19	3.11	0.20	60	n.s.
Distributive justice	2.45	2.93	−2.29	61	0.05
Procedural justice	2.82	2.86	−0.23	61	n.s.
Team commitment	4.07	3.47	3.24	61	0.01
Organizational commitment	3.53	2.91	3.78	59	0.01
Continuance commitment	2.77	2.50	1.25	59	0.10
Exit	2.92	3.61	−2.70	61	0.01
Voice	3.38	3.02	2.04	61	0.05
Loyalty	3.05	2.67	1.91	61	0.05
Neglect	1.67	2.38	−2.94	61	0.01
Labor market activity*	0.41	0.60	−2.07	61	0.05
OCB (Supervisor rating)	3.91	3.49	2.41	56	0.01

Note: * the scale labor market activity runs from 0 to 3

employees, and there is a similar, but marginally significant result for continuance commitment.

With regard to the behavioral measures, the contingent workers show less positive behaviors and more negative behaviors towards the organization than core employees do. That is, contingent workers display relatively less voice and loyalty, and more exit, labor market activity and neglect. In line with these results, supervisors also evaluated the behavior of the contingent workers more negatively: in their opinion, contingent workers displayed less OCB than did core employees.

Correlational Analyses

As can be observed in Table 12.2, there are a number of significant correlations between trust and the other attitudinal and behavioral variables for the overall sample. As expected, trust is correlated positively to the commitment and justice variables. Furthermore, trust is positively correlated to positive behaviors such as loyalty and OCB, but the correlation with voice is not significant. Trust is clearly negatively correlated with the negative behaviors, exit and neglect. Thus, the expectations about the role of trust for the organization as a whole were corroborated. The correlations are substantial, indicating that trust is a relevant variable in this context. In a comparison of the relative strength of the correlations in the table, trust shows somewhat higher correlations with most behavioral outcomes than the justice measures. The correlations between the justice variables and the behaviors are relatively weak. The only significant correlations are between distributive justice and labor market activity, and between procedural justice and exit, although the correlation with OCB approaches significance.

However, an interesting result is that team commitment tends to be even somewhat higher correlated to the behavioral measures than trust. Team commitment also is generally more strongly correlated to the behavioral measures than is organizational commitment, which is in line with results reported in Ellemers et al. (1998). Employees who are highly committed, show less destructive behaviors (exit and neglect) and more constructive behaviors (voice, loyalty, OCB).

Exploratory Correlational Analyses

An important goal of this study was to explore whether trust plays a different role for contingent workers in comparison to core workers. For this purpose, separate correlation tables are made for the two groups of workers. Table 12.3 shows the correlation table for core employees only, whereas Table 12.4 shows the results for contingent employees. When the results are

Table 12.2 Correlations among the dependent variables

	1	2	3	4	5	6	7	8	9	10	11	12
1. Trust	(0.82)											
2. Team commitment	0.35	(0.87)										
3. Organizational commitment	0.33	0.53	(0.76)									
4. Continuance commitment	0.26	0.23	0.40	(0.68)								
5. Distributive justice	0.41	-0.10	-0.16	0.18	(0.88)							
6. Procedural justice	0.58	0.00	0.10	0.11	0.42	(0.64)						
7. Exit	-0.56	-0.63	-0.44	-0.22	-0.05	-0.26	(0.80)					
8. Voice	-0.16	0.32	0.25	0.28	-0.20	-0.19	-0.09	(0.77)				
9. Loyalty	0.50	0.63	0.41	0.44	0.12	0.21	-0.72	0.16	(0.67)			
10. Neglect	-0.35	-0.65	-0.29	-0.12	-0.02	-0.04	0.54	0.00	-0.45	(0.89)		
11. Labor market activity*	-0.17	-0.19	-0.12	-0.35	-0.35	-0.14	0.37	0.01	-0.36	0.28	(0.68)	
12. OCB	0.27	0.37	0.35	0.24	-0.13	0.22	-0.42	0.07	0.34	-0.47	-0.24	(0.86)

Note: Correlations higher than $r = 0.25$ are significant at the $p < 0.05$ level (two-sided)
Reliabilities (alpha coefficients) are reported in parentheses along the diagonal

Table 12.3   Correlations among the dependent variables for core employees

	1	2	3	4	5	6	7	8	9	10	11	12
1. Trust												
2. Team commitment	0.44											
3. Organizational commitment	0.52	0.42										
4. Continuance commitment	0.19	0.02	0.41									
5. Distributive justice	0.52	0.07	0.15	0.12								
6. Procedural justice	0.68	0.00	0.13	0.14	0.44							
7. Exit	-0.58	-0.49	-0.44	0.01	-0.18	-0.43						
8. Voice	-0.23	0.06	-0.27	0.03	-0.06	-0.21	0.24					
9. Loyalty	0.55	0.50	0.44	0.16	0.42	0.29	-0.70	-0.06				
10. Neglect	-0.42	-0.63	-0.40	-0.29	-0.05	-0.20	0.48	0.30	-0.39			
11. Labor market activity*	-0.33	-0.10	-0.14	0.15	-0.36	-0.37	0.58	0.09	-0.64	0.21		
12. OCB	0.42	0.05	0.19	-0.15	0.18	0.36	-0.36	-0.23	0.28	-0.17	-0.40	

Table 12.4 Correlations among the dependent variables for contingent workers

	1	2	3	4	5	6	7	8	9	10	11	12
1. Trust												
2. Team commitment	0.30											
3. Organizational commitment	0.14	0.43										
4. Continuance commitment	0.36	0.33	0.33									
5. Distributive justice	0.38	-0.04	-0.18	0.12								
6. Procedural justice	0.41	0.02	0.17	0.11	0.43							
7. Exit	-0.59	-0.68	-0.21	-0.23	-0.14	-0.07						
8. Voice	-0.08	0.46	0.70	0.38	-0.24	-0.14	-0.38					
9. Loyalty	0.42	0.74	0.23	0.50	-0.04	0.11	-0.69	0.36				
10. Neglect	-0.39	-0.61	-0.01	-0.09	-0.19	0.04	0.54	-0.03	-0.48			
11. Labor market activity*	0.07	-0.10	0.10	-0.13	-0.53	0.13	-0.02	0.07	0.11	0.22		
12. OCB	0.07	0.52	0.31	0.01	-0.24	0.09	-0.33	0.29	0.28	-0.56	0.09	

studied, some interesting differences can be observed in the strength of the correlations between trust and the other variables of this study.

The first observation is that correlations between trust and most of the other variables are generally higher for core workers, indicating that trust is a more important guide to the attitudes and the behaviors of the core employees than to contingent workers. When taking a closer look, the differences are especially large with regard to Labor market activity, Organizational commitment, and OCB. However, relations between trust and the variables Team commitment, Distributive justice, Procedural justice, and Voice also tend to be higher for core employees. Therefore, it can be concluded that the role of trust depends on the type of contract.

A second observation is that trust is not the only variable that has a different impact on contingent and core workers. Most notably, the results for team commitment seem to mirror those of trust, as team commitment seems to be a more important determinant of the job behaviors of contingent workers. 'Voice' by the core employees is not significantly correlated to the attitudinal measures, whereas voice by the contingent workers is highly dependent on organizational commitment. OCB by core employees is strongly and positively related to trust ($r = 0.42$) but is not related to team commitment ($r = 0.05$). OCB by the contingent workers, on the other hand, largely depends on team commitment ($r = 0.52$) and not on trust ($r = 0.07$). These results suggests that the emergence and development of employees' behavior in organizations is indeed different for core employees and contingent workers.

It should be noted, however, that the results are not in line with the hypotheses of McLean Parks and Kidder (1994). McLean Parks and Kidder (1994) suggest that the psychological processes underlying work-related behavior may depend on job status. They suggested that contingent workers would base their attitudes and behavior on their evaluation of distributive justice, whereas core employees would focus on procedural justice. However, in this study there was no clear support for this hypothesis, although procedural justice evaluations by core workers were correlated somewhat higher with OCB ($r = 0.36$) than with contingent workers' OCB ($r = 0.09$). Procedural justice therefore may be more important for core employees in comparison to contingent workers, but the role of distributive justice considerations does not depend on job contract.

DISCUSSION AND RESEARCH AGENDA

The results of this study show that job status may influence attitudinal and behavioral responses towards the organization. Thus, people who perform the same jobs, but who have different contracts with their organization, may differ in their attitudes and behavior. In the study presented here, contingent workers showed relatively low affective commitment to the team and to the organization. Moreover, they displayed less constructive and more destructive behavior towards the organization, in comparison to employees hired on a permanent basis. Contrary to the expectations, distributive justice was higher for contingent workers than for core employees. The levels of trust and procedural justice did not depend on job status.

Furthermore, the results disclosed that team commitment and trust had special roles in their correlations with behavioral measures. Most notably, trust was relevant for the prediction of OCB for core employees but not for contingent workers, whereas team commitment was the strongest predictor of OCB for contingent workers, while there was no significant relation between team commitment and OCB for core employees.

Despite the positive correlation between team commitment and OCB, it should not be forgotten that the attitudes and behaviors of contingent workers were often less favorable than those of core employees. As contingent workers showed more neglect and exit and less OCB, this may harm the effectiveness of the organization. When there is a high turnover of contingent workers, new contingent workers have to be hired and have to be settled into the job, which may be very costly to the organization (Cascio, 1991). In this specific organization, the level of service is very important to the customers. It could be argued that the customers might be less likely to get a high level of service from contingent workers than from core employees. But in other organizations as well, neglect and lack of OCB are generally considered to be detrimental for the organization.

One of the results was somewhat surprising, as contingent workers were evaluating distributive justice as higher than the core employees did. However, objectively, their outcomes, both financial outcomes and fringe benefits, were lower than the outcomes of core employees. One explanation for this result might be that the contingent workers knew they were well off in comparison to fellow contingent workers in many other organizations. Feldman (1990) argues that temporary employees might not feel entitled to the same pay as core employees get, and that they might take temporary workers in other organizations as their frame of reference. In any case, it could be argued that the highly positive evaluation of distributive justice by contingent workers in this study actually underlines that good pay (high outcomes) cannot compensate for the lack of relationship between the contingent workers and the organization. Even if there is distributive justice or even relatively favorable pay, it still might not evoke the behavior wanted by the organization. In general, the results suggest that the evaluation of justice and trust may not differ for employees with a different contract, but the psychological meaning of justice and trust in the organization, and its behavioral consequences, may differ very much (compare McLean Parks and Kidder, 1994).

The data presented here do not give any definitive answers to the question whether or not the relevance of trust generally differs for employees with different job contracts. Several circumstances may be pointed out that may have led to the specific findings of this study. For instance, the research has been performed in hotels only, where the type of work may be different than in many other jobs. It might be important that the tasks of the employees involved dealing with customers, and can be considered tasks with a rather large variety and autonomy. Although the employees in the hotels did have supervisors monitoring their activities, the content of the interaction with the customers cannot easily be observed. Moreover, the nature of the work is such that the supervisors also co-operate with the regular employees. Many other contingent workers work in industries, doing more monotonous tasks, where monitoring of task performance may be more strict.

Most of the contingent workers in the hotels were attending some kind of education and probably did not pursue a career in this line of work. Also in this respect, the participants in this study may differ from contingent workers in other organizations. As stated earlier, people who choose to do temporary work may have more positive attitudes towards their work and the organization than people who dislike temporary contracts. It is not unlikely that temporary employees who would prefer a permanent contract with the current temporary employer would behave more similarly to the permanent employees, as they might take the perspective that the relationship with their employer might continue. Finally, it should be noted that the sample size of this study is limited, thus leading to caution with regard to conclusions about the stability of the results.

Although it is necessary to make cautionary remarks with regard to the stability and generalizability of the results, there are several pleas possible for the worth of the study presented here. The least convincing one is that the other studies performed on differences between contingent and core workers usually suffer from the same difficulties. It probably means we need a lot of small steps to get firmer ground on this topic. One strength of the current study is that the contingent workers and permanent employees performed the same tasks in the investigated organizations, making it possible to make pure comparisons between the two contract types. The use of data from different sources, self-reports and OCB judgments by the supervisor, is another strength. Furthermore, the results are very much in line with other studies that more or less measured the same variables. The strength of the intercorrelations among trust, justice variables and job attitudes were quite similar to those reported by Dirks and Ferrin (2002). The pattern of results with regard to the relation between commitment and OCB, no correlation for core workers, a strong correlation for contingent workers, is identical to that reported by van Dyne and Ang (1998; trust was not measured in that study). Thus, there is clearly some stability in findings.

Clearly, a lot of work remains to be done, and this study hopefully contributes to a further exploration of this topic. I wish to conclude this chapter with a number of suggestions for further research on the relevance of trust for contingent and core workers. I thereby focus on the potential worth of different conceptualizations of trust, as well as the role of characteristics of – and individual differences among – contingent workers.

WHAT RELEVANCE OF WHICH TRUST?

In making a statement that the relevance of trust may differ among employees with different job contracts, some important conceptual issues are evaded. In the meta-analysis on trust in leadership, Dirks and Ferrin (2002) argue that the trust concept needs refining. On a measurement level, trust in leadership is often highly correlated with justice variables, and there is a risk that there is a conceptual overlap among the measures. Furthermore, as in many attitude measurements, the operational definitions of trust can have two components: cognitive and affective (McAllister, 1995; Cummings and Bromily, 1996). The cognitive aspect of trust refers to rather cool, transactional considerations in dealing with other parties, based on information and on estimates of the reliability and integrity of the other party. Affect-based trust refers to a special relationship with the referent other, on expected mutual consideration when dealing with each other. It is hypothesized that affect-based trust is a stronger predictor of job performance and OCB than cognition-based trust (Dirks and Ferrin, 2002). Similar results actually have been reported in research on identification and affective commitment, where cognition-based identification tends to be a weaker predictor of behavioral measures than affective commitment (Mael and Ashforth, 1992).

It is widely expected that contingent workers take a transactional perspective towards the contract with their employer (McLean Parks and Kidder, 1994; van Dyne and Ang, 1998; McLean Parks et al., 1998). McLean Parks et al. (1998) argue that this may be a consequence of the tangibility of their contract, where tangibility is 'the degree to which the employee perceives the terms of the contract as unambiguously defined and explicitly specified, and clearly observable to third parties' (ibid., p. 708). When a contract becomes more tangible, workers are likely to work to the letter of the contract. McLean Parks and Kidder (1994) propose that, because the contract of the contingent workers is transactional in nature, contingent workers would only pay attention to distributive justice. As there often is simply no time to develop a warm, affective, relationship with the employer, they supposedly tend to look, coolly, at whether the employer lives up to the contract. If true, this might imply that cognition-based trust may be more predictive of contingent workers' behavior, whereas affect-based trust may be more important for regular employees.

In a similar vein, contingent workers may have a different perspective towards trust in leadership. Although transformational leadership is related more strongly to trust in leadership than transactional leadership, and is generally seen as relatively more predictive of the follower's behavior (Dirks and Ferrin, 2002), this does not mean necessarily that this is also true for contingent workers. A rather provocative proposition would be that if contingent workers only perceive their contract as transactional, a transactional leadership style by their supervisor may suffice to get the most out of the contingent workers. Transactional leaders may even display better results than transformational leaders, as they may better meet the needs of the contingent workers. Transformational leaders may be seen as manipulative, as leaders who want to get more out of the contingent worker than is required according to their contract.

In the study presented here, the relations among trust and several attitudes and behaviors depended on the type of job contract. In general, the correlations tended to be lower for contingent workers. The correlations with trust were somewhat higher for distributive and procedural justice, team commitment and voice, and clearly higher for organizational commitment, labor market activity and OCB. These results suggest that, indeed, trust may play a different role for workers with different types of contract. In contrast with these results, the correlation tables suggest that, for contingent workers, team commitment is relatively more important. For instance, trust was relevant for the prediction of OCB for core employees but not for contingent workers, whereas team commitment was a strong predictor of OCB for contingent workers, while there was no significant relation between team commitment and OCB for core employees. The pattern with regard to commitment is identical to the findings of van Dyne and Ang (1998), who also found a relatively lower commitment of contingent workers.

As an explanation for these results, I again refer to the different relationship core employees and contingent workers have with their employer. In this case, the contingent workers considered the employer as equally trustworthy, equally high on procedural justice and even higher on distributive justice. However, one may wonder how relevant these judgments were for the contingent workers. When contingent workers take a transactional perspective towards their employer, they might argue that they do not profit from the employer's just and trustworthy behavior as much as core employees do, at least not in the long run. It is not worthwhile to display OCB for the employer. However, they may still do so if they are committed to the group they work in on a day-to-day basis, their team. Their colleagues are people they might relate to, or even identify with. They work with them on a daily basis, but they might have few contacts with their employer. Although OCB is positive behavior that contributes to organizational effectiveness, the primary goal of the contingent worker might not necessarily be to help the organization. In other words, their OCB might not be directed at helping their organization but at helping their colleagues. In relating to their colleagues, they are likely to see a direct effect of their helping behavior by getting respect and amicability. This is something contingent workers do profit from, if only by creating a satisfying work environment. Most notably, their colleagues consist for a significant part of fellow contingent workers, a group they probably can easily identify with.

It should be noted that these results again point at the necessity to articulate the type of trust that is investigated. In this study, trust was measured at the level of the organization or management, whereas team commitment was directed at the colleagues. It is not far-fetched to assume that, for contingent workers, trust in – and trust received from – colleagues, would be more important than trust in management. In fact, it may compensate for a certain level of distrust towards the organization and/or leader. As a team, contingent and core workers are interdependent and workers don't let their colleague down without good reason. This may also be true in other organizations where the supervisor is not immediately involved in daily work routines and in situations where workers have different supervisors, such as in shift work in industries and hospitals.

In one respect, most of the contingent workers differ in a unique way from regular employees: the involvement of a third party, the temporary agency. The role of the temporary firm in influencing contingent workers has received little attention, but there is some evidence that commitment to the agency may spill over to the host organization (see McLean Parks et al., 1998). Unfortunately, having two employers may also lead to role conflicts (Rogers, 1995). Whether or not trust in the temporary agency by contingent workers is an important issue, can only be a matter of speculation. Nevertheless, it is conceivable that the relationship with the agency is at least as important as the relation with the host organization, if only because the relationship with the agency is likely to be lengthier. While working for the host organization, the contingent workers have to consider their relationship with the agency. As the agency has power over the assignment of new jobs elsewhere, the contingent worker risks worse or less assignments when s/he gets a negative review from the host organization. This 'threat' may restrict negative behaviors such as exit and neglect by the contingent worker. However, the temporary agency is also a potential source of support when there is some kind of conflict between the contingent worker and the host organization. When the relationship between the agency and the worker is well-established, some kind of mutual, knowledge-based trust (Lewicki and Benedict Bunker, 1996) may emerge between agency and worker. Although the contingent worker is likely to be asked to protect the interests of the agency while working at the host organization, it would be important to know there is a backing from the agency when the host organization treats the worker badly. It does not mean the worker can remain in the host organization when there is a conflict, but it may also mean that s/he does not have to accept every action by the employer and stay there, because s/he runs the risk of not getting assignments elsewhere. The agency can gain in trustworthiness towards 'their' contingent workers when they take the bad experience with the host organization into account when sending other contingent workers to the same organization, for instance by informing them about their past experiences and by asking them to report irregularities and injustice in host organizations.

THE TRUSTING CONTINGENT WORKER

By now, the reader might think that contingent workers are at the mercy of their temporary employers and of their agency. This clearly would be an exaggeration, as contingent work may have advantages as well for groups of contingent workers. For a number of workers, the temporary contract may be the preferred type of contract. For inexperienced workers it may give the opportunity to gain experience and to get a broader perspective on the jobs they might be interested in in the long term. Contingent work may be ideal for students who have their study as their main activity, as they have few obligations towards the organization, but may work more in quieter times. For parents with young children, contingent work may contribute to the family income, while flexible working hours at the same time may give the opportunity to do care-taking and child-rearing tasks at home as well. However, there are also groups of contingent workers that depend on contingent work for their family income.

It is reasonable to assume that the voluntariness of contingent work may affect job attitudes and work behavior. In fact, there is some empirical evidence that contingent workers who would prefer a permanent job over temporary work may have lower job satisfaction and job performance (Ellingson et al., 1998) and, likewise, that people whose preferred employment status is to be temporary workers may have higher job satisfaction and commitment than permanent workers and involuntary workers (Lee and Johnson, 1991). In (parts of) countries with low unemployment rates, where it is easy to get a permanent labor contract, one could assume that contingent work is only performed by people who choose to do so. It is expected that in such countries, the job attitudes of contingent and core workers may be more similar than in countries where contingent work is often involuntary, for instance when the preferred permanent position is not available (van Dyne and Ang, 1998). One additional caution is in order here, as job level may be associated with voluntariness. Contingent workers who would prefer temporary work may be more highly skilled (Marler et al., 2002), as is generally the case with freelancers, which might mean that positive attitudes of contingent workers are at least partly caused by differences in job level and not by voluntariness alone.

There may be at least one implication with regard to the role trust plays for voluntary versus involuntary contingent workers. Whatever the situation on the labor market, the voluntary contingent worker is likely to have higher expectations from the relationship with the employer than the involuntary worker. It could be argued that the trustworthiness of the employer may become more important, because the voluntary contingent worker has alternatives, either by switching jobs or by deciding to stop working (for some period). The contingent worker is likely to have more self-confidence and self-esteem if his/her life does not depend on the job. The relationship between employer and employee is more in an equilibrium, whereas the employer clearly has more power when the contingent worker has no alternatives on the job market and depends on having a job.

There are other differences among contingent workers that may influence the role of trust in the employer–employee relationship. There are individual differences with regard to the propensity to trust, a kind of personality characteristic (Rotter, 1967). Although meta-analytical results are not very hopeful with regard to the importance of the propensity to trust (Dirks and Ferrin, 2002), it may be that its role is more important for contingent workers, as they have less information about the trustworthiness of the employer than the core employees, and therefore let themselves be guided by their general inclination to trust or distrust.

In conclusion, it should once again be noted that the heterogeneity among contingent workers remains a serious problem in all research on contingent workers when comparing them with regular workers. The differences in pursued goals, labor market conditions, voluntariness and job level, may all contribute to obscuring the true effects of job contracts. It is my hope that these inherent difficulties will not restrain other social scientists from pursuing a better understanding of the way the growing group of contingent workers operates in organizations around the world.

REFERENCES

Allen, N.J. and J.P. Meyer (1990), 'The measurement and antecedents of affective, continuance and normative commitment to the organization', *Journal of Occupational Psychology*, 63, 1–18.

Beard, K.M. and J.R. Edwards (1995), 'Employees at risk: contingent work and the psychological experience of contingent workers', in C.L. Cooper and D.M. Rousseau (eds), *Trends in Organizational Behavior*, Vol. 2, New York: Wiley, pp. 109–26.

Boon, S.D., and J.G. Holmes (1991), 'The dynamics of interpersonal trust: resolving uncertainty in the face of risk', in R.A. Hinde and J. Groebel (eds), *Cooperation and Prosocial Behavior,* Cambridge: Cambridge University Press, pp. 190–211.

Cascio, W.F. (1991), *Costing Human Resources*, Boston: PWS-Kent.

Cummings, L.L. and P. Bromiliy (1996), 'The Organizational Trust Inventory (OTI): development and validation', in R.M. Kramer and T.R. Tyler (eds), *Trust in Organizations*, Thousand Oaks, CA: Sage, pp. 302–30.

Dirks, K.T. and D.L. Ferrin (2002), 'Trust in leadership: meta-analytic findings and implications for research and practice', *Journal of Applied Psychology*, 87, 611–28.

Dyne, L. van and S. Ang (1998), 'Organizational citizenship behavior of contingent workers in Singapore', *Academy of Management Journal*, 41, 692–703.

Ellemers, N., D. de Gilder and H. van den Heuvel (1998), 'Career-oriented versus team-oriented commitment and behavior at work', *Journal of Applied Psychology*, 83, 717–30.

Ellingson, J.E., M.L. Gruys and P.R. Sackett (1998), 'Factors related to the satisfaction and performance of temporary employees', *Journal of Applied Pyschology*, 83, 913–21.

Feldman, D.C. (1990), 'Reconceptualizing the nature and consequences of part-time work', *Academy of Management Review*, 15, 103–12.

Folger, R. and R. Cropanzano (1998), *Organizational Justice and Human Resource Management*, Thousand Oaks: Sage.

Gilder, D. de (2003), 'Commitment, trust and work behaviour: the case of contingent workers', *Personnel Review*, 32, 588–604.

Gilder, D. de, H. van den Heuvel and N. Ellemers (1997), 'Het 3-componenten model van commitment' [A three component model of organizational commitment], *Gedrag en Organisatie*, 10, 95–106.

Guest, D.E. (1998), 'Is the psychological contract worth taking seriously?', *Journal of Organizational Behavior*, 19, 649–64.

Hackman, J.R. and G.R. Oldham (1980), *Work Redesign*, London: Addison Wesley.

Hartley, J. (1995), 'Challenge and change in employment relations: issues for psychology, trade unions, and managers', in L.E. Tetrick and J. Barling (eds), *Changing Employment Relations*, Washington, DC: APA, pp. 3–30.

Hirschmann, A.O. (1970), *Exit, Voice and Loyalty: Responses to Decline in Firms, Organizations, and States*, Cambridge, MA: Harvard University Press.

Kalleberg, A.L., B.F. Reskin and K. Hudson (2000), 'Bad jobs in America: standard and nonstandard employment relations and job quality in the United States', *American Sociological Review*, 65, 256–78.

Kramer, R.M. and T.R. Tyler (eds) 1996), *Trust in Organizations*, Thousand Oaks, CA: Sage.

Lee, T.W. and D.R. Johnson (1991), 'The effects of work schedule and employment status on the organizational commitment and job satisfaction of full versus part time employees', *Journal of Vocational Behavior*, 38, 204–24.

Lepak, D.P. and S.A. Snell (1999), 'The human resource architecture: toward a theory of human capital allocation and development', *Academy of Management Review*, **24**, 31–48.

Lewicki, R.J. and B. Benedict Bunker (1996), 'Developing and maintaining trust in work relationships', in R.M. Kramer and T.R. Tyler (eds), *Trust in Organizations*, Thousand Oaks, CA: Sage, pp. 114–39.

Mael, F. and B.E. Ashforth (1992), 'Alumni and their alma-mater: a partial test of the reformulated model of organizational identification', *Journal of Organizational Behavior*, **13**, 103–23.

Marler, J.H., M. Woodard Barringer and G.T. Milkovich (2002), 'Boundaryless and traditional contingent employees: worlds apart', *Journal of Organizational Behavior*, 23, 425–53.

Mathieu, J.P. and D.M. Zajac (1990), 'A review and meta-analysis of the antecedents, correlates and consequences of organizational commitment', *Psychological Bulletin*, 108, 171–94.

McAllister, D.J. (1995). 'Affect- and cognition-based trust as foundations for interpersonal cooperation in organizations', *Academy of Management Journal*, 38, 24–59.

McLean Parks, J. and D.L. Kidder (1994), '"Till death us do part…" Changing work relationships in the 1990s', in C.L. Cooper and D.M. Rousseau (eds), *Trends in Organizational Behavior*, Chichester: Wiley, pp. 111–33.

McLean Parks, J., D.L. Kidder and D.G. Gallagher (1998), 'Fitting square pegs into round holes: mapping the domain of contingent work arrangements onto the psychological contract', *Journal of Organizational Behavior*, 23, 697–730.

Mowday, R.T., R.M. Steers and L.W. Porter (1979), 'The measurement of organizational commitment', *Journal of Vocational Behaviour*, 14, 224–47.

Nollen, S. and H. Axel (1996), *Managing Contingent Workers*, New York: American Management.

Organ, D.W. (1988), *Organizational Citizenship Behavior: The Good Soldier Syndrome*, Lexington, MA: Lexington Books.

Pearce, J.L. (1993), 'Toward an organizational behavior of contract laborers: their psychological involvement and effects on employee co-workers', *Academy of Management Journal*, 36, 1082–96.

Podsakoff, P.M. and S.B. MacKenzie (1997), 'Impact of organizational citizenship behaviour on organizational performance: a review and suggestions for future research', *Human Performance*, 10, 133–51.

Rogers, J.K. (1995), 'Just a temp: experience and structure of alienation in temporary clerical employment', *Work and Occupations*, 22, 137–66.

Rotter, J.B. (1967), 'A new scale for the measurement of interpersonal trust', *Journal of Personality*, 35, 651–65.

Rousseau, D.M. (1995), *Psychological Contracts in Organizations: Understanding Written and Unwritten Agreements*, Newbury Park, CA: Sage.

Rousseau, D.M. and S.A. Tijoriwala (1998), 'Assessing psychological contracts: issues, alternatives and measures', *Journal of Organizational Behavior*, **19**, 679–95.

Rusbult, C.E., D. Farrell, G. Rogers and A.G. Mainous III (1988), 'Impact of exchange variables on exit, voice, loyalty, and neglect: an integrative model of responses to declining job satisfaction', *Academy of Management Journal*, 31, 599–627.
Taylor, F.W. (1911), *The Principles of Scientific Management*, New York: Harper.
Whyte, W.H. (1960), *The Organization Man*, Harmondsworth: Penguin.

13. Trust under pressure: afterthoughts

Katinka Bijlsma-Frankema and
Rosalinde Klein Woolthuis

Although trust is a much debated topic, empirical research on trust relations that are not sustained by institutional mechanisms and 'taken-for-granted' rules of the game have so far received relatively little attention (Child 1998; Humphrey 1998; Reed 2001). The studies presented in this book focused on exactly those relationships in which partners have little to fall back upon to build trust, that is, to make their 'leap of faith' (Bradach and Eccles, 1989). The studies described situations in which actors are members of different organizations, tribes or countries; relationships are not embedded in a shared institutional structure, common culture, or networks; and/or transactions are not backed up by contracts, monitoring or sanctioning systems. Other factors, such as the increasing importance of intangible resources and the pace with which technologies develop, also contribute to the complexity of governing cooperative relations. This book aimed to shed some preliminary light on trust and trust building in situations where several institutional, taken-for-granted, or rational bases for control and trust are lacking. The question this book broached is: how do actors build and sustain trust in these situations; how do actors deal with 'trust under pressure'?

The empirical studies presented in this book were conducted by scholars with a wide variety of disciplinary backgrounds, employing insights from many fields, including organization theory, knowledge management, sociology, psychology, economics, management, human resources management and communication sciences. Empirical data were gathered in twelve different countries, including Eastern European countries, Mexico and Tanzania as well as Western European countries. The studies were conducted in a variety of contexts: relations within and between organizations, and within and across countries. Characteristic of all studies was that relationships had to be built, coordinated and/or controlled under uncertain circumstances, in contexts in which institutional, taken-for-granted or rational bases for control and trust were weak or lacking.

While exploring new ground, the studies produced some fresh observations that gave rise to the afterthoughts presented here. Some of these insights point to new directions for research or to alternative conceptualizations of trust that seem valuable enough to pursue, however fragile and thin the support for these insights is at the moment.

FOCUS OF EXPLANATION: RISK REDUCTION VERSUS VALUE CREATION

A first observation, based on several studies in this volume, is that trust can be built in circumstances where actors, at first sight, have very little in common and where many sources of control and trust are absent. An example of this is the study by Kühlmann on German–Mexican business partnership formation. In these partnerships, actors come from different (cultural) backgrounds, have no exchange history or information on reputation, and the relationship is embedded in different institutional structures (laws, regulation, arbitration) simultaneously. As a result, actors have a very narrow basis on which to built trust. If a situation like this were looked at with the insights on trust gathered in stable contexts, scholars would probably expect cooperation to fail because of the high risks involved and the lack of means to reduce these risks. However, parties *do* engage in those partnerships and build up trust, and manage to do so successfully. Two possible explanations of this puzzling phenomenon may prove to be valid in future research. First, it can be argued that in the research conducted in stable contexts, the focus has predominantly been on the reduction of risk and transaction costs, while shedding little light on the part played by value creation possibilities and transaction benefits (Johannisson, 2001). If the value of the goal that can be reached by working together is seen as high enough by actors, it can be expected that they will engage in trust building, despite the thin ice they stand on. This would imply that in different situations, different mixes of perceived risks and envisioned value creation may lead to different strategies and different ways to deal with matters of trust and control.

The study by Rus on the relationship between trust and SME development in Bosnia, Macedonia and Slovenia, provides a first cue that this idea is not too far-fetched. He found that while growing firms tend to rely on trust, firms in their decline make more use of formal contracts to manage their relationships. This suggests that trust and reaping opportunities may go hand in hand, whereas in situations of decline, parties focus on defensive action and safeguarding, to hold on to what is left. In the study by Busacca and Castaldo on trust building between firms and customers, the focus is on value creation. A central idea in this study, based on a 'resource-based view' (RBV) perspective, is that trust does to external relationships what knowledge does internally for the firm, that is, creates value. They examine the value creation role of trust by comparing marketing relationships in several, highly differing markets (financial services, meat, undergraduate training at a university and consumer electronic appliances) and find that in all markets trust enables stable customer–firm relations, thereby increasing shareholder value and firm profitability.

The study by Hoecht shows that in some situations risk and value creation go hand in hand because the most promising value-creating strategies are the most risky as well. The study focuses on collaborative R&D projects in the flavor and fragrance industry in the UK. In these industries, external linkages are needed to promote creativity and innovation, while these linkages also increase the risk of intentional or accidental disclosure of sensitive information. Still, motivated by the perceived possibility of value creation, actors find ways to construct a basis for governance with some control and some trust elements that in their eyes suffice to make their leap of faith. Based on these cues, a direction for future research may be to take both the risk and the value creation that partners envision into account in explaining cooperation, trust and control. Future research may show that jointly perceived opportunities work as a positive factor in trust building under pressure, because they can create a willingness to actively look for what one has in common with a partner-to-be. In this process actors may emphasize the positive and use that to build trust, rather than focus on risks and costs.

UNDEREXPOSED SOURCES OF TRUST

A second explanation of trust building in circumstances where actors, at first sight, have very little in common and where the basis for control and trust are narrow, is that there are sources of trust that, in previous literature, have not been recognized as such. It is possible that in trust research so far, the focus has been more on trust based on formal and tangible means, than on more informal, intangible and abstract sources of trust building, thus underexposing the latter. It can be conjectured that if a base for formal control is absent or ineffective, more abstract, intangible sources come to the fore as playing an important part in trust building, as is shown in the studies by Blomqvist and Kühlmann.

The study by Blomqvist sheds light on how fast trust can be created in collaborative projects between large and small firms in the high-tech ICT industry. In this sector, the market does not allow actors to slowly build up trust before they engage in IT partnerships, while the future is also uncertain due to the high complexity and uncertainty of technological and market developments. Still, trust is claimed to play an important role by the actors that actually do business and collaborate in these highly volatile markets. Blomqvist illustrates how personal intuition and shared excitement triggers fast trust. Respondents in her study state that they try out potential partners by engaging in a brainstorm about the proposed project. They sharply examine the other's reactions and attitudes during the process. If the personal chemistry is there, they feel confident that this partner can solve unexpected problems with them in the course of the temporary project. So, what they do is go through a series of imaginary exchanges, creating instant, virtual exchange experiences. If these exchange experiences are positive, fast trust is built. The basis for trust thus created proved to be strong enough to make the leap of faith in this high velocity market.

In the study by Kühlmann, German–Mexican sales relationships are examined. He emphasizes that in international/intercultural business cooperation, mutual trust is of particular importance because explicit contractual agreements are often difficult to make and enforce given different legal systems. But, in such situations, trust is also difficult to establish due to cultural differences, the costs related to regular face-to-face contacts, and the lack of possibilities to monitor the partner's behaviors. So, the parties have to find other ways to create a basis for trust to enable fruitful inter-firm relationships. Kühlmann finds, surprisingly, that both the Mexicans and Germans try to build this basis by mimicking each other's behaviors and preferences. The Mexicans provide the Germans with strong signals on their competence, reliability and openness of information sharing to counteract the prevailing stereotype signifying that they are sloppy, unreliable and corrupt. The Germans, on the other hand, invest in the personal side of the relationship, show support and share information, as if to counteract the German stereotype of cold businessmen who live agreements to the letter. All in all, the studies by Blomqvist and Kühlmann are fine examples of how in the interaction between almost strangers, meanings are actively constructed to build the notion of sharing understanding of a situation. In these studies, these abstract, partly imaginary and intangible sources of trust proved to be viable alternatives to more traditional sources. The studies also indicate that there may hardly be a limit to the degree of abstraction or symbolism in these processes of meaning construction: if people seem not to share a thing, their creativity may be triggered to produce unexpected results.

A second, so far underexposed source of trust is what actors who – at first sight – have nothing in common, do share. The Mexican and German businessmen that Kühlmann studied, and the ICT entrepreneurs in the study by Blomqvist, may actually have shared enough to have good reasons to trust each other and to engage in cooperation. First, they may have shared a vision on potential value that could be created, transaction benefits (Johannisson, 2001) to reap, collective success to be proud of, or the joy of reaching a common goal. Chester Barnard (1938) coined the term 'common moral purpose' to explain the value attached to working together over working as an individual, because of what can be accomplished in cooperation with others and the joy inherent in a common enterprise. Sharing as a source of trust may encompass widely different similarities, as the studies in this volume suggest, like sharing commitment to a team of colleagues (De Gilder), perceived organizational support (Bijlsma et al.), affinity with a product made or a technology used (Rocco), or sharing knowledge of the institutional rules that are diffused within a specific sector (Rus).

A third underexposed source of trust that surfaced in this volume is the sharing of codified rules and systems. Besides providing a tangible set of rules that is often used as a basis for control, codified rules and systems can provide the common ground on which a more abstract feeling of sharing can be developed and on which trust and cooperation can be built, even between strangers. This phenomenon was described before by Child and Mollering (2003) in their empirical study of Hong Kong managers' trust in the management of Mainland Chinese subsidiaries. They found that the introduction of codified business systems enabled a process of familiarization in a context where other institutional sources of trust were weakly developed. In this volume, the study by Tillmar on small business cooperation in Tanzania shows that from knowing and using a book-keeping system, a notion of sharing is constructed, on which trust can be built across tribal borders. Furthermore, in the study by Rocco, a set of codified rules is recommended as a shared vocabulary in a virtual, multinational, multicultural team that has no common culture, language, nor face-to face contact on which to base mutual trust.

In future research on trust under pressure more attention may thus be paid to sharing codified rules and systems, to sharing commitment to a common endeavor and to sharing based on meaning construction in interaction. In the process of meaning construction, actors can also define new 'communities' to which they both belong, thus creating new similarities. There seem to be few limits to this mode of trust building since many kinds of symbolic communities can be imagined on which sharing can be based, for instance sharing affinity with a product (Busacca and Castaldo), or with a brand (Kerkhof et al.) on which customer trust can be built. The idea that processes of meaning construction can be very powerful in building trust under pressure has also given rise to the next afterthought, that is that in building trust actors can be conceived of as bricoleurs.

BUILDING TRUST: BRICOLEURS AT WORK

In studying trust and trust building under pressure, the conceptualizations of trust used by most authors in this volume are rather open ended, in accordance with the exploratory nature of the studies. It can, however, be noticed that studying trust building under pressure has produced a stronger conceptual focus on the idea that trust can be actively constructed through interaction between actors. In several of the studies actors appear to construct 'common ground' between them, while the nature of this common ground differs between contexts. The common ground found or constructed ranges from codified rules and systems to processes of familiarization with a high symbolic loading. In the first chapter, Möllering coins the term 'active trust' to conceptualize the process of trust construction between strangers. By getting to know each other and discover or construct similarities, actors gradually achieve common ground. The empirical studies of Tillmar and Hoecht show how in different contexts this process of familiarization or common ground formation works, and what sources of trust are employed in this process. Actors seem to build trust with whatever is available and relevant to the common project.

The study by Tillmar offers an interesting example of this idea. She investigated cooperation between entrepreneurs in Tanzania. In Tanzania, institutional sources of trust were absent, and business exchange across clan borders was hard to accomplish because of deep-rooted mutual distrust. Yet, cooperation and sharing resources such as transportation facilities are necessary conditions for the firms to survive. The study describes the various building blocks that actors assemble to build trust. Shared knowledge and use of a book-keeping system, joint attendance of a course on entrepreneurship, and membership of a newly founded Savings and Credit Cooperative Society helped the actors from different tribes to build mutual understanding, friendship and trust. But, next to these more abstract forms of sharing, there were also rather concrete safeguarding mechanisms that supported the development of trust. The Chamber of Commerce provided 'cross-tribe' arbitration, and the ability to obtain a loan from the newly founded cooperative bank was restricted to those businessmen/ entrepreneurs that had a house, children and a good business reputation. In other words, mechanisms were built in to reduce the room for opportunism – in the Tanzanian context the risk of people 'running away' with the money. The picture that the study sketches hence is one in which actors actively build trust with those measures available and suitable to their specific situation. Those measures involve both trust and control mechanisms, which are put together in a mutually enforcing manner.

The study by Hoecht shows how social control mechanisms, especially in the form of reputation as a 'self-disciplining' mechanism for knowledge workers, complement contractual sources, and reward structures as a basis for control. The study elaborates on the various strategies that companies adopt to reduce the risk of information leakage while keeping their organization open for external consultants to enable innovative ideas to grow. Incremental trust building is a major strategy. External consultants must prove their reliability with minor projects before they are assigned to more important work. Another building block for trust is the external consultant's reputation: the fear of losing a good reputation as a result of gossip or information leakage, and therewith the loss of potential new work, will make the consultant want to behave and appear trustworthy. A third building block is the strategy to pay consultants even when their services are not strictly needed to ensure permanent access to their expertise and to curb opportunistic behavior, that is keep them away from competitors.

The metaphor that fits these descriptions is that of human beings as bricoleurs, who take the building blocks that are relevant and within reach and combine them into the 'good reasons' (Lewis and Weigert, 1985) for trusting others with whom they want to cooperate to pursue a common goal. Given the role of meaning construction in trust building, the studies also mirror the idea that the process of getting to good reasons – good enough reasons may be a more adequate term – is not a purely rational, nor an entirely conscious process, but is better viewed as a 'constitutively semi-conscious process', as Bachmann (1998, p. 307) contended. A direction for future research is to pay more research attention to the processes of meaning construction, to gain insight into the sensemaking of actors involved, as several authors (Weick, 1995; Kramer, 1996; Bijlsma and van de Bunt, 2002) advocate. By studying sensemaking (Weick, 1995), more light can be shed on the process of trust formation and the building blocks used in different situations or relations.

BUILDING BLOCKS OF INTERPERSONAL TRUST

To work upon the idea that the metaphor of bricolage fits many cases of trust building under pressure means that future research may profit from a more systematic treatment of different sources of trust, how these are related and how these can be combined by actors. Although most authors in this volume seem to broadly agree on what trust is, there is no trace of agreement on sources of trust. In the literature, authors also diverge when it comes to the discussion of the bases of trust, depending on their view on human motivations (Lane and Bachmann, 1998; Nooteboom and Six, 2003). In comparing several categorizations of trust sources that could be suitable for studying trust under pressure, the classical typology of Zucker (1986) fitted well with the studies in this volume. Zucker distinguishes 'three central modes of trust production: (1) process-based, where trust is tied to past or expected exchange; (2) characteristic-based, where trust is tied to person, depending on characteristics such as family background or ethnicity; (3) institution-based where trust is tied to formal societal structures, depending on individual or firm-specific attributes (e.g. certification as accountant) or intermediary mechanisms (e.g. use of escrow accounts)' (Zucker, 1986, p. 53).

The two sources of interpersonal trust Zucker distinguishes, mirror the two modes of solidarity Durkheim ([1893] 1960) distinguished over a century ago: mechanic solidarity, based on sharing, and organic solidarity, based on exchanging. Exchanging as a source of trust is based on positive exchange experiences or positive exchange expectations, which can be based on several grounds, ranging from highly specified contracts to the norm of reciprocity which according to Gouldner (1960), is universal in nature. Sharing as a source of trust rests on the idea that the other, like yourself, is bound to adhere to, to 'take for granted', or to morally value, being part of a community that functions by a set of rules known and respected by its members. Shared membership of a community (group, category), binds people to the rules of that community, thus giving the trustor good reasons to expect that the trustee will abide by the rules. As Garfinkel (1963, p. 190, cited in Zucker, 1986) notes:

> so that an individual (or organization) knows what the expectations are, knows that the other(s) know the expectations, and knows that the other(s) know that the individual (or organization) knows the expectations, even when the content of the expectations varies by social position, individual attribute and so on.

Related to the theme of trust under pressure, it was noted before that in the absence of shared membership of a flesh-and-blood community like family or ethnicity, actors can share membership of, or a feeling of belonging to, more abstract or symbolic 'communities'. Such abstract communities may be defined by participants on a wide variety of characteristics, such as shared sector-specific knowledge, shared preferences for practices, shared affinity with a product, similar style of problem solving and so on. In a similar vein, Rocco uses the concept of common ground as a 'sharing' source of trust in her study on a virtual team. Common ground is defined as a sum of mutual ideas, beliefs, assumptions and suppositions upon which a group of individuals coordinates actions and makes choices. She argues that common ground can be based on: being a member of the same

community (community membership), being able to communicate using
the same language or vocabulary (linguistic co-presence), or by actually
meeting each other in person to be able to optimally communicate and
develop mutual understanding (physical co-presence). It can be concluded
that if physical co-presence and membership of a concrete community
cannot be realized, a shared vocabulary does offer alternative possibilities
for active trust building.

The two sources of interpersonal trust, sharing and exchanging, can be
distinguished analytically, but they must not be conceived of as mutually
exclusive sources of trust. Zucker clearly argues that the three sources of
trust she distinguishes can be seen as mutually supportive in building trustful
relations. Yet, authors tend to focus predominantly on sharing as a source of
trust, or on positive exchanges: the focus on sharing being mainly embraced
by sociologists and the focus on exchanging by economists. Powell (1996,
p. 62) repudiates both views as equally unappealing. 'Trust has been viewed
in two ways: 1) as a rational outcome of an iterated chain of contacts in
which farsighted parties recognize the potential benefits of their continued
interaction, and 2) as a by-product of the embeddedness of individuals in
a web of social relations such that values and expectations are commonly
shared.' He argues that while the rational view, mostly found in economics,
tends to be under-socialized, the social norm-based view, mostly found in
sociology, tends to be over-romanticized:

> Social norm based conceptions of trust miss the extent to which cooperation
> is buttressed by sustained contact, regular dialogue and constant monitoring
> ... Similarly, the rational or calculative view overstates the extent to which the
> continued success of a relationship is based on the ability of parties to take a
> long-term view and practice mutual forbearance. (Powell, 1996, p. 63)

Creed and Miles (1996, p. 19) also notice that experiences of reciprocity as
well as shared norms of obligation and co-operation further trust: 'trust
can be influenced by increasing perceived similarities and the number of
positive exchanges'. Yet, only a few theorists have specifically referred to
sharing and exchanging and the nature of the interaction between these
sources of trust. March and Olsen (1975) do refer to both and propose a
cyclic dynamic between the two, in which satisfactory exchange experiences
lead to trust, which in turn creates a tendency to share perspectives and
preferences with trusted others, thereby creating sharing which promotes
the chance of positive exchange experiences. Several studies in this volume
seem to reflect a step within this dynamic cycle.

Sharing and exchanging as building blocks of trust not only go hand in
hand, they are mutually supportive as well, as the studies by Rocco and
de Gilder illustrate. The study by Rocco sheds light on the question which

sources of trust are available for building trust in an international virtual team of ICT professionals, that has to perform under conditions of tight coupling of activities and high time pressure. In such circumstances, trust building is difficult because parties seem to have little in common, apart from their professional knowledge and skills. The team members studied are located in three different nations with rather different cultures, they do not meet face-to-face and, given the high time pressure of projects, cannot gradually build up trust. Rocco shows that distance weakens the possibilities of common ground based on community membership and physical co-presence, and shows how this affects trust between project team members in a negative way. She argues that if the organization introduced a restricted set of codified rules, for instance regarding answering terms for email and voice mail, these negative effects could be curbed. The rules could function as common ground for trust building and as a set of mutual expectations, worded in a single vocabulary, on which positive exchanges could be built. Rules that apply to all can thus promote clear mutual expectations, which means that sharing of rules can further positive exchanges, which, together with the common ground created, support trust building.

In the study by de Gilder, relations between co-workers must be built from scratch. In his study, differences in trust, commitment and justice perceptions were investigated between contingent and core employees in two hotels, as well as their effects on work behaviors. Contingent workers showed lower commitment to the team and to the organization, and displayed less constructive behaviors towards the organization than core employees. Team commitment and team trust had special roles in relation to behavioral measures. Team trust was relevant as a predictor of organizational citizenship behavior (OCB) for core employees but not for contingent workers, whereas team commitment was the strongest predictor of OCB for contingent workers, while there was no significant relation for core employees. These findings do support the idea that sharing with others, in this case commitment to the team, is a positive factor that supports positive exchange behaviors.

INSTITUTIONAL SOURCES OF TRUST

The idea that sharing can be stretched to membership of symbolic communities touches upon the relation between interpersonal and institutional sources of trust. The metaphor of bricolage, which is used to describe how actors draw on available sources to construct good enough reasons to trust, points to the importance of the institutional environment in which actors operate, which may support sharing or exchanging as a source of interpersonal trust, or both.

The third base of trust building Zucker (1986) distinguished, the socio-institutional environment, has by now been typified as a rather undifferentiated, encompassing set of rules and mechanisms that is in need of further exploration. Bachmann (1998, p. 319), for instance, argues that many elements of the institutional framework should be taken into consideration in examining how social actors engage in economic exchange, but that insight into the nature of the relations between these factors is scarce: 'As yet we equally know little about how different elements of the institutional framework such as legal regulations, the status and role of trade associations, the financial system, etc. interact with each other. These issues need to be studied very thoroughly through comparative research.' The comparative study by Rus supports the relevance of this endeavor. The study focuses on processes of de-localization in three countries, of which two have institutions that are less developed or corrupt. He reports on an SME development survey in Bosnia, Macedonia and Slovenia in which he examines the relationship between trust, conceived of as social capital, and SME development. He distinguishes three types of trust, each of which relates to a mode of tie strength. First, interpersonal trust that depends on information which travels through strong ties; second, network trust that depends on information which is passed through weak ties; third, institutional trust that depends on public information which requires no ties. He finds support for the hypothesis that well-functioning formal institutions can form a basis to start building trust from and thereby contribute to economic development. In Slovenia, where institutions are relatively well developed, he finds higher levels of trust and longer term relationships. He also finds that SMEs that have more inter-firm relationships grow faster.

A first step proposed in differentiating the socio-institutional framework, which operates within organizations and in the wider societal context, is to distinguish between institutional rules and mechanisms that support characteristic-based interpersonal trust (sharing) and those which support process-based interpersonal trust (exchanging). Zucker (1986) herself did not follow upon the insight of Durkheim ([1893] 1960) that institutionalized rules, the collective conscience in his words, can be defined as supporting sharing or supporting exchanging between actors. Yet, drawing upon the distinction in sources of interpersonal trust, sharing and exchanging, it seems not too far-fetched to distinguish institutional sources of trust that support sharing and institutional sources that support exchanging. This idea is sustained by the study by Busacca and Castaldo. They found that the bases on which customer trust is built, and hence value is created, differs greatly with the product sold. For instance, buying meat was found to be a typical experience good. Consumer trust was mainly based on sharing emotions with the sales person, whereas consumer trust in the financial consultant was mainly based on competencies and exchange-based. In other words, the relevance of specific antecedents of consumer trust with regard to specific products may be regulated by cultural rules within the socio-institutional framework, that define the legitimacy of meaning giving to products by customers. Whether exchanging or sharing is the dominant source of trust customers can legitimately rely upon, may thus differ between the socio-institutional structures of countries, or even sectors. By distinguishing institutional sources that support sharing from sources that support exchanging, a first step is made in exploring how elements of the socio-institutional frame can be used as building blocks in building interpersonal trust.

Codified and Non-Codified Sources of Institutional Trust

A second step that would fit the studies in this volume is to distinguish formal, codified sources of trust from informal, non-codified sources. This distinction mirrors an often made analytical distinction between, for instance, contract and 'beyond contract', formal and informal rules and regulations, and formal and informal relations within and between organizations. The distinction fits an earlier observation made, that is that sharing of codified rules and systems is an underexposed source of trust that surfaced in this volume. Besides providing a tangible set of rules that is often used as the basis of the control, codified rules and systems can provide common ground on which former strangers can develop a more abstract feeling of sharing, on which trust and cooperation can be built.

Furthermore, distinguishing codified and non-codified institutional sources that support trust building allows for a link to insights gained on the dispersion modes of knowledge and rules from small groups to larger populations. This seems interesting because in this volume it is found that processes of de-localization and globalization bring shifts in the sources available for trust building. This raises the question which sources of trust are best fitted to serve in global contexts, but also whether sources of trust can be transformed to function in wider contexts. Throughout this volume cues can be found that sharing as a source of trust can range from common membership of a local flesh-and-blood community to common membership of highly symbolic communities, that may be defined in an interaction-based process of meaning construction. This insight is in line with the theoretical work of Boisot (1995). In discussing how local knowledge can be dispersed in larger communities, he defines two principles that enable local knowledge to be diffused effectively within a large population: codification and abstraction. The other side of the coin of the 'McDonaldization of society' (Ritzer, 1993) is that a codified system can provide common ground to former strangers, teaching them the rules regarding expected exchanges on which positive expectations can be built. Abstraction, the second principle, is better fitted to disperse values, norms and meanings, through, for instance, mission statements. The anti-globalist movement is an example of how abstract views can build trust between people and unite them into a community based on a newly constructed shared meaning. Since in this volume codified rules or systems, and shared membership of abstract communities, were found as sources of trust in globalized or de-localized trust building, it can be concluded that the two principles of dispersion Boisot presented, codification and abstraction, can be also be validly applied to de-localization of trust sources.

Distinguishing between codified and non-codified sources of trust may help understand how different principles of dispersion may be involved in developments like globalization and related shifts in sources of trust that actors draw upon in trust building. The four institutional sources of trust thus distinguished are shown in Table 13.1.

Table 13.1   Institutional sources of trust

Sharing	Exchanging
Codified rules, regulations and systems supporting sharing	**Codified rules, regulations and systems supporting exchanging**
– Formal organizational rules and sanctions	– Formal positions within organizations
– Criminal law and courts	– Contract law and courts
– Standards	– Contracts
– IT/accounting systems	– Certification
	– Escrow accounts
	– Insurances and safeguards
Non-codified rules, regulations and systems supporting sharing	**Non-codified rules, regulations and systems supporting exchanging**
– Culture, norms, values	– Psychological contract
– Shared frames of meaning construction	– Temporal embeddedness (shadow of past/future)
– Membership of informal groups	– Embeddedness (reputation, obligation, retaliation)
– Identification	– Norm of reciprocity

To support this line of inquiry, another step in differentiating institutional sources of trust would be to do justice to the layered nature of institutional frameworks, by distinguishing socio-institutional frameworks at the level of organizations, (organizational) fields, nations and the world as a whole.

If these different layers are distinguished, then codified rules or systems at different levels must be distinguished. At the level of the organization, codified organizational rules can form a basis for sharing, as well as form a basis for exchanging in employment contracts. Non-codified rules can have the same function. Within an organization, a mission statement and implicit and informal rules that form the organization's culture support sharing, whereas implicit expectations regarding leader–member and organization–individual exchanges can be found in the psychological contract.

At the inter-organizational level one can, likewise, find codified and non-codified sets of rules that guide relationships. Codified rules may be found in project plans and formal contracts alike, with the former probably emphasizing joint goals as a basis for sharing and shared expectations, the latter often more focused on controlling and safeguarding the exchange. Non-codified rules to support sharing are built as partners build up a shared commitment to the common endeavor, and when routines and shared meanings become part of their interaction, which will also positively affect exchanging, next to positive exchange experiences and the norm of reciprocity.

At the level of a society, codified rules in the form of, for instance, the constitution, criminal law and courts, support sharing throughout the nation based on rules that apply to all, and contract law, courts and certification systems support exchanging as they provide a framework for designing and safeguarding concrete exchange relationships between business partners. In a society, non-codified rules boil down to culture, language, symbols, and meaning structures. These institutions form a basis for sharing as parties from the same country know which norms and values they adhere to, as well as for exchanging, as this knowledge makes it easier to know what to expect from the other. At the global level, international criminal law and the universal use of codified business systems support sharing, while international contract law, escrow accounts and safeguards used in e-commerce support exchanging around the globe. Abstract forms of sharing meaning structures, as anti-globalists do, might be the start of evolving non-codified rules that form a basis for sharing and exchanging in international trade and collaboration.

Although the non-codified institutional sources of trust have been touched upon, it is less easy to distinguish precisely at which level they function. Sharing may be based on shared membership of informal groups, symbolic communities, shared norms of conduct, common values, shared cognitive frames, common modes of meaning construction, shared cultures, tacit knowledge, and so on. These may all function at each of the levels distinguished. Non-codified institutional sources that support exchanging include: codes of conduct regarding exchanges, arbitration, reputations, network position, formats of psychological contract that are seen as legitimate and norms of reciprocity. These sources may likewise function at the level of the organization, the organizational field, the nation or the universal level. Future research may produce answers to many questions that can be asked regarding the different sources of institutional trust distinguished and how these sources are drawn on in processes of trust building. In such research, attention should also be given to how the different institutional layers feed into each other in various manners. In a collaboration, built up between two individuals from two different countries, they bring with them all the codified and non-codified rules of their country, industry and organization. Furthermore, their joint enterprise is related to international institutions. It would be interesting to explore how the rules for sharing and exchanging that those actors construct, are influenced by the different institutional layers they are embedded in.

SOCIETAL AND ORGANIZATIONAL DEVELOPMENTS AFFECTING TRUST AND TRUST BUILDING

By distinguishing sources of interpersonal and institutional trust, new questions can be asked that may be addressed in future research. Given the theme of this volume, a question that comes to the fore is whether the societal and organizational developments that were discussed in the introduction would bring shifts in the importance of trust as a mechanism of governance, or in sources of trust available and suitable for trust building in situations where these developments have materialized.

Creed and Miles (1996) address the question whether organizational developments have changed the relevance of trust as a mechanism of governance. They propose that trust demands are rising with the different organizational forms developed over time. They argue that in network forms of organizing, performance is more dependent on high levels of trust than in other organizational forms that preceded the network form. In the study by Bijlsma, Rosendaal and van de Bunt an empirical test of this statement is presented. The study examines to what degree perceived organizational support (POS) indirectly via vertical and horizontal lines of trust (that is trust in managers and colleagues), selfish behaviors of colleagues, and heedful interrelating, affects team performance. The authors compare two organizational forms, a divisional form and a network form organization.

Two structural equation models were fitted to the data. The results support the argument of Creed and Miles. In both forms, perceived organizational support enhances trust in managers and colleagues. In the network form trust in managers and colleagues promotes heed and, through heed, performance. In the divisional form, these effects are either absent or less prominent. The authors conjecture that the combination of POS, trust in managers, and two factors that are related to trust and to the reward system, that is shared commitment to the team project and heedful interrelating, models a favorable condition for team performance within a network form. The study thus supports the idea that in new organizational forms, trust is of pivotal importance to performance and adequately dealing with contingencies.

Rus, however, finds that there can also be disadvantages of trust when relationships become too close. He finds that the interpersonal trust that can only travel through strong ties is in fact too sticky. It cannot be transferred and thereby can become a hindrance for a company's growth and development. He finds that institutional trust, that is being transferred through public information, contributes much more to a firm's development, and that SMEs that have more and looser inter-firm relationships grow faster. So while loose and transferable forms of trust contribute to economic prosperity, interpersonal, strong and sticky forms of trust even show a slightly negative effect. The study thereby is an illustration of the argument of Durkheim ([1893] 1960) that, to put it shortly, it is better to relate to contemporaries than to intimates. So, trust is more important nowadays, but the form of trust, and the sources it is built upon, must be suited to the situation and the socio-institutional context to function well.

A second question that comes to the fore is whether organizational developments are affecting the relation between sharing and exchanging as sources of trust. Over a century ago, Durkheim ([1893] 1960), expected that, given the advancing division of labor, sharing-based forms of solidarity would diminish in favor of exchange-based forms, which are based on dissimilarity between actors. Based on the work of Durkheim, it can be conjectured that in a contemporary organizational form, like the network form, purely sharing-based trust does not promote performance as well as a balanced combination of both sources of trust does. In the study by Bijlsma, Rosendaal and van de Bunt heedful interrelating, which according to Weick and Roberts (1993) is based on a collective mind and trust between colleagues, is shown to be the main factor affecting performance. These results suggest that a specific balance between sharing-based trust and exchange-based trust may be needed to support the specific combination of collective mind and heedful interrelating.

Another interesting matter is which shifts in sources of trust occur in trust building between actors at increasingly large distances, either physically, cognitively or culturally. Since in this volume codified rules or systems and shared membership of abstract communities were found as sources of trust building in globalized or de-localized contexts, it can be conjectured that the two principles of dispersion Boisot (1995) presented, codification and abstraction can also be validly applied to de-localization of trust sources, but research is needed to test this proposition.

A last theme, related to trust under pressure, that deserves more scholarly attention in future research is the transferability of trust. This theme is addressed in the study by Kerkhof, Vahstal-Lapaix and Caljé. They analyse how reputation and trust relate in situations where there is no face-to-face contact between buyer and seller in Internet shops. In most of these situations there is no common ground, nor a shadow of the past, to base trust on. They studied the effects of the reputation of an Internet store and the reputation of advertisers on the website of the store on consumer trust in the Internet store. The results confirm both effects. Trust can still be built by transferring it through credible cues or signals. In this manner, unknown parties can gain credibility and legitimacy through association with known and trusted others. This mechanism enables the firm to 'borrow' the trustworthiness and reputation that is necessary to sell their products over the net. Trust in the Internet store was shown in the relation between the reputation of the store, the perception of risk buying at the store and the intention to buy.

Given the freshness of the questions asked, the thin ice on which most propositions in these afterthoughts rest, and the shadows of support gathered so far, it can be concluded that a lot of promising research lies ahead.

REFERENCES

Bachmann, R. (1998), 'Conclusion: trust – conceptual aspects of a complex phenomenon', in C. Lane and R. Bachmann (eds), *Trust Within and Between Organizations: Conceptual and empirical applications*, New York: Oxford University Press, pp. 298–322.

Barnard, C.I. (1938), *The Functions of the Executive*, Cambridge: Harvard University Press.

Bijlsma-Frankema, K.M. and G.G. Van de Bunt (2002), 'In search of parsimony, a multiple triangulation approach to antecedents of trust in managers', *Research Methods Forum*, 7. http://aom.pace.edu/rmd/2002forum.html

Boisot, M.H. (1995), *Information Space: A framework for learning in organizations, institutions and culture*, London: Routledge.

Bradach, J.L. and R.G. Eccles (1989), 'Price, authority, and trust: from ideal types to plural forms', *Annual Review of Sociology*, 15, 97–118.

Child, J. (1998), 'Trust and international strategic alliances: the case of Sino–foreign joint ventures', in C. Lane and R. Bachmann (eds), *Trust Within and*

Between Organizations: Conceptual and empirical applications, New York: Oxford University Press, pp. 241–71.

Child, J. and G. Möllering (2003), 'Contextual confidence and active trust development in the Chinese business environment', *Organization Science*, **14**(1), 69–80.

Creed, W.E.D. and R.E. Miles (1996), 'Trust in organizations: a conceptual framework', in R.M. Kramer and T.R. Tyler (eds), *Trust in Organizations: Frontiers of theory and research*, London: Sage, pp. 16–39.

Durkheim, E. ([1893] 1960), *The Division of Labor in Society*, Glencoe, IL: Free Press.

Garfinkel, H. (1963), 'A conception of and experiment with "trust" as a condition of stable concerted actions', in O.J. Harvey (ed.), *Motivation and Social Interaction: Cognitive determinants*, New York: Ronald Press, pp. 187–239.

Gouldner, A. (1960), 'The norm of reciprocity: a preliminary statement', *American Sociological Review*, 25, 161–78.

Humphrey, J. (1998), 'Trust and the transformation of supplier relations in Indian industry', in C. Lane and R. Bachmann (eds), *Trust Within and Between Organizations: Conceptual and empirical applications*, New York: Oxford University Press, pp. 214–40.

Johannisson, B. (2001), 'Trust between organizations: state of the art and challenges for future research', Plenary presentation at EIASM workshop on 'Trust within and between organizations', Amsterdam, November 29–30, 2001.

Kramer, R.M. (1996), 'Divergent realities and convergent disappointments in the hierarchical relation: trust and the intuitive auditor at work', in R.M. Kramer and T.R. Tyler (eds), *Trust in Organizations: Frontiers of theory and research*, Thousand Oaks: Sage, pp. 216–46.

Lane, C. and R. Bachmann (1998), *Trust Within and Between Organizations: Conceptual issues and empirical applications*, Oxford: Oxford University Press.

Lewis, J.D. and A. Weigert (1985), 'Trust as a social reality', *Social Forces*, **63**(4), 967–85.

March, J.G. and J. Olsen (1975), 'The uncertainty of the past: organizational learning under ambiguity', *European Journal of Political Research*, **3**(2), 149–71.

Nooteboom, B. and F. Six (2003), *The Trust Process, Empirical studies of the determinants and the process of trust development*, Cheltenham, UK and Northampton, MA, USA: Edward Elgar.

Powell, W. (1996), 'Trust-based forms of governance', in R.M. Kramer and T.R. Tyler (eds), *Trust in Organizations: Frontiers of theory and research*, Thousand Oaks, CA: Sage, pp. 51–67.

Reed, M.I. (2001), 'Organization, Trust and Control: A Realist Analysis', *Organization Studies*, **22**(2), 201–28.

Ritzer, G. (1993), *The McDonaldization of Society*, Thousand Oaks, CA: Pine Forge Press.

Weick, K.E. (1995), *Sensemaking in Organizations*, Thousand Oaks, CA: Sage.

Weick, K.E. and K.H. Roberts (1993), 'Collective mind in organizations: heedful interrelating on flight decks', *Administrative Science Quarterly*, **38**(3), 357–82.

Zucker, L.G. (1986), 'Production of trust: institutional sources of economic structure', in B. M. Staw and L.L. Cummings (eds), *Research in Organizational Behavior*, Vol. 8, Greenwich, CT: JAI Press, pp. 53–111.

Index